C0-DAN-449

# UNDERWOOD THROUGH THE YEARS

## A Portrait of Life In Underwood, Washington

By

Mary Olsen Kapp

*Mary Olsen Kapp*

And

Kathleen LaMotte

*Thank You,*
*Kathy L.*

**Copyright © 2013**

2$^{nd}$ printing

For information about the book
Contact

Mary Kapp   509-493-1679   jmkapp@gorge.net
Kathy LaMotte   509-493-3813   salmon@gorge.net

Printed in the U.S.A.
By
Mira Digital Publishing
A Division of Graphic Connections Group
Chesterfield, MO

ISBN:
978-0-615-86016-9

# ACKNOWLEDGEMENTS
# TO

Underwood residents who shared their family histories and photos,
Especially Hannah Haselton May, who at age 102 remembers Underwood in the
early years

Ralph Brown for contributing archived news items, obituaries and
genealogy related to Underwood

Darla Johnston and Sally Stillman for contributing information

Cheryl Mack for researching and writing the Amos and Edward Underwood family
history

Jeffrey Elmer for finding, typing and offering a notebook full of
Underwood news items from local papers as well as *The Oregonian*

Marilyn Murray for careful proof reading

Underwood news reporters from the past and the newspaper offices and librarians
who kept nearly every issue

Anne Markgraf Ward for contributing three notebooks worth of research on
Underwood from newspaper articles, saving us countless hours of searching
through microfilm, although we also spent a fair number of hours looking for news
articles about Underwood

The Gorge Heritage Museum in Bingen for the numerous photos obtained through
its archives

The Gorge Interpretive Center Museum in Stevenson for photos

# Table of Contents

**PART ONE**

# INTRODUCTION

Although perhaps not official, we have used the following general designations for the layers of civilization on Underwood Mountain:

**Old Town** – On the river level at the confluence of the White Salmon and Columbia Rivers. Existing on this level were the historic landing for boats, the mercantile store, the hotel, saloon, gas stations, and the Indian fishing village.

**Flats** – From Cooper and Larsen Roads to Newell Road

**Heights** – Laycock- Kelchner Road to the top of the Mountain

> (Note- we believe the street sign for Laycock-Kelchner Road is misspelled, so we have changed it throughout this book. We assume the road was partly named after the Laycock family, who lived in the area before 1930.)

Many of the early Underwood Mountain settlers acquired land through the Homestead Act of 1862. In the appendix is a list of those who acquired land in this way. The list also includes those who bought the land outright and also Indian allotment acreage.

Much of the history in this book is based on accounts from local newspapers regarding the Underwood Mountain vicinity. We have mentioned the month and year, but not always the day and name of the newspaper. If anyone wants to know the exact reference, we have kept notebooks full of the news articles by date. Contact the authors for this information. A problem with early news accounts is that they used initials for the first names of men and the spouses were usually just Mrs. so and so, making it difficult to identify people accurately.

Although we made an attempt to include many of the Underwood residents in the family history part, we realize there are some who have been missed. If some of you have a family story or photos you want to share, give it to one of the authors and we will keep it for the next Underwood historians, perhaps at a local museum.

If you have an update, additional information or corrections to the information in this book, let us know. Perhaps readers may be able to answer some of the questions mentioned throughout the book about our history.

The authors have found the history of Underwood and its inhabitants to be fascinating. We hope you will too.

Mary Kapp – jmkapp@gorge.net          Kathy LaMotte – salmon@gorge.net

# Part One

# CHAPTER ONE

# GEOLOGY OF UNDERWOOD MOUNTAIN

**Underwood Mtn. looking north from Oregon**

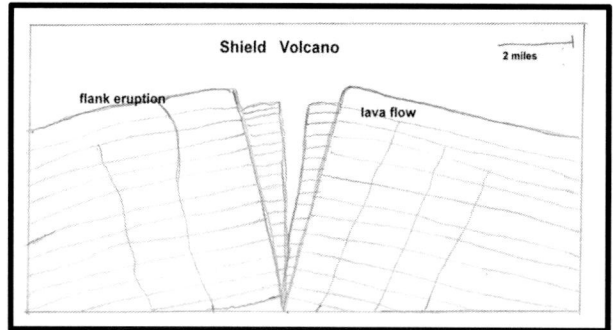

Underwood Mountain, on the Washington side of the Columbia River Gorge, reaches an elevation of 2,700 feet above sea level. Lying between the White Salmon River valley on the east side and the Little White Salmon River valley on its west side, it is five miles in diameter. Underwood Mountain is an early Pleistocene shield volcano. Pleistocene means it was formed anywhere from 11,700 to approximately 1.8 million years ago. Some shield volcanoes are still active today, such as Kilauea in Hawaii. Two other local shield volcanoes are Mount Defiance west of Hood River, Oregon and Larch Mountain, east of Portland, Oregon. It is believed Underwood Mountain erupted 20,000 to 850,000 years ago. It is not likely to erupt again.

Volcanic mountains are formed due to accumulation and solidification of lava, ashes and debris erupted from the earth's interior. A shield volcano, such as Underwood Mountain, is formed by liquid lava emitted from a central vent. It is like a warrior's shield. When the highly fluid lava

erupts, it travels farther than lava from more explosive volcanoes. As with Underwood Mountain, there were steady accumulations of broad, thin sheets of lava.

There are three principal geologic units in this area: Grande Ronde Basalt, Frenchman Springs Wanapum Basalt, and Basalt of Underwood Mountain. The Grande Ronde Basalt is composed of Miocene flows of the Columbia River Basalt Group. The Miocene period took place 5.3 to 23 million years ago. The Grande Ronde is the thickest formation in the Columbia River Basalt Group and it commonly exceeds 1,000 feet in thickness. The Frenchman Springs Wanapum Basalt overlies the Grande Ronde Basalt. In this area, the Frenchman Springs Basalt crops out in the cliffs above the Spring Creek Fish Hatchery. The hatchery springs discharge from the Wanapum Basalt. The Frenchman Springs Basalt is 250 feet thick. The Basalt of Underwood Mountain overlies the Frenchman Springs and is widely exposed on Underwood Mountain and Underwood Heights. The Basalt of Underwood is composed of numerous blocky, jointed flows each about 10 to 30 feet thick. The total thickness of the Basalt of Underwood Mountain layers is about 590 feet.

## Geology of Underwood Mountain (cont.)

Underwood Basalt crossed, and at one time temporarily dammed the Columbia River, as remnants of Underwood flows can be found on the Oregon side. Another temporary lake behind a natural dam on the Columbia River occurred about 100,000 years ago when a large debris slide removed the summit and north flank of Mt. Hood. The volcanic debris (a lahar or mudflow) flowed down the Hood River valley, across the river and several miles up the White Salmon River valley on the north shore.

**Round river rocks embedded in the cliff just west of the Old Town Underwood along Highway 14.**

Rick Thompson, President of the Lower Columbia Chapter, Ice Age Floods Institute, believes these tumbled quartzite river rocks probably came from Montana. The standard explanation for them is "ancestral Columbia River."

In a March 1955 publication of the Washington State Fruit Commission, author Bill Hoard talks about the soil on Underwood Heights. He says that although the soil varies, much of it is known as Chemawa Shot Soil. It is 30 feet deep in places and ideal for holding moisture. The "Shot Soil" or "Buckshot Soil" gets its name from hard, round pellets of partially decomposed rock, about the size of a shot-gun shell shot, mixed with the loam, sand or clay. These little "BB" sized balls do not dissolve in water and were possibly caused from hot volcanic basalt reacting with water.

The lower town of Underwood, and the former town of Hood lie at the base of Underwood Mountain. If these places were inhabited during the last ice age, 14,000 to 16,000 years ago, they would have been flooded multiple times by the releasing of Glacial Lake Missoula. Sheets of ice flowed southward from Canada and blocked the Clark Fork River in Idaho with a 2,000 foot high ice dam. This caused a huge lake behind it, covering western Montana. When the ice dam would break, the water drained out of it in two or three days, moving at up to sixty miles an hour, leaving 300 foot high gravel bars along the way. At Bonneville the water crested at 650 feet. The floods must have caused quite an upheaval to anything in the way. Some geologists estimate this cataclysm occurred perhaps five times, with many smaller floods from various glaciers not affecting areas below The Dalles.

Sources:
*The Magnificent Gateway by John Eliot Alle, 1979.*
*Website: USGS – The Volcanoes of Lewis and Clark, 1806.*
*Website: USGS - Volcano Hazards*
*Website: USGS – The Geological History of the Columbia River Gorge.*
*Website: The Columbia River – Underwood and Underwood Mountain.*
*Rick Thompson*

## Geology of Underwood Mountain (cont.)

The rock cliffs have posed problems caused by gravity and erosion. Here are two news articles to illustrate that geological occurrence:

*Albert Schey of Lyle was working on the end of a sling rope over 200 feet up the side of the rock cliff above the Underwood Fruit and Warehouse company, raking loose rocks off the cliff and rolling them down to the road in preparation for the coming winter's weather. When loosening a small rock, a huge boulder also rolled loose and pinned Schey's leg between another boulder, causing a compound fracture. Schey hung on the cliff for several hours while a rescue crew, headed by Gardner's ambulance service fought to reach him and tie him onto the stretcher before bringing him down the hill. It was raining every minute of the operation. The boulders are removed every fall by the highway commission for the prevention of falling rock.*
Mt. Adams Sun *November 26, 1937*

**The rock cliffs just west of Old Town Underwood, showing a layer of round river rocks above layers of gravel.**

### The Bluff is a Dangerous Shortcut

*Young Butch Sterrett and the two Hore boys attempted to descend the bluff at Underwood and were trapped on the steep hillside. Oscar Sterrett, Butch's father, and Don Reed, superintendent at Underwood Fruit and Warehouse, pulled the boys to safety with a rope.*

The reporter conjectured that the boys would wait a few years before attempting to climb down the bluff again.
Mt. Adams Sun, November 1, 1951

The next week this letter to the editor appeared in the paper:

*I DO NOT intend to stop climbing mountains. I will try to find an easier way down. Yours Truly, Lee Sterrett (Butch).*

Lee was about age 10 at the time.
\*\*\*\*\*\*\*\*\*\*\*\*\*\*\*\*\*\*

Do we have earthquakes in this area?

The *Pioneer* of September 22, 1961 reported earthquake shocks of 5 to 6 on a Mercalli scale of 12. They started Friday night and lasted until Sunday. The quakes occurred along a well-defined fault extending from Puget Sound to Skamania County. The tremors were heavy enough to move furniture, ripple plate glass windows and shake items off shelves.

# CHAPTER TWO
# UNDERWOOD  BEFORE 1900

## Native  People

When the first Caucasian explorers entered this region, they found it was inhabited by people who had been here awhile, actually for thousands of years. The first residents called themselves Chilluc-kittequw, living along the mouths of rivers that ran into the Columbia between Beacon Rock and Hood River County. They spoke a dialect described as the Upper Division of Chinookan and could communicate with other tribes along the Columbia from The Dalles to the Pacific Ocean.  American settlers named them Cascade Indians. Living near spawning inlets, the natives included fish in their diets, as well as game, Wapato bulbs, Camas roots, nuts and huckleberries.

*www.historylink.org* – *Skamania County*

## Lewis and Clark Expedition

The following was taken from the Lewis and Clark Journals – as they wrote (*in their own short hand and spelling*) on the return trip about stopping in the village located near Old Town Underwood:

*April 14,1806 – at 1 P.M. we arrived at a large village situated in a narrow bottom on the N. side a little above entrance of canoe creek [Big White Salmon R.]. their houses are rather detached and extent[d] for several miles. they are about 20 in number. These people call themselves We-ock-sock, Wil-la-cum. they differ but litt[l]e in appea[ra]nce dress &c. from those of the rapids. Their men have some leging and mockersons among them. these are in a stile of [the] Chopunnish. they have some good horses of which we saw ten or a douzen. these are the fi[r]st horses we*

*have met with since we left this neigh-borhood last fall,  in short the country below this place will not permit the uce of this valuable animal except in the Columbian vally and there the present inhabitants have no uce for them as they reside immediately on the river and the country is too thickly timbered to admit them to run game with horses if they had them. we halted at this village and dined. purchased five dogs, some roots, shappalell, filberds and dryed burries of the inhabitants. here  I observed several habitations entirely under ground; they were sunk about 8 feet deep and covered  with strong timber and several feet of earth in a conic form. these habitations were evac-uated at present. they are about 16 feet in diameter, nearly circular, and entered through a hole at the top which appears to answer the double purpose of a chimney and a door. from this entrance you decend to the floor by a ladder. the present habitations of these people were on the surface of the ground and do not differ from those of the tribes of the rapids. their language is the same with that of the Chilluckkittequaws. these people appeared very friendly.*

## Other Explorers

In addition to Lewis and Clark, the natives of the Cascades region must have encountered or were affected by some of these other early explorers:

1792 - The American **Robert Gray** sailed his ship the *Columbia* into the mouth of a great uncharted river, named it the Columbia River after his ship and claimed the area for the United States.

## Other Explorers (continued)

1792 – Shortly after Gray, British **Lieutenant William Broughton** sailed the *Chatam* through the treacherous mouth of the Columbia River and up the river as far as the present Vancouver, Washington. Before turning back, he formally claimed possession of the river and surrounding land for the British Empire. Broughton was under the command of **Captain George Vancouver**, who waited outside the Columbia bar in his ship the *Discovery.* Broughton named the Vancouver area after his commander.

1811 – **Wilson Price Hunt** was the leader of an overland expedition to connect with the Pacific Fur Company at the mouth of the Columbia River headed by John Jacob Astor of New York. In January of 1812 Hunt and his party rode horses on a trail through present-day Benton and Klickitat counties. Below The Dalles rapids, the countryside became more hilly and the trail more rugged. Hunt decided to continue the journey by dug-out canoe. In February they reached the Cascades of the Columbia, (now flooded by Bonneville Dam) . Here they found an Indian fishing village. Hunt noted that the Indians preferred to trade goods for blue glass beads. On their way downriver they *"frequently encountered huts of Indians who sold us dogs, dried salmon, beaver skins, and root of the ouapatou (wapato)"*
*www.historylink.org Astorian Wilson Price Hunt*

1824 – **Dr. John McLoughlin** became the factor (manager) of the British Hudson Bay Trading Company at Fort Vancouver. At that time the Columbia River was the boundary between the American and the British governments. Dr. McLoughlin kept the peace with the native population of the area, so the Cascades tribes probably had dealings with him.

1825 – **David Douglas** was another explorer important to this area. He was an English naturalist who named the Cascade Mountains. The fir tree so abundant here is named after him. He was sent by the London-based Horticulture Society to gather specimens and seeds of the Northwest Coast.

1830 – **American pioneers** started the overland trek to the Oregon country. In 1843, 700-1000 Americans travelled the Oregon Trail. Many of them abandoned their covered wagons in The Dalles and travelled the Columbia River by boat or raft. By 1846, the land north of the Columbia River to the 49th parallel became an American territory.

1850s – **Benjamin Bonneville** was born in France, but came with his parents to the United States in 1803 at the age of seven. In 1832 he led an American expedition to reach the Willamette Valley but finally had to turn back because the British John McLoughlin had given orders for no Indians or traders to supply the American party. By 1834 his men had reached a point on the Columbia River where he attempted to trade with the Sahaptins, but without success. The Sahaptin tribes were from the plateau region, so he supposedly did not reach the Cascades on that trip. In the 1850s Bonneville was appointed as a colonel at the Columbia Barracks, next to Fort Vancouver, which had become a U.S. Army post in 1849. In 1861 Bonneville was called to duty during the Civil War. Bonneville Dam and the Bonneville Power Administration are named for him, as well as the town of North Bonneville.
*www.Wikipedia.org Benjamin Bonneville*

# PREHISTORIC STONE FIGURE

**Oregonian** article discovered by Jeffrey Elmer

The Oregonian, Portland, OR.
October 3, 1906, page 4

## CURIOUS STONE IMAGE UNCOVERED BY RAILROAD EXCAVATION

Head of Dog With Horns of Sheep.

HOOD RIVER, Or., Oct. 2.— Workmen engaged in excavating for the North-Bank railroad near Underwood, Wash., recently unearthed a curiosity that is now in the possession of Edward Underwood and has been the subject of much interest and comment by the few that have seen it. It was found by Emil Anderson who had charge of constructing a station on the new road, who says it was discovered at a depth of over 25 feet and was embedded in 18 feet of gravel from the top of which had been removed several feet of rock.

In appearance it resembles an animal, half dog and half sheep, with the features of the former and horns of the latter. The image has been carved out of the hard basalt rock found along the Columbia River at this point and is as hard as iron. In height it is about two feet, but originally was probably somewhat higher as it has evidently been broken off at the bottom as can be seen by the picture.

While Underwood, who is a pioneer of 1853 in this region, seems to think that it is the work of Indians who formerly camped in great numbers at the mouth of the White Salmon River, near where it was found, engineers who have examined it say that its antiquity is so great that it may antedate them and that the fact that it is of stone indicates that it is not the work of their handicraft as almost without exception their images are of wood. They are inclined to think that it was the figurehead of a galley or boat of some kind in the remote ages. Underwood has been offered various sums of money for the image, but so far has refused to part with it. The photo gives a profile view and was taken on the porch of his dwelling.

## Prehistoric Stone Figure (continued)

The whereabouts of the stone figure on the previous page had been a mystery to the authors until it was located in 2010 at Maryhill Museum near Goldendale. It is on display in the Native American section. Maryhill Museum acquired many Indian artifacts from Mary Underwood Lane, so perhaps that is how the statue came to be there.

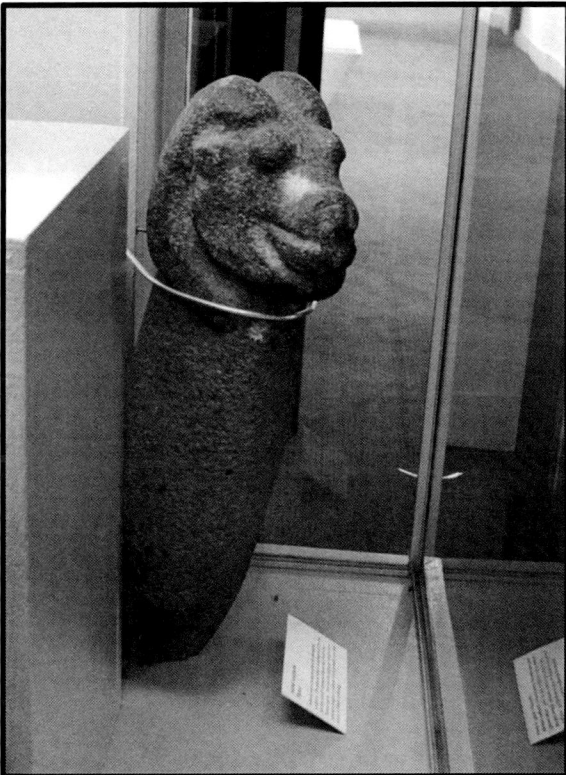

**Prehistoric stone carving found at Underwood 1906**
Photo by Mary Kapp

Note: Although the stone carving was found after 1900, it surely was deposited in the gravel at Underwood Landing long before that. Perhaps it washed down with the Missoula floods of some 15,000 years ago or maybe it was carved by local stone-age natives.

There are samples of ancient American stone carvings on display at the Portland, OR Art Museum. These have been found in archaeological sites along the Columbia River. They were carved from the abundant basalt rock found in the area and some are similar to the stone carving found in Underwood. The carvings depict humans and also animals found in the area, such as bighorn sheep, condors, beavers and owls. Bowls were also carved of stone. Below are samples of photos of these stone figures and bowls which can be viewed on the website www.dailykos.com .

**Underwood Area Before 1900** (continued)

Underwood is located at the Eastern edge of Skamania County, Washington. Skamania County was created in 1854. The county seat moved to Stevenson from North Bonneville in 1890. In the early days it was difficult to get to the county seat over trails or by boat. It was even difficult to get to White Salmon, so the settlements most closely associated with the people of Underwood were Hood River, across the Columbia River by boat and Husum, up the White Salmon River. Underwood has never been an incorporated town with a mayor and city government.

Before 1900, the history of Underwood largely centered around Amos Underwood and his brother Ed and their families. A timeline compiled in 1994 by Ed's wife Isabella Underwood's descendants, Charlotte Barnes and Martha Holcomb, highlights these pre-1900 occurrences:

*1857 – Amos Underwood married Ellen Chenowith Lear.*

*1860 – Amos acquired land near the mouth of the White Salmon River using his personal military land bounty for a free homestead on railroad land claims along the north shore. He also bought a settler's homestead, so that his land totaled 320 acres.*

*1861 – Amos operated a ferry from his homestead to Hood River. He owned two freight scows, a saloon and 10 gold mines near Mt. Adams.*

(Ed Underwood, younger brother of Amos, came to the area in 1865 and filed for a homestead on the bluff above the Columbia River.)

*1869 – Edward had a store and a wood camp which sold cord wood to river boats. His farm had a hundred head of cattle.*

\*\*\*\*\*\*\*\*\*\*\*\*\*\*

Other early settlers came to the Underwood area. The U.S. census of 1900 lists these heads of families besides Amos and Ed Underwood: Herman Bueche, Henry Debo, John Dark, Herman Friedrich, Alma Haynes, Harry (Wilhelm) Kellendonk, Christian Larsen, Emmett Locke, Harry Olsen, Isadore Rice, Charles Rosencrantz, Charlie and Edgar Thornton, and William Wendorf. (See information about these people and other early settlers in the **Family Histories** section of this book)

Some pre-1900 events that might have affected those living in the vicinity:

1850 – The Donation Land Claim Law allowed settlers to receive title to their land, up to 640 acres for a married couple.
*Web site: HistoryLink.org*

1851 – Francis A. Chenoweth began operating the first railroad on the north bank of the Columbia River as a portage around the Cascades rapids. It was a simple wood flat car pulled by a mule over fixed wood rails mounted on planks. This was an improvement over carrying freight and passengers by foot or hoof over a land trail, the rapids, being too treacherous for boats to negotiate. The steam paddle wheel boats generally stayed either upstream or downstream of the rapids at what was known as Cascades. The contraption was sold to Daniel and Putnam Bradford in 1853.
*Web site: HistoryLink.org File #8726 Theodore Winthrop, "Winthrop's Northwestern Journal" (spring 1853)*

1853 – The Donation Land Claim provision of free land if lived upon and cultivated for four years was reduced to 160 acres or 320 if a married couple.
*Web site: HistoryLink.org*

**Underwood Area Before 1900** (Continued)

1854 – Felix Iman built the steamer <u>Wasco</u>, to travel between Cascades and The Dalles, following the <u>Allen</u> and the <u>Mary</u>.

1855 – Treaty forming the Yakima, Warm Springs and Umatilla Indian reservations.

Spring, 1856 – Hostile Klickitat and Yakima Indians attacked settlers from the Joslyn acreage in what is now the Bingen area to the Cascades between what is now Stevenson and North Bonneville.

1862 – Homestead Act brought more settlers to the area.

1863 – A six-mile long steam train, the "Ann," on steel rails, went into service on the Bradford Brothers line on the north bank of the Columbia River. Now travel down river became easier.

1867 – A road opened for wagon travel between The Dalles and Hood River.

1882 – OWR and N Railroad completed, on the Oregon side of the Columbia River linking the area with the East Coast.

1887 – An act of congress to split Indian lands into individual allotments, with remaining lands becoming public and therefore up for sale.

1889 - President William Henry Harrison declared that Washington be admitted as the 42nd state of the union.

1896 – The Cascade Locks and Canal opened to river traffic, taking nearly 20 years to complete at a cost of $3.7 million. The U.S. Army Corps of Engineers accomplished this improvement to travel and freight, allowing navigation around four miles of rapids.
*Web site: HistoryLink.org File #7815*

Boat landings in the Underwood Mountain area were at Cook, Drano, Galligan and Underwood.

**Paddle Wheeler Bailey Gatzert (built in Ballard, Washington in 1890) at the Cascade Locks**
Photo from Gorge Heritage Museum archives

11

# CHAPTER THREE
# OLD TOWN UNDERWOOD

The early business establishments clustered together at the confluence of the Big White Salmon River and the Columbia River. This was close to the means of travel, which was by trail, primitive roads, railroad, or boat. Amos Underwood had been running a ferry to Hood River since 1861. Thus the name:

## Underwood's Landing

The development of the docks, ferries and paddle-wheelers can be learned from newspaper accounts about Underwood.

*Hood River Glacier January 1905*
*A public meeting was called at the school house to discuss a steamboat dock at or near Captain Olson's landing. At present, no steamboat will make regular landings. A committee was elected to determine the cost of the dock and road from C.T. Robard's store to the dock site. Those elected are: William Frost, R.D. Cameron, William Kellendonk, Fred Luthy, Henry Olson, C.H. Cromwell and P.I. Sather.*

*Hood River Glacier May 1905*
*A. Underwood, pioneer ferryman, was granted a license for one year for conducting a ferry between Hood River and Underwood. Captain Harry Oleson will have personal charge of the ferry business, Amos Underwood retiring after 50 years of ferry service on the middle Columbia. Captain Oleson has secured a gasoline launch and a large sailboat. Captain Olsen was kept quite busy with his big gasoline boat Sunday taking and bringing passengers to and from Hood River. Quite a few went to the baseball ball game from here.*

(Note: The spelling of Harry Olsen varies from Olsen to Olson to Oleson in news accounts. He is also sometimes referred to as Henry.)

*Hood River News-Letter September 1906*
*Charlie Davidson returned to Portland on the Spencer, which now lands at our Underwood dock, which will be completed in the sweet by and by. Mr. and Mrs. Vincent and Frank Thornton and lady friend were aboard the Kellog on their return from the hop fields.*

*Hood River Glacier May 1908*
*The J.N. Teal, Capitol City, and Dalles City boats are all now making regular stops at Underwood.*

*Hood River Glacier April 1909*
*Captain Harry Olsen now has his new boat the Seal in commission. He has also arranged a new landing float on the Oregon side, which cuts down the walk across the sand bar by about half.*

Otis Treiber operated the Underwood to Hood River ferry from 1910 to 1917, buying half interest from Captain Harry Olsen. (*See the Treiber information in the family history section of this book.*)

*The White Salmon Enterprise February 1911*
*The Beaver is the name of the new boat that has arrived at Underwood and will go into commission the first of March for services between that place and Hood River and for excursions up and down the river. Built by Frank Smith at Astoria, it is 51 feet long with an 11 foot beam. The boat is equipped with a 50-horse power engine and is fitted with electric lights. It is built of eastern oak, ironwood and Portland cedar. The boat will easily seat 75 passengers. It will be in the charge of Captain Olson, who has had thirty years' experience on the Columbia.*

**Underwood's Landing** (continued)

_Oregonian_ article discovered by Ralph Brown:

## FERRYMAN LASSOES DEER

### Young Buck Captured From Launch on Venturing Into River.

**The Oregonian, Nov 20, 1913**

HOOD RIVER, Or., Oct. 19.—(Special.)—A young buck deer swimming in the Columbia was lassoed yesterday by Captain Otis D. Trieber, proprietor of the Underwood-Hood River ferry system.

"While I was on the Washington bank I saw the deer enter the water, and when he was about a third of the way across I slipped around behind him in my launch," said Captain Treiber. "The deer was as quick in the water as a duck and it kept me busy to head him off from the shore. I was alone in the boat and had to steer and cast my rope. The buck dodged the noose until I was pretty well discouraged. Several times in trying to turn him from the bank I ran the boat entirely over him."

The deer is now tied to a tree in Underwood, Wash.

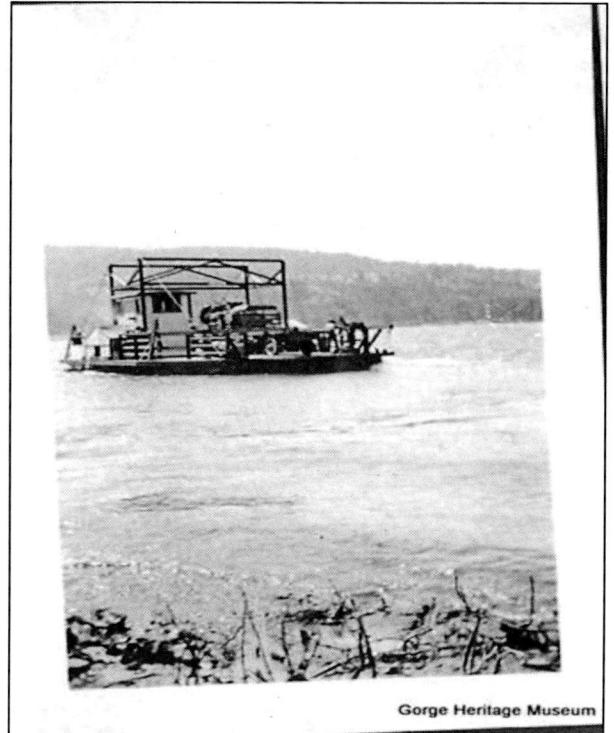

Gorge Heritage Museum

The ferries transported passengers, goods and vehicles from Underwood Landing to Hood River Landing and to the White Salmon Landing.

The Underwood-Hood River ferry schedule of April, 1914 advertised nine round trips starting at 6:45 a.m. and ending at 5:35 p.m. The Bear, a 65 foot ferry boat was built by Capt. Treiber at the mooring of his houseboat near Underwood.

In March of 1923 Frank Hogue bought the Underwood Ferry system from R. Johnson.

In November, 1924 the bridge across the Columbia to Hood River opened, soon ending the need for a ferry across the river. In 2024 the bridge will be 100 years old.

**Hood River Bridge, built 1924**

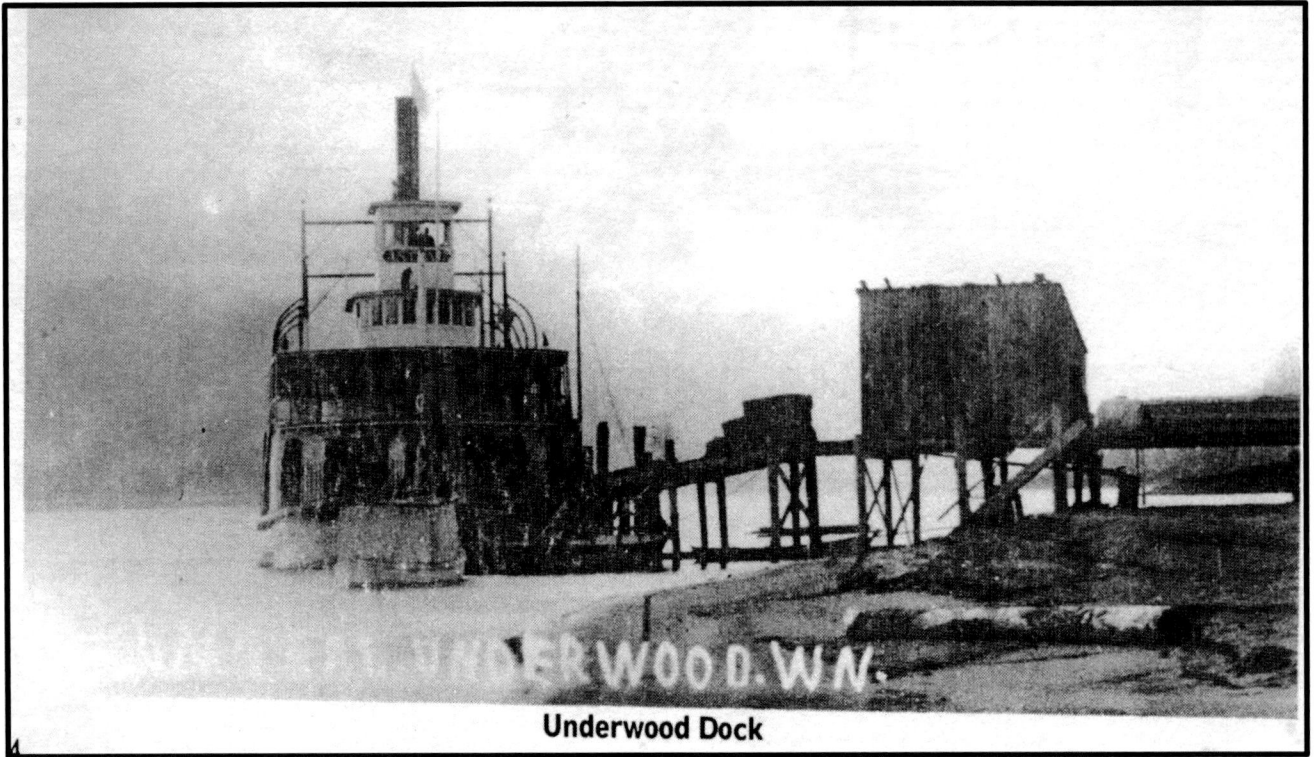
Underwood Dock

The landing at Underwood

163-33

Photos from Gorge Heritage Museum archives.
Otis Trieber collection.

14

**Underwood's Landing** (continued)

**The dock pilings are still seen across from the Underwood Mercantile Building**

In May 1938, the rising waters backed up from the new Bonneville Dam changed the landscape of lower Underwood. The dock pilings became partly submerged instead of stretching along a sand bar and the Indian village at the mouth of the White Salmon River was temporarily completely washed out. Lake Bonneville backed up the White Salmon River for nearly a mile.

## Historic Business Establishments

The business establishments of "Old Town" Underwood grew along the river, where as the people mostly lived above on the flats or heights. Local news items tell the story of early merchant enterprises.

### Blacksmith Shop
*Skamania County Pioneer* August 1911

*Wm. Carstens recently purchased the blacksmith shop at Underwood and moved up there from Stevenson. He has Grandpa Pugh*

*with him and both men are kept very busy in this shop.*

### Livery Stable
*Skamania County Pioneer* December 1911

*L.J. Stuart (or Stewart) has sold half interest in the livery business to Will Laycock who will take charge the first of this year.*

*Mt. Adams Sun* August 1962

*The old "Horses Home and Livery Stable" at Underwood burned to the ground August 23. Cause of the fire is unknown. The blaze was observed at 9:50 p.m. by Mrs. Jack Laurence who lives in a trailer home parked just west of the Underwood Mercantile store. The alarm was answered by firemen from Bingen, White Salmon, Hood River, the U.S. Forest Service and Broughton's Mill.*

*The old livery stable was built about 1908 and managed by a man named James (Lundy) Stewart. Later it was the center of some of Underwood's liveliest square dances and bottle tipping, according to early residents. From 1915-1917, Bill Underwood staged dances in the old barn's loft. The orchestra included two violins and an organ.*

*Claude Ackley recalls riding his saddle horse from the top of Burdoin Mountain to the Eyrie (on the east bluff of the White Salmon River) where he tied his horse, walked down an old Indian trail and across the railroad bridge to call the dances.*

*The fiery sky-glow from the burning stable was visible for many miles. Sparks fell at the George Baker place on Underwood Heights. Had the wind been from the west instead of north, it would have been difficult to save the Underwood store, service station and café, Laurence says.*

*The building was owned and insured by Henry Kapp of White Salmon who stored hay, lumber, farm equipment and other materials in the building. Antiques lost included a 1908 Maxwell car and a Model T.*

15

## Store/Mercantile Building

*Hood River Glacier* September 1904
*C.T. Robards of Hood River is constructing a store building 20' X 40', fronting the river and next to the Saint's Rest (saloon?) It will soon be filled with a stock of general merchandise.* (Mr. Robards was the postmaster in 1904, so the post office must have been located in the store.)

The *Hood River Glacier* of June 1905 reports that Myron S. Smith and W.L.Clark took possession of the store at Underwood. The Underwood section of the newspaper in July states:

*Mr. Smith, our merchant, is adding to the stock of merchandise and putting an addition to the store, an upper story hall. Mr. Smith had for many years been connected with the Wind River store. Mr. Clark is superintendent of the government property at the Cascade Locks. An addition was placed in the rear of the building to warehouse the flour and feed department. The telephone exchange is in the store and Mr. Smith has been made postmaster, adding new fixtures for the Post Office and renting boxes. The store stock includes dry goods, groceries, boots and shoes, clothing, notions, tin ware, fishing tackle, tobacco, cigars, and rough and dressed lumber*

By November of 1905 Smith and Clark, postmasters and general store keepers, were having a third floor put in above the warehouse for a dance hall and meeting room. In December, the upper story room was open for a social dance, with supper served in the Underwood hotel.

In July 1907 Smith and Clark added a cooler to the warehouse. Mr. Rosenkranz was doing the carpenter work.

In January 1910 about 25 couples attended the New Year's Eve party at Smith's Hall and a very enjoyable time was had by all. By this time the SP&S railroad had been servicing the town of Underwood and M.S. Smith had the ticket agency in the store.

*White Salmon Enterprise* March 1911
*M.S. Smith has sold his store to a Hood River merchant.*

In June of 1918 The Underwood Mercantile Company was incorporated and took over the store from the D.G. Jackson Company. The incorporators were M.S. Smith, H.S. Adams and Dr. H.L. Geary. Both Mr. Smith and Mr. Adams had been engaged in the mercantile business in the Skamania County district. Mr. Smith and Mr. Geary were owners of extensive orchard interests.

*The Oregonian* November 29, 1921
*The roof of the Underwood Mercantile company store fell from the weight of snow, causing damage amounting to several thousand dollars. The noise made by the spreading of the walls warned those within and everybody escaped just as the crash came. Many roofs of barns have fallen in and one sawmill has been wrecked.*

The store changed hands again in January of 1923, this time to a cooperative of Underwood men, among them Messers Hamlin, Haynes, Geary and Gibbs.

*Skamania Pioneer* January, 1926
*The Underwood Mercantile company installed a soda fountain.*

The Underwood Mercantile Company was sold to Glover Brothers of Cascade Locks, Oregon in January 1927. The store was owned by a stock company formed of local people and carried a large general line of merchandise. E.E. Claypool had been manager of the company for some time, but he had gone to Portland to work for the Allen-Lewis company.

In April 1936 a fire destroyed most of the roof of the store. The White Salmon fire department quickly arrived and put out the

## Store/Mercantile Building (continued)

blaze, which could have destroyed most of the town. About 50 feet of the roof burned.

In March 1939 H.I. Scherrie was the new proprietor of Underwood's general store, recently having bought it from Mr. Glover. In April the news was that Mr. and Mrs. Wallace Glover had charge of the grocery store again.

*The Enterprise May 1944*
### White Salmon's Fire Boys Save Store at Underwood

*Timely arrival of the White Salmon fire department saved the large two-story building of the Glover store at Underwood. They were able to control and put out the roof fire which had burnt through and was being fanned by a heavy breeze. Only ten by twelve feet on each side of the roof was burned through. The building houses the general store and post office on the ground floor and several apartments on the second floor.*

In January 1946 George E. Balsiger owned the Underwood store, advertising Hotpoint appliances, union suits, vests, coveralls, rain coats and boots.

On May 5, 1946 another fire started in the roof of the store, destroying the three story frame building. This time the fire departments from Bingen, White Salmon and Hood River could not save the other buildings in the town of Underwood. Also burned were the Texaco station, a tavern, the three story Underwood hotel, the Kapp meat market and gas station, a few cabins, two residences and some Indian dwellings. The Underwood Fruit warehouse and the railroad depot were not burned. The store and post office resumed business in the railway depot building, returning to Balsiger's store in the late 1940/early '50's. The store was rebuilt with only two stories.

*News from the May 10, 1946 issues of The Enterprise and The Pioneer*

*May 10, 1946 –Ad in The Enterprise:*
*All records of orders for appliances were destroyed in the fire and I will appreciate it if patrons will attempt to help us correctly place their names on our new list. I have leased the Underwood Depot and can be contacted there and will appreciate it if all outstanding accounts are paid as promptly as possible. Phone 923, Underwood Mercantile Co., Geo. E. Balsiger*

In October 1952, George Balsiger's Underwood Mercantile Company store was broken into and robbed of a total of $312.80 worth of cash, guns, ammunition and other merchandise. At about 3 a.m. Mrs. Balsiger was awakened by a crash but at that time a freight train came through and she thought nothing about it. A broken window in the front of the store smashed in by the robbers made possible the entry.

In June 1964, George and Ted Balsiger, father and son, sold their Underwood Mercantile Store to Al and Nadine Chisholm of White Salmon.

The Mercantile building housed the post office until 1997. However, from time to time the post office was located in the railroad depot.

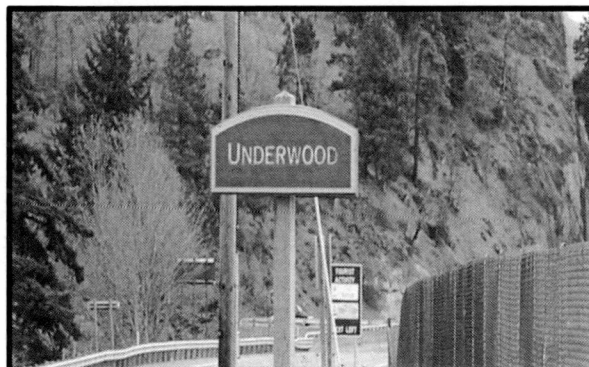

**Store/Mercantile Building** (continued)

Photo from Gorge Heritage Museum archives

**Smith and Clark store, saloon, hotel in back**
    **Between 1905 – 1911**

Bad luck again! On July 5, 1990 a blaze gutted the Underwood Auction building, formerly the mercantile store. The fire was reported about 11:20 p.m. Monday and sparked out of control by midnight. The building also housed the Underwood Post Office. Postmaster Wilma McCarthy was able to retrieve most of the mail.

October 1990 – The post office was refurbished in the former mercantile/auction house building and reopened there.

July 1995 –Tim Cummings of Dallesport, owner of the historic mercantile building in Underwood, had decided to sell. He did not want to provide the Postal Service with an on-going lease because a new owner might want to use the whole building. Therefore the Underwood Post Office was forced to vacate the building.

**Mercantile, hotel, livery stable (on river) before the road for vehicles. After 1906.**

**Fruit warehouse to the west, saloon to the east.** Photos from Gorge Heritage Museum.

**Below: Three story mercantile on road.**

**Youth's BVDs**
Regular 85c
Now 40c

**MISSES SIZE 12**
**Union Suits**
Regular $1.00
Sale Price 50c

**BOYS RIBBED**
**Union Suits**
Size 10, Regular $1.25
Sale Price 60c

**LADIES**
**Union Suits**
$1.45 to $2.00 at
75c

**HOT WATER** FOR EVERY NEED AT LOW COST

Everyone is happy with a Hotpoint Electric Water Heater in the home. Just install it and forget it. Hot water always at the turn of a faucet. Safe and dependable. Get full details today.

HAVE ALL THE HOT WATER YOU WANT
WITH A
**Hotpoint**
AUTOMATIC
ELECTRIC WATER HEATER

**LADIES**
**Under Vests**
the Lot at
15c each

**BOYS**
**Coveralls**
Regular $2.00 at
98c

INFANTS and CHILDREN'S
Woolen, Cotton and Rayon **STOCKINGS**
Regular 50c pair at          Regular 25c
25c pair          2 pr. for 25c

SPECIAL Men's Alligator Rain Coats, Knee Lengths $2.50 each

All Children's RUBBERS at ½ Price

We are Authorized Agents for Hotpoint Line of Appliances.

•

GET YOUR ORDER IN EARLY

**GEO. E. BALSIGER** UNDERWOOD STORE
Phone 923, Underwood, Wash.

Your **Hotpoint** Dealer

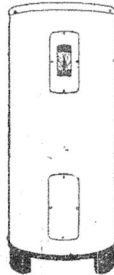

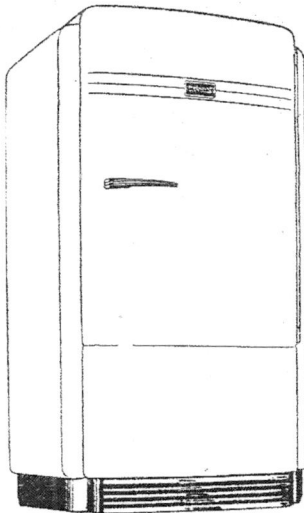

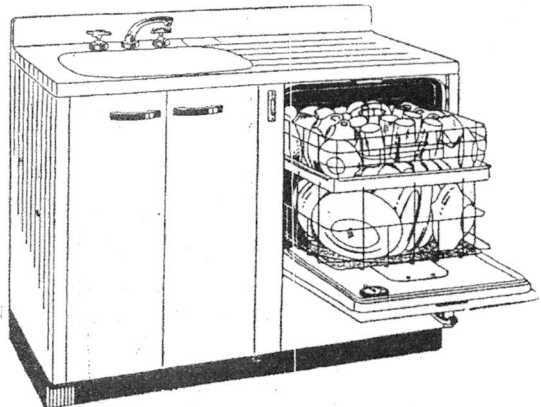

## Old Town Underwood

**Six men and one dog waiting for the train in front of the Underwood Mercantile building. Heinrich Kapp, Sr. in butcher's apron on far left. The Fruit Grower's Union packing house to the left. It is believed the packing house building survived the 1946 fire and is still standing, used now as a residence. The Underwood hotel is in the background. The railroad track was much closer to the mercantile than it is now. There is a little boy standing on the porch. The photo was taken after 1908 and before 1930.**

Photo from the Gorge Interpretive Center Museum in Stevenson.

## The Underwood Hotel

Another business establishment in "Old Town" Underwood was the Underwood Hotel. It was an impressive, big, square, three-story tall building with a porch supported by large brick posts surrounding the first floor. One entered the hotel from the south side. As you entered, the lobby was on the left, the dining room was straight ahead. The dining room contained a long table where meals were served family style. The area beyond the dining room, on the left, were the managements' living rooms. The kitchen was on the north side of the building, with a large screened-in porch to the outside. A few feet outside the screened porch was a rock wall about 4 feet tall. Beyond the wall was a steep hillside, leading up to Underwood Heights.

The rented rooms were on the second floor and the stairway to get there was off the lobby. The managers' bedroom was on the third floor. There was a bathroom built on the end of the east porch near the lobby entrance.

*Virginia Charters*

### Local Newspaper Notes about the Underwood Hotel

**From the Hood River *Glacier***

1905, Feb 9 - *A new hotel is the future prospect for Underwood.*

1905, April 6 - *Mrs. Olson* (Amos and Ellen Underwood's daughter Mary) *expects to build a hotel at the landing and be ready to accommodate the visiting public.*

1905, June - *The ring of the hammer can be heard and it is sweet music to all who live in the hustling little town of Underwood. Captain Harry Olson has commenced work on his new hotel. It is the intention of Captain Olson to erect one of the best hostelries along the river. It will mean much to Underwood, for already the travel is heavy and new faces are seen daily near the settlement.*

1905, July 13 - *Work was resumed Monday on the Olson Hotel. Mr. Mickelsen and Mr. Fordyce are the carpenters.*

1905, July 27 - *Captain Harry Olson, the Underwood ferryman believes in the future of Underwood and is erecting one of the finest hotels along the river. This will be a great improvement to the hustling town when it is completed.*

1905, Aug 10 - *Captain Olson has about completed his hotel.*

1905, Aug 17 – *Mrs. Olson's new hotel is nearing completion.*

1905, Oct 26 - *Mrs. Henry Olson, who was over from Underwood yesterday, reports her new hotel nearing completion.*

1905, Nov 23 - *A new hotel was just completed, which is well built upon a solid rock foundation. It is most beautifully situated on the banks of the Columbia River and nestled in amongst tall pines and firs. It is picturesque and a true type of the cottage hotel as we read about in magazines, having a beautiful and spacious veranda all around it from which visitors can obtain a beautiful view of the river and the magnificent steamers that majestically pass by. Also on the opposite bank of the Columbia can be seen the iron horse traveling over the steel road and the thriving city of Hood River and the famous Mount Hood. At the rear of the hotel are towering bluffs several hundred feet high. The cottage hotel is very tastefully built and painted in color harmonizing with its surroundings and its accommodations are equally tasteful. The rates are based on the principle of "live and let live." The proprietor Mrs. Olson endeavors to make all guests feel at home and provides them the very best she can for what she charges. Any guest visiting this Cottage Hotel will leave feeling that they've received full value for their money. Miss Elsie Underwood who has charge of the dining room will do her best to please and wait upon the guests at the hotel.*

**The Underwood Hotel** (continued)

1905, Dec 28 - *Supper was served in the Underwood Hotel.*

1906, July 12 - *Margarite is the new room girl at the Cottage Hotel.*

1906, July 26 - *Mrs. Olson served ice cream Sunday at the Cottage Hotel for the public benefit.*

1906, Aug 2 - *The Cottage Hotel affords a new piano.*

1906, Aug 16 - *Mr. Amos Underwood has succeeded in securing another saloon license. We understand there was a request for a license to run a bar in the hotel.*

(A name change:)

1907, June 11 – Advertisement in The Oregonian – *Hotel Rockhaven, Underwood, Wash; fishing, boating, hunting, home cooking, fine scenery; a delightful place to rest. Take train or boat to Hood River, then Underwood Ferry. If notified, will meet trains. Terms very reasonable, Mrs. Mary V. Olsen, proprietor.*

1908, Mar.12 - *Rock Haven mistress, Mrs. Olson, visited Husum friends Saturday.*

1908, April 2 - *H. Taylor reported on trip to Underwood. Had a very fine dinner at the hotel in Underwood, and got acquainted with Mrs. Olson, the proprietor.*

1908, April 9 - *Charlotte Underwood's wedding was in the Underwood Hotel.*

1908, July 30 - *Mrs. Olson is building an addition to her hotel, putting in two new bathrooms.*

1946, May10 – (About the Underwood fire) - *There were 15 residents in the 18 room hotel, operated by Mary Lane and owned by Frank Hunsaker of White Salmon.*

**From the Stevenson *Pioneer***

1905, Sept 14 - *Work is progressing on Captain and Mrs. Olson's 20-room hotel which is nearing completion. Mrs. Olson has had years of successful catering to the traveling public, has traveled extensively and is of the thorough painstaking and genial disposition calculated to please. In fact*

*press of travel has compelled the adding of tent after tent till they are already doing a good business in advance of opening. The "Rockhaven." From its basement, hewn from solid rock throughout, light, health, breeziness, comfort and handiness draw from Mrs. Olson's experience has been planned and worked out in substantial detail.*

1906, Oct 18 - In a letter to the editor, Amos refers to the hotel as "his hotel"

1909, Dec 16 - *Amos Underwood celebrated his 75th birthday and in the company of others enjoyed a spread at the hotel.*

1910, Mar 17 - *The Olson Hotel has been remodeled throughout and has been fitted up with a fire escape.*

**Underwood Hotel, three story building in far back**

**Underwood Hotel Memory**

Charlotte Horn Barnes (great granddaughter of Isabelle and Ed Underwood) remembers the Underwood Hotel because of the trips with her mother Martha to visit her relatives as the children were growing up. After Martha's death and the year of mourning had been completed, Charlotte remembers a ceremony conducted by Mary in the Underwood Hotel to commemorate Martha. Charlotte's final visit was to see Aunt Mary and show Mary her newly born twins. The hotel burned in 1946.

## The Underwood Hotel (continued)

Charlotte remembers the lobby in the SE corner. An upright piano was against the stairway wall. The lobby had lots of rocking chairs. In the hot summer evenings, they would be taken out to the porches so the guests could enjoy the breeze and summer views of the Columbia River.

The kitchen was in back at the NE corner. Charlotte's memories are of a large wood stove with pots hanging on the wall. There was a back door that went onto a screened porch. Smoked salmon was hung here and the cement floor was hosed down to keep it cool. She remembers the aroma of pork roast.

A small bedroom was on the first floor in the SW corner. It was called Mary's bedroom. Charlotte's memories only include "a bed and clothes."

The fourth room on the main floor was the dining room. There was a long table across the middle of the room surrounded with straight chairs. There was always a white table cloth on the table. The room was kind of dark, and the walls were finished with wooden planks similar to ship-lap. Charlotte associates the dining room with ceremonies of Isabella's Shaker religion which included bells.

The lower level included the stairway to the second floor which had the bedrooms. During a remodel of the hotel, a section of the outside porch was converted into a bathroom. The bathroom contained a toilet, sink, and tub, but the entrance was out the hotel door, onto the porch, and then into the bathroom. Charlotte remembers that it was cold to use.

She remembers the stone retaining wall along the driveway and the swing hung in the oak trees at the side of the hotel. The only "out" buildings she remembers is the row of outhouses. There was a concrete path on the east side of the hotel to get to two rows of outhouses. The men's were on the left and the women's were on the right. They were painted green and each stall had its own roof. The hotel itself was painted yellow and trimmed in white.

The adults would visit inside the hotel; the kids would play around outside. There were no "toys" at the hotel. Both rivers were off limits. The kids stayed away from the Indians who lived by the river, "we couldn't understand them anyway." We never played on the boulders behind the hotel. Poison oak and rattlesnakes, "the scourge of the Gorge" were there. The kids used the swing and dug holes in the sand bank between the hotel and the road. The visits usually included lunch, and then "we went back home to Hood River."

Guests at the Underwood Hotel included Buzz Gather. When he was principal of the Butler Acres School in Kelso during the 1950's, he talked with Charlotte about living there and knowing Mary Underwood (Olsen) Lane.

*Anne M. Ward Correspondence –Dec 17, 1994*

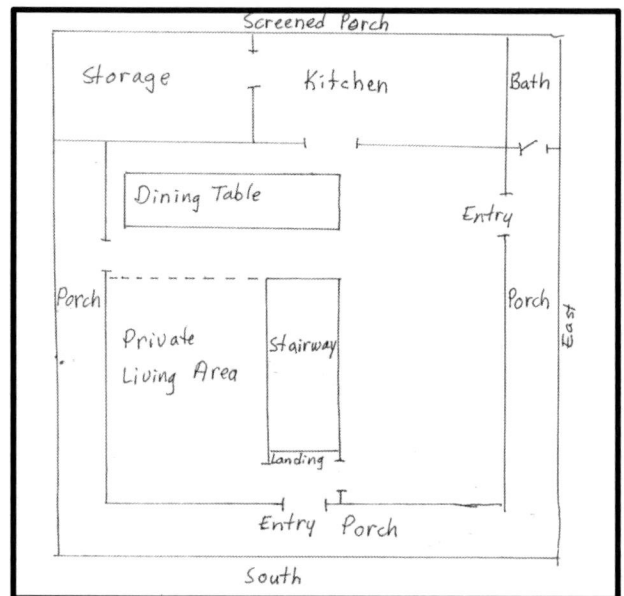

**Drawing of the Underwood Hotel**
*(Notice addition of bathroom added on outside porch in upper NE corner. )*

24

## The Underwood Hotel

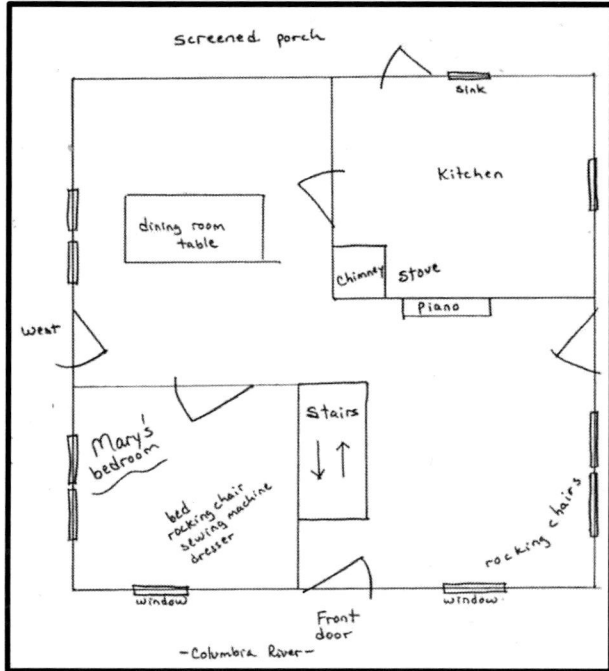

**Before bathroom addition**

\*\*\*\*\*\*\*\*\*\*\*\*\*\*\*\*\*\*\*\*

### Underwood Hotel Memories
By Everett W. Arnold

(*Arnold's parents, Grace and Wilford, operated the hotel from 1929-1933. Memories of the Underwood Hotel are shared in this article written by E.W. Arnold as he describes his life in Underwood.) From Gorge Heritage Museum archives and the Anne Ward collection.*

While our family lived in and operated the Underwood Hotel, I was between the ages of eight and twelve. The local children I played with were my brother Calvin, who was three years younger; my sister Virginia, who was five years younger; and Vernon Meigs, who was two years younger. Vernon lived across the highway, where his parents operated a service station-store.

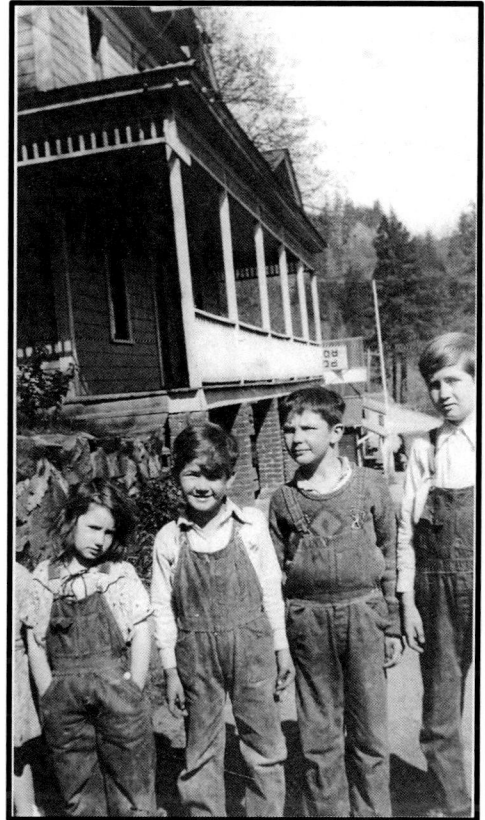

**Left: Virginia Arnold, Calvin Arnold, Raymond Meigs, Everett Arnold. In the background is the hotel.** Photo from Gorge Heritage Museum archives

The hotel was impressive because it was the first time I had lived in such a large facility. It was a big square building three stories tall, with a porch completely surrounding the first floor. One entered the hotel lobby from the east side. As you entered, the lobby was on the left and the dining room straight ahead. The room contained an extremely long dining table; at least to me it was extremely long. Meals were prepared by Mother and served family style. The area beyond the dining room and to one's left was our family living room. The kitchen was on the north side of the building, with a large screened-in porch to the outside. A few feet outside this porch was a rock wall about four feet tall, upon which were placed the garbage cans. Beyond the

25

## The Underwood Hotel (continued)

wall was a steep hillside, leading up to Underwood Heights.

**This rock wall is all that remains of the hotel**
Photo by Mary Kapp

There must have been skunks living in that hillside, for we experienced their coming to raid the garbage cans for food. I remember hotel guests coming out to the screened-in porch to watch the skunks. Once in a while the skunks would get into a fight and cause quite a stink for us and our guests.

To get back to the hotel, all the hotel rooms were on the second floor. Our family slept on the third floor. There was a bathroom built (as an afterthought, I would guess) on the end of the east porch, near the entrance to the lobby. I remember the bathroom being a real luxury, since I had not been exposed to too many inside toilets or bathrooms before coming to the hotel.

We would play hide-and-seek and kick-the-can around the hotel and under the huge porch that surrounded the main floor of the hotel. The porch was supported by large brick posts, one of which we would use as "home base". I remember quite sharply one game of hide-and-seek when I was running to base while looking for the person who was "it", and ran full steam into one of those brick posts, striking my right forehead. I carried a very tender lump for

many years as a result of that impact. (I am certain that the accident was a contributing cause of my extreme nearsightedness.I was unable to get much-needed glasses until the summer between the eighth grade and high school. I finally made enough money to buy them myself.)

I loved to visit Vernon Meig's home because he had so many interesting toys to play with. His older brother made logging trucks and other vehicles with wheels from the conveyors that carried boxes of apples and pears through the packing and cold storage warehouse. We would build roads all over the dirt bank, behind their place, to pretend we were hauling logs to the river, where they could be rafted, just like the adults were doing on the White Salmon River at Underwood.

Two American Indian families lived on the river bottom land, just below where all the Underwood businesses were located. I remember that one of the families was named Quiemps. They had two boys who were near my age, so we went to school with them, and we also played with them occasionally. There was a lot of activity in the Indian area, near the White Salmon River, when the salmon run was on. The Indians would net the salmon, filet them out and lay the fish on wooden racks to dry in the sun. I recall that the government fish hatchery men would have a trap in the river and haul the salmon out to get the eggs and milk the male sperm into the containers of eggs. They would then give the fish to the Indians to process. I have an impression that the fish were so thick in the water that one could almost walk across the river on fish.

There was a grocery store on the highway, just below the hotel. It seemed, at the time, to be a huge store with all kinds of good things to explore and to eat. I remember going there often to shop with Mother and being very much impressed with all the fascinating items on display. I believe it was not only a grocery store, but a hardware and soft goods store as well.

## The Underwood Hotel (continued)

My parents operated the Underwood Hotel from 1929 to 1933. They were fortunate to have the hotel during those years, for that was the period when the water-level highway was constructed between Underwood and Carson. Also, I remember that the meals at the hotel were so good that the freight train crews would stop at Underwood to take their meals with us. During this time, I attended a two-room public school on Underwood Heights from the second through fifth grades. There are advantages to having four grades to a room. You get more than one chance to learn. A good example was when I was in the fifth grade. The fifth grade row of desks were right next to where the teacher held all the class recitations. When the eighth grade class was learning the Gettysburg Address, I had it mastered long before most of the eighth graders.

Some incidents remembered about going to school on Underwood Heights: We were warned not to talk in assembly. Once I was talking to the boy next to me and all of a sudden I was rising out of my seat into the air, due to the principal grabbing me by the overall suspenders. He took me to the cloakroom where he had a switch which he used to impress upon me the value of not talking in assembly. Some of us were participants in a traveling show that was put on at our school. The only thing I now remember is that we stuck our heads through a canvas scenery. Another time we were involved in a black face minstrel show at the school.

In the spring, the fields would be full of wild flowers in full bloom. I remember walking home from school, so that I could pick wild flowers to take to the pretty wife of the local butcher shop owner, Heinie Kapp. The butcher shop was just down the street from the hotel. I went there a lot, owing to the crush I had on the butcher's pretty wife. (By the way, he became the principal owner of the Bank of Stevenson and in later years offered me a job in the bank, but my wife Jane, did not want to live in the area.)

Mr. Thun had a large strawberry farm on Underwood Heights. He allowed me to pick strawberries each spring, even though I was quite young, compared to others. My memories of strawberry picking are riding to work and back in his model-T Ford pickup; that it was a hot, tiring, and dirty job; being teased by the older kids for being so slow, and how proud I was of the money that I earned. Of course, the strawberries were delicious!

There was a big apple-pear packing house along the railroad tracks, just west of town; and what a treat it was when I could find my way there. I recall the man who made all those wooden boxes that the ladies wrapped and packed fruit into, before it was placed into their cold storage and then later shipped out by rail. The box maker was a "hero" to me. He made those boxes with great skill. I enjoyed watching him hammer those boxes together, quickly and rhythmically, with a hatchet and thinking how much I would enjoy having a job like that.

Of course we had a radio. My father could not miss listening to Lum and Abner, Amos and Andy, and I, Little Orphan Annie and Jack Armstrong. I lost faith in the radio station when I realized that the Lucky Strike ad "not a cough in the carload" may not be all that truthful. We had a boarder in the hotel who always woke up coughing, and coughing, and coughing. Then I noticed that the cigarettes he smoked were Lucky Strikes. It was then that I realized that I shouldn't take everything I hear at face value.

> *The meals at the hotel were so good that the freight train crews would stop at Underwood to take their meals with us.*

**The Underwood Hotel** (continued)

**The Underwood Hotel, finished in November 1905.** Photo from Gorge Heritage Museum archives.

## The Underwood Hotel (continued)

**Underwood Hotel in back, behind the three-story mercantile building.**
Photo from Gorge Heritage Museum archives

## The Saloon and Alcohol Issues in Underwood

There was a saloon in "Old Town" Underwood, which the loggers enjoyed after a day of hard, dangerous labor.

*(Excerpt from article titled:* Log Drive on the River – 1905.)

*When the logs got to the mouth of the river they were taken to the mill. There at the mouth, the logs were first held. The logs would be twenty or thirty feet high in a jam or a quarter of a mile long. When they wanted to move them they would take two or three men and go out and pull a line back on the key log. Some you couldn't pull and you'd have to shoot them out. You would hook one out and get out of the way. Break them loose and get maybe one or two. Sometimes you'd get a good haul of close to fifty logs.*

*After a drive we'd all go into Amos Underwood's saloon and celebrate. Some would get ugly, but most of us had all kinds of fun – laugh and play jokes.*

A taped interview with Ivan Donaldson, given by Roy C. Chubb for The History of Skamania County publication.

In August 1906 A.J. Haynes built a wood shed onto the saloon building for Amos Underwood.

But some people opposed the saloon:

*The booze joint has opened in Underwood, a board of county commissioners having been elected who are favorable to the "dispensary of liquid headaches." Some of the ranchers up the valley say that it means another fight in an attempt to close it as it is an intolerable nuisance, especially in the fruit picking season. The people of Underwood flats do not want it; neither do the people along this side of the river, and Skamania county commissioners will again be petitioned to close it. There is no police marshal to regulate things and a saloon under these circumstances is bad business.*

The Enterprise April 14, 1911.

## Underwood Up In Arms

*Now is the time of year when strawberries take a good deal of attention. A great many of the people are up in arms over the granting of a saloon license there by the commissioners. They say they will be unable to get strawberry pickers there this year if the saloon is allowed to run; they say also that reckless driving on narrow grades of that section by drunken drivers has almost resulted in several accidents and that the people living up the White Salmon River are preparing to ship their berries from White Salmon instead of Underwood, as a result. It is claimed that at least 90 per cent of the people there are against the saloon and they do not see why they have to send in a remonstrance against it every time the commissioners meet in order to keep it out. There is movement on foot there to have an extra meeting of the commissioners called to revoke the license at an early date. They say if they must have a saloon they must also have a police officer and a jail. A meeting has been called for Saturday evening to take action in the matter.*

Skamania County Pioneer April 27, 1911.

*Twenty-six people came down from Underwood yesterday, bearing a petition signed by 104 residents, asking the commissioners to close up the saloon at that place. They claim that this petition is signed by fully 90 per cent of the voters of the precinct.*

Skamania County Pioneer July 6, 1911

*The county commissioners have revoked the saloon license of Amos Underwood, at Underwood, and given him 90 days to dispose of his stock. Both sides put up a hard fight before commissioners yesterday, and the decision, which was rendered this morning, is in the nature of a compromise between the two factions.*

Skamania County Pioneer – July 6, 1911

## Saloon and Alcohol Issues  (continued)

**Amos Underwood – on right- in his saloon along with Lundy Stewart**
Gorge Heritage Museum Archives
\*\*\*\*\*\*\*\*\*\*\*\*\*\*\*

**Prohibition** in the United States was a national ban on the sale, manufacture, and transportation of alcohol, in place from 1920 to 1933. The dry movement was led by rural Protestants in both political parties, and was coordinated by the Anti-Saloon League. The ban was mandated by the Eighteenth Amendment to the Constitution, and the Volstead Act set down the rules for enforcing the ban and defined the types of alcoholic beverages that were prohibited. Private ownership and consumption of alcohol was not made illegal. Prohibition ended with the ratification of the Twenty-first Amendment which repealed the Eighteenth Amendment, on December 5, 1933.
*Wikipedia definition of Prohibition*

\*\*\*\*\*\*\*\*\*\*\*\*\*\*\*\*\*\*\*\*\*\*\*\*\*\*\*\*\*\*\*\*

Washington State was ahead of its time.

## Prohibition Law Constitutional
*Washington State goes dry January 1, 1916. The people so voted on initiative bill No. 3 at the general election in 1914.*

*The Supreme Court sustained the constitutionality of the initiative and referen-dum amendment to the state constitution in 1912.*

*As a result the 1200 saloons in Washington, or as many of them as are still open, will go out of business, also all breweries, and the 8,000 or more men engaged in the liquor business will seek new employment.*
*Skamania County Pioneer – Dec. 16, 1915*

\*\*\*\*\*\*\*\*\*\*\*\*\*\*\*\*

## Hospitalized 51 Years
*A prohibition agent shot George Walther in the neck in 1924. George Walther, now 71, has spent the last 51 years in a Portland hospital paralyzed from the waist down.*

*Officials at Good Samaritan Hospital and Medical Center decided long ago to let Walther stay because of his long tenure as a patient (partially supplemented by a special congressional allowance) and later as a quasi-employee.*

*Congress did not vote an allowance for him until 1934, but the $100 a month came regularly for many years. Later he was awarded about $80 a month in Social Security because of his employment period.*

*Walther was a 20-year old farm boy near Underwood, Wash, walking down a hill with another youth, when federal agents moved in to investigate a still or illegal cache of liquor.*

*One of the agents, G. J. Montgomery, carried a new gun with which he was not familiar. He tripped over a log, the weapon discharged and the bullet struck Walther in the back of the neck.*

*Fred Wise, Walther, and the other youth, Reuben Quarnstrom, were indicted by a federal grand jury in Tacoma, Wash., four days after the shooting.*

*Wise was convicted. Quarnstrom died before he was brought to court to answer the charges. The case against Walther was dismissed, and Rep. Charles H. Martin and Sen. Charles L. McNary convinced Congress that Walther was not a bootlegger.*
*Portland Oregonian (AP) – 1975*

31

## Saloon and Alcohol Issues (continued)

George Walther lived in Good Samaritan Hospital in Portland until he died at age 76. He is buried at Chris-Zada Cemetery in Underwood.

### Fred Wise Sent To Penitentiary

*Fred Wise of Underwood, arrested last week by Deputy Sheriff Edick, was sent to Salem to serve out an unexpired 3-year term in the penitentiary. In 1922 Wise was convicted by a jury here on a charge of murderous assault on officers who apprehended him while he was bringing a load of moonshine across the Columbia. He was paroled on the unanimous petition of the trial jury.*

*Wise last week was convicted in federal court of Washington for illicit liquor operations and sentenced to 14 months at McNeil Island. He had appealed his case. District Attorney John Baker, on receipt of the news of the federal conviction, secured a bench warrant from Judge Wilson. Sheriff Johnson and Deputy Edick took Wise to Salem.*

<u>Hood River News</u> – May 1, 1924.

\*\*\*\*\*\*\*\*\*\*\*\*\*\*\*\*\*\*\*\*\*\*\*\*\*\*\*\*\*\*\*\*\*\*\*\*\*\*

Back to the business establishments of Old Town:

At one time there were three gas stations in Old Town Underwood – a Signal station at the mercantile building, a Union 76 at the Kapp meat market and a Texaco owned by Frank Hunsaker.

### Hunsaker Texaco Station

When there was a town at the bottom of Underwood Mountain along Highway 14, Mr. Frank Hunsaker bought up a piece of property in the 1930s. This parcel was located right on the corner when coming down Cook/Underwood Road and turning right into the business area. Frank was the distributer for Texaco for a number of service stations in the area.

Mr. Hunsaker had three children, a daughter Francis, and two sons, George and Dan. The business was intended as a service station and a restaurant. Mr. Hunsaker bought this with the intent of his daughter running the business. His daughter, Francis Hill and her husband, Bob, ran the service station and restaurant from 1946 to 1950. In 1946 most of the old town of Underwood burned in a fire, including the Hunsaker-owned gas station and café. Frank Hunsaker rebuilt the facility and his daughter Francis Hill ran the restaurant. It was a three story building. The living quarters were in the basement level and included three bedrooms to rent to truckers. During the winter of 1949, truckers were stranded at Underwood so Bob Hill pulled a sled to White Salmon for supplies to feed the stranded men.

*Reference: Mr. Frank Miller Hunsaker, grandson of Frank Hunsaker*

Ray Meiggs and his wife Frieda operated the filling station and Auto Supply store in Underwood from 1921 until 1939, when Ray died. He sold the garage part of the business to John Van Carnop in 1928.

**UNDERWOOD SERVICE STATION HAS NEW FACILITIES** – *Wm. R. Harms, proprietor of the Underwood Service Station, announces remodeling his lunch and barroom run in connection with the service station and that now he has facilities for small dancing parties with music being provided by a large phonograph.*

*He has had the floor sanded and refinished, new booths put in, a new bar top and many other improvements making his establishment one of the most modern along the river.*

*Mr. Harms will continue to serve light lunches, beverages, ice cream, and confections and reports that he will remain open from 8:00 A.M. until 1:00 A.M. There will be dancing every night except Sunday.*

<u>Mt. Adams Sun</u> February 9, 1940

### Texaco Service Station

*Mr. and Mrs. Roy Holman, former Stevenson residents, have (leased) and are oper-*

## Service Stations (continued)

*ating the Texaco Service Station at Underwood. The deal was made with Robert Hill, who continues to operate the café which adjoins the station.*

*Pioneer, December 24, 1948*

In 1958 Bruce (Bud) and Jean Cuffel took over management of the Richfield station, formerly the Hunsaker Texaco station. Janell Harvey was operating the restaurant business.

Ruth Brown, Frank Hunsaker's granddaughter, recalls that in the 1950s her parents took her to the café in Underwood every Friday night for a chicken dinner. Even though others leased the business, the Hunsakers retained ownership of the building. After Frank and his wife died in the 1960s their son George inherited the property. The building suffered another fire in the 1970s and was never rebuilt.

**Hunsaker gas station burning during the Underwood fire of 1946.** Photo from Gorge Heritage Museum archive.

## Underwood Café

The *Mt. Adams Sun* reported that in December of 1964 Jerry Eccles and Sam Hollamon held an open house in their newly opened Underwood Café. They took over from the previous operators, Harry Smith and Margaret Fournier, leasing the building from owner Mrs. Mary Hunsaker. Lola Pothier, Smith's cook and manager continued on with the new owners. Jerry's mother, Mrs. Guy Eccles, was the baker, specializing in home-made pies.

\*\*\*\*\*\*\*\*\*\*\*\*\*\*\*\*\*\*\*\*\*\*\*\*\*\*\*\*\*\*

## Underwood Post Office

Another establishment that existed in the old town of Underwood (until 1996) was the Post Office.

The first United States Post Office in Underwood was established in 1900. Grace Underwood Dark, wife of John Dark, was the first postmaster.

Prior to having a post office in Underwood the mail was brought over by boat from Hood River. The mail was picked up and then distributed throughout the Underwood, Chenowith, Mill A, Willard area. This occurred perhaps twice a week depending on the weather. In bad weather mail might arrive only every couple of weeks.

Jack Kapp recalls as a young boy in the 1940s going over to pick up the mail at this building and bringing it back to his father, who owned the butcher shop in Underwood.

Robert Morby, a lifetime resident of the area shared the following procedure the railroad had with the post office: If no other business needed to take place, a railman would simply hang the mail bag on a big hook as the train passed through Underwood.

**Post Office** (continued)

**Underwood railroad station/post office**

The post office was housed in the Mercantile (Balsiger's) store from 1904 to 1946, when a fire destroyed most of downtown Underwood. The town proper was located at the bottom of Underwood Road along State Highway 14. George Balsiger did rebuild his store.

When the building was renovated (about 1957), the post office was relocated into its own space with its own outside entrance. This is the same building known today as the Underwood Mercantile or in later years, the Underwood Auction. This building is located just west of the White Salmon River along HWY 14. The building still stands today.

Mail service continued at the site for 38 years. However, there was a brief break in

the routine. On July 3, 1990 there was another fire. This fire destroyed much of the Underwood Auction building.

Residents had to pick up their mail in Bingen. After renovation was completed the post office reopened at the same location in October of 1990.

The Underwood Post Office remained at this location until June 29, 1995. The building was up for sale and a new lease could not be agreed upon. Wilma McCarthy was postmaster at the time, having held the position since 1985. She was temporarily reassigned to the post office in Husum, and Underwood residents again had to pick up their mail in Bingen.

The dilemma now was, where to move the post office. Area residents became active in stressing the importance of reopening a post office in Underwood, and how it serves as a bonding point within the community. Sites were suggested such as the Rec Center a mile up the hill from the river. A modular unit was also suggested. If a solution could not be quickly obtained there was a good chance the Postal Service would determine it was easier to simply let the consolidation with Bingen stand.

Finally the Underwood Fire Hall meeting room was investigated as a possible new location for the post office. The Fire Department site began to look most favorable. The Underwood fire hall was owned by the White Salmon Valley School District, and was leased by Skamania County. If agreed, the county would sub-lease to the Postal Service.

Agreement was finally made between all agencies involved. The fire department generously gave up their meeting place and this area was quickly converted into the new Underwood Post Office.

Finally, after more than eight months without a post office in Underwood, the new facility was completed. On March 4, 1996, doors to the new post office were opened to

**Post Office** (continued)

the public. There were now 202 boxes at the new office.

Underwood has one of the few post offices that are open for business on Saturday.

The following is the list of Postmasters for the town of Underwood, Washington.

| Name<br>Date Appointed | Title |
|---|---|
| Grace Dark<br>05/25/1900 | Postmaster |
| Charles T. Robards<br>12/13/1904 | Postmaster |
| Myron Smith<br>06/13/1905 | Postmaster |
| Herbert S. Adams<br>04/22/1911 | Postmaster |
| Charles S. Brannon<br>05/16/1923 | Acting Postmaster |
| Omar C. Claypool<br>11/09/1923 | Acting Postmaster |
| Kendall E. Schweitzer<br>03/19/1924 | Postmaster |
| Omar C. Claypool<br>08/11/1926 | Acting Postmaster |
| O.C. Larsen<br>12/31/1926 | Acting Postmaster |

(Another source – Attwell, has:)

| | |
|---|---|
| Julia Kapp<br>12/31/1926 | Postmaster |
| Clifford W. Cordier<br>05/19/1927 | Postmaster |
| Ruby D. Sooter<br>05/25/1943 | Acting Postmaster |
| Ruby D. Sooter<br>12/24/1943 | Postmaster |
| John J. Roberts<br>10/08/1976 | Office-in-Charge |
| Mary G. Ziegler<br>01/13/1977 | Office-in-Charge |
| Mary G. Ziegler<br>04/21/1979 | Postmaster |
| Wilma E. McCarthy<br>04/15/1983 | Office-in-Charge |
| Wilma E. McCarthy<br>11/09/1985 | Postmaster |

Services temporarily suspended from July 26, 1995 to March 5, 1996

| | |
|---|---|
| Diane Lee Neils<br>04/27/2000 | Office-in-Charge |
| Janice L. Reily<br>09/09/2000 | Postmaster |
| Elizabeth A. Phillips<br>01/12/2001 | Office-in-Charge |
| Stephen M. Chambers<br>05/04/2002 | Postmaster |
| Lee A. Roia<br>04/29/2005 | Office-in-Charge |
| Lee A. Roia<br>07/09/2005 | Postmaster |

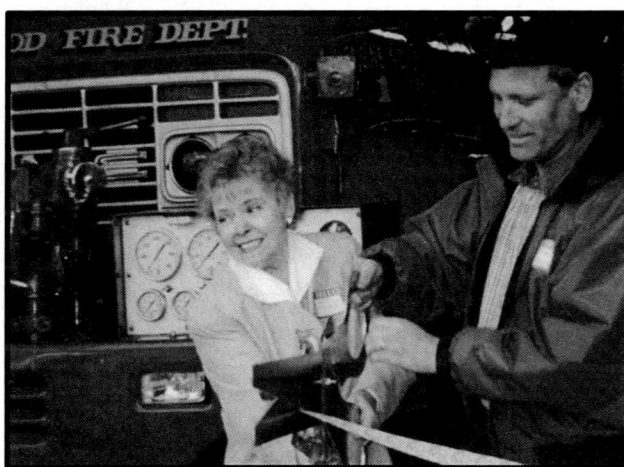

**Wilma McCarthy – Postmaster and Tim Newell – Underwood Fire Chief cutting ribbon at opening ceremony of the new building. Spring of 1996.**

In May 1973 Mrs. Thomas Crego interviewed Mrs. Ruby Sooter for Postal Recognition Week and found that the Underwood Post Office has served the community for 73 years, having been established April 1, 1900, with the first postmaster coming from the Underwood family.

*Ruby has been our post master since 1943, the longest term held since this post office was established. Betty Baker has served as clerk since 1952. Since 1949, the Newell family has carried the mail to the star route customers,*

**Post Office** (continued)

*first Paul Newell, then his daughter-in-law Betty Newell, followed by granddaughter Sharon Newell Bryan.*

*Skamania County Pioneer*, May 4, 1973

Paul Newell took over the mail delivery route from Charles Thornton who died in January of 1949.

*Photo by Jesse Burkhardt*

**SHOULDN'T BE LONG NOW** — A construction crew is working to complete interior renovations in a portion of the Underwood Fire Hall to accommodate a new post office. Skamania County Commissioner Al McKee is hopeful the facility, which will replace the former location on SR 14, will be open for business sometime in February. Underwood has been without its own post office since the end of June.

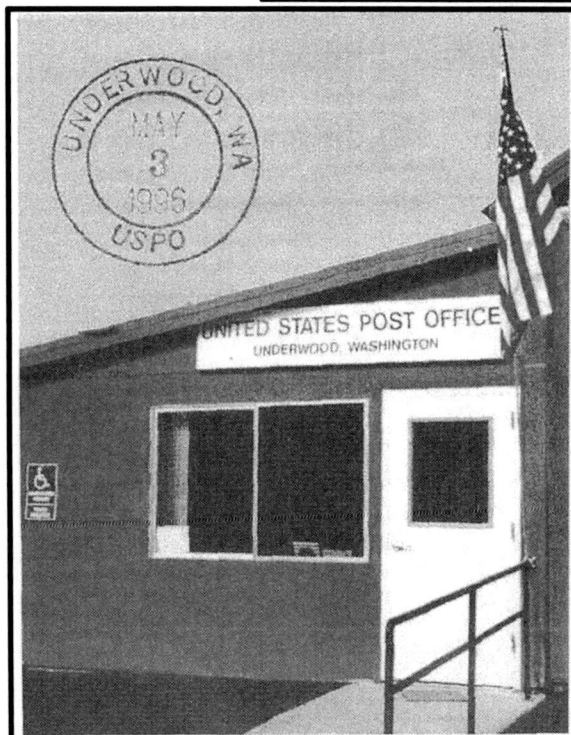

**The Underwood Post Office has been in this location on Schoolhouse Road since 1996. The outside walls were changed from barn red to beige soon after opening.**

References:
The Enterprise – numerous editions
Skamania County Pioneer
Odd's n' Ends by Keith McCoy
Jack Kapp
Robert Morby
Columbia River Gorge History. Vol. two by Jim Attwell
Ralph Brown

## Underwood Fruit Warehouses

A chronology derived from local news reports tells the story of the fruit warehouses located in historic lower Underwood. There were also fruit packing houses on Underwood flats and heights.

April 1908 – Mordicai Jones (of Husum area) has secured 100 X 100 feet adjoining the railroad track on which he will erect a cold storage plant. His immense orchard has only commenced to bear, but it is believed and hoped that he will erect a sufficiently large plant to care for the hundreds of acres of other orchards soon to come into bearing.

October 1910 – the Apple Growers Union have their new warehouse completed and filled with apples. They are now loading the railroad cars for shipment east.

April 1923 – Underwood, Wash., has developed into one of the heaviest apple-shipping points in the mid-Columbia vicinity. Three large warehouses, with a combined storage capacity of 160,000 boxes have been constructed by the Underwood Fruit and Warehouse association, the Mount Adams Orchards company and Dan Wuille Co.

August 1924 –The Underwood Fruit and Warehouse Company has just completed a cold storage warehouse with a capacity of 50,000 boxes of fruit. A large refrigerating plant has a capacity of manufacturing 22 tons of ice every twenty-four hours. The warehouse occupies 350 feet of frontage along the S.P.& S. railroad tracks.

October 1924 – Underwood suffered a $75,000 loss by fire which broke out in the new fruit warehouse. It was believed a short-circuit in the wiring is responsible for the fire. Fire trucks from Hood River could not save the big new building, but were able to save the surrounding property.

April 1925 – The Underwood Fruit and Warehouse Co. began immediately to rebuild and enlarge its refrigerated warehouse. The following Underwood, Husum and Gilmer, Wash. growers operated the company: The Mt. Adams Farm Co., J.E. Slade, A.J. Haynes, F.W. Ariss, H.K. Love, C.W. Gibbs and Dr. H.L. Geary. The Mt. Adams Farm Co., which had the largest acreage of d'Anjou pears in the northwest, put an estimated 100,000 boxes of pears through the new refrigerated plant.

May 1925 – Work of rebuilding the Underwood Fruit Growers Warehouse was delayed on account of the inability of the company to secure a satisfactory lease from the railroad company.

July 1928 – The Underwood Fruit and Warehouse Co. elected the following officers at their annual meeting: B.A. Perham, Yakima, Pres., F.W. Ariss, Portland, Vice Pres., J.E. Slade, Hood River, Sec.-Treas., Roy Anthon, Underwood, manager. They are building an addition to their plant, making the length of the building about 650 feet.

June 1929 – Papers were filed in Olympia naming local people as the incorporators and owners of the Growers Service Company, Inc. W.L. McCutchan and Mrs. McCutchan of Underwood and Ira E. Hyde of White Salmon, the incorporators, are all well known to the growers of the Underwood, White Salmon and Husum localities. The properties included in the deal were the McCutchan packing plant and warehouse at Underwood, the McCutchan packing plant at Husum and the cold storage plant and packing house at Bingen, formerly owned by Baker and Coe.

July 1931 – The Underwood Fruit and Warehouse Co. increased its cold storage space by 40 percent because of the increasing pear production in this district.

June 1936 – A new storage room was being built at the Underwood Fruit and Warehouse Co. Foreman Floyd Turk says the building is to be 200 feet long.

*The Enterprise*, August 21, 1942 – Manager Roy Anthon, due to a labor shortage, called for full or part time help so the fruit would not go to waste.

*"Local people, no doubt, will want to help save the fruit crop of this district, and those who are busy during the day can be of great help to us by working on shifts of three hours in the evening."*

## Underwood Fruit Warehouses
(continued)

**Fire at the Underwood Fruit and Warehouse**

Photo from Gorge Heritage Museum Archives

June 30, 1955 – *Fire, which broke out shortly before mid-night Monday night still flared late Wednesday after having wiped out all except 150 feet of a 1000-foot-long warehouse of Underwood Fruit and Warehouse Co. H.D. Couch, manager of the fruit warehouse said there was no fruit in the structure which was 40 feet wide, extending along the Spokane, Portland & Seattle railroad tracks. Sawdust insulation in the walls of the cold storage section gave a hundred firemen a stubborn battle. A 20-mile-an-hour easterly wind helped drive the flames through the plant. Firemen dealt with heavy smoke, a brush fire on the bluff and burning railroad ties.*

*The loss was estimated so far at $600,000 by John Bloxom, Yakima, one of the owners. The plant is owned by the Bloxom family and it is fully insured. The bulk of the operation was pear packing, serving a number of smaller orchards and the mammoth Mt. Adams Orchards Co. winter pear orchard*

*north of White Salmon, also owned by the Bloxom family. All records of the plant operation since 1923 were destroyed, since the office was completely burned.*
  *The Enterprise*

By 1957 the Underwood Fruit and Warehouse Company had built a plant in Bingen, Washington and moved away from Underwood.

A warehouse building apparently remained in Underwood, because there is this report of another fire:

October 19, 1989 – The Underwood Fruit and Wholesale Warehouse, located near Underwood, was destroyed by fire which was started by sparks from railroad grinding equipment. Smaller brush fires threatened homes on the bluffs overlooking the burning building, but no major damage was reported.
  *The Enterprise*

**Fruit Warehouses** (continued)

Above from Helen Paulus
Below from Bob Miller & Sally Newell

**Early fruit box labels**

## Spring Creek Fish Hatchery

Spring Creek National Fish Hatchery is located on State Highway 14, two miles west of the White Salmon River and Cook/Underwood Road.

In 2001 the hatchery celebrated its 100th anniversary. The history of the hatchery begins even earlier. In 1871, Congress organized the U.S. Bureau of Fisheries to study the fishery stocks, which were already declining due to the demise of commercial overharvesting in the 19th Century.

People throughout history have valued the worth of Columbia River salmon for a variety of reasons--cultural, economical, recreational, ecological and as a food source. However, people made choices that detrimentally affected salmon and their aquatic habitat. Hatcheries were established to mitigate the effects of human activities on salmon and by supplementing declining populations. Federal fish hatcheries have operated in the Pacific Northwest for more than 100 years, with fisheries managers and biologists constantly learning and improving the process of propagating salmon.

Native Americans along the Columbia believed that the salmon represented supernatural beings who sacrificed themselves to feed the people. The salmon's bones were returned to the water so the beings could return the next season. For this reason, Native Americans placed a spiritual value on salmon, relying on the returns for the nourishment of life. The symbolic value of salmon is seen in native art, and heard in story and song.

Concerns about over-fishing along the Columbia River led to the building of salmon-breeding stations to supplement declining salmon returns through artificial propagation. In the fall of 1896, streams on both sides of the Columbia River between Viento and Celilo Falls were surveyed as possible sites for auxiliary stations for taking and eyeing salmon. The Big White Salmon River showed good prospects. The Big White Salmon River historically contained both spring and fall chinook salmon runs.

**SALMON CAPTURED** – Chinook salmon were trapped at the White Salmon River beginning in the fall of 1897 and eggs were collected and incubated.

A hatching station had been set up at the mouth of the Little White Salmon River, and in the fall of 1901, two large racks and a downstream trap were constructed at the mouth of the Big White Salmon. Spawned eggs were brought by rowboat to Spring Creek, two miles down-river, because it had a clean and cold spring-water supply. Temporary troughs were set up under tents at Spring Creek and incubation began. The hatching site was known as the Big White Substation. In 1944, the name changed to Underwood Station, and in 1951 was renamed the Spring Creek National Fish Hatchery.

In the late spring of 1902, the first offspring of chinook salmon reared in Spring Creek water were released as fry into the Big White Salmon River. However, an undetermined number of fry accidentally escaped into Spring Creek. Three or four years later, fall chinook were observed trying to enter Spring Creek, but were unable to do so because of a rock ledge which prevented their entry into the creek

**Spring Creek Fish Hatchery** (continued)

channel. The crew hastily surrounded the few salmon that were there and placed them in the creek. Spawn was collected and that began the first of the Spring Creek stock.

**FIRST BUILDINGS** The earliest known structures were a hatching house and a mess house. By 1919, the forms were set for the first known residence on site called the cottage.

It is uncertain exactly when permanent structures were constructed at the Big White Substation along Spring Creek. Likely they were erected around 1910. The railroad along the north bank was finished in 1908, and a highway was completed in 1920. Prior to that, most transportation was accomplished by boat. According to the 1915 log book, a hatching house and mess house were on site.

By 1922, a foreman's house referred to as the cottage, was being lived in. The cottage was finally finished between 1927 and 1929 but electricity didn't arrive until 1933. With the completion of Bonneville Dam in 1938, the pool behind the dam began to rise and caused many flooding problems at the hatchery. Bonneville Dam

engineers re-established the station by moving the hatchery building, constructing a new fishway into Spring Creek, and rearranging ponds, grounds and equipment.

**EARLY YEARS – This aerial shot was taken during its early years. The facility has undergone many changes over the last 100 plus years. The round ponds were removed during 1968-1972 reconstruction project.**

The 1948 flood damaged buildings and washed silt and gravel into the concrete ponds. In 1953, the construction of four residences, ten circular rearing ponds with water supply and circulation systems, and a new fish ladder was completed. By 1960, a power crowder, a fence-like mechanism used to force fish into a spawning building, and lift were installed to facilitate handling adult salmon. In 1968, the Army Corps of Engineers began developing plans for enlarging Spring Creek NFH as part of the mitigation program associated with The Dalles and John Day dams. The construction project included 44 rearing ponds, a mechanical building, a spawning-visitor center and food storage facility, filtration beds for the water reuse system, and installation of 176 Heath incubators. The project was completed by 1974, and except for minor modifications remains the same today.

**Spring Creek Fish Hatchery** (continued)

Spring Creek is the only hatchery in the Pacific Northwest that raises a genetically pure Tule fall chinook that originated in the Big White Salmon River. Today the production capacity at Spring Creek is 15 million smolts.

Photos: **SPRING CREEK NFH - as we see it today.**

Sources:
100 Years of Hatcheries Along the Columbia River by Gaelyn L. Olmsted. Research assistance: Cheri Anderson, Debbie Hogberg, Ed LaMotte

## Western Fish Nutrition Lab

While the fish lab at Willard is not located in Old Town Underwood, it is related to the Fish Hatchery and Dr. Halver and his family lived in Underwood for many years.

### Willard Fish Lab
By Dr.John Halver

The Western Fish Nutrition Laboratory was established by the US Fish and Wildlife Service in 1950 to determine the nutritional requirements of Chinook Salmon as part of the mitigation process for loss of spawning areas by construction of the Columbia River Dams.

Economic diets were required to rear the millions of salmon being reared by the many hatcheries involved in the Columbia River Development program of the US Army Corps of Engineers. Exact dietary requirements were not known at that time. Therefore the WFNL had the task, the equipment and the staff to determine the qualitative and quantitative requirements of the salmon for the vitamins, amino acids, proteins, fats, minerals and carbohydrates needed to raise healthy fish. The lab was constructed on the Little White Salmon River site at Willard beginning in 1950 and was put into operation in the summer of 1953. In the interim, work was begun at the University of Washington until the final staff and equipment was available at the Willard site. A team of scientists expert in the various nutrition fields was assembled and research projects yielded data on the dietary needs of the salmon. After 7 years, enough data were discovered to allow guidelines for the manufacture of effective economical diets for the many federal hatcheries involved. The data and diets made were soon adapted for use with other species of salmonids, and then extended to other fish types as well.

Then in 1960 a major outbreak of liver cancer occurred in trout in the USA and in Europe. The cause was not known and the WFNL was given the task of solving that problem. The facilities were expanded and the team discovered that the cause was a mold toxin in the feed ingredients. Results of this discovery were applied world-wide, and the techniques developed are still used today to eliminate this cancer causing compound in animal and human foods.

Field stations of the WFNL were established at Hagerman, Idaho to use the amply constant temperature water of the Thousand Springs area, and a salt water station was built at Marrowstone Point on Puget Sound.

In the period of 1953 to 1975 over 150 scientific papers were published on the discoveries made at the laboratory by the many scientists who worked together to determine the nutritional requirements.

In 1975 it was decided that enough nutritional work had been completed to warrant focus of the laboratory in other areas of biology. As a result the WFNL was moved to the Hagerman Site, and the Willard site soon became the central Columbia biological laboratory, which is now operated by the US Geological Service. The Hagerman laboratory was then turned over to the University of Idaho to continue research in this area.

**Fish Nutrition Laboratory at Willard**

John Halver was promoted to Senior Scientist in Nutrition for the US Fish and Wildlife Service with an office at the University of Washington in Seattle for the period of 1975 - 1978, when he was then recruited

43

as Professor of Nutrition in the College of Fisheries, and remained in Seattle to teach and conduct research.

Research findings at the WFNL and in John's projects in Seattle and around the world have formed the basis for understanding and applying nutritional biochemistry to both practical and health related phenomenon. Results have been used in formulating effective diets for raising many species of fish and shrimp. Other work has provided recommendations for vitamin, protein, fat and mineral dietary levels for animal and human health. A recent study has identified a modified fat oil that can be used to stop brain cancer growth.

\*\*\*\*\*\*\*\*\*\*\*\*\*\*\*\*\*\*\*\*\*\*\*

### Fire of May 5, 1946

In a matter of hours nearly all the buildings in the lower old town of Underwood were destroyed by fire. Those structures along the river side of the highway were spared – the railroad station, the livery building, the fruit warehouses, and the fish hatchery west of town. The greatest loss perhaps was the historic 1905 three-story Underwood hotel.

From *The Enterprise* May 10, 1946:

*An uncontrolled fire burned the town of Underwood to the ground Sunday morning. Fire departments from Bingen, White Salmon and Hood River fought the blaze for three hours but seven large buildings, including a large general store, post office, hotel, two service stations, and a beer tavern were all consumed by the huge conflagration which was fanned by a strong west wind.*

*Fire also destroyed four Indian shacks, two residences in Underwood and three cabins. The upper floor of the general store, owned by George Balsiger was composed of apartments and Balsiger stated the fire started in the roof of the store near the chimney. The blaze also destroyed one car.*

*Traffic on the Evergreen highway was stalled for one hour when pumper lines were*

*laid across the highway into the Columbia. A huge crowd of some two or three thousand persons watched the conflagration.*

*Brush fires were started on the Underwood side of the White Salmon River and burned to the top of Underwood Heights hill and sparks started a bad brush fire on the White Salmon side of the river, endangering three homes.*

*The largest loss was the Balsiger store, a three story building, a frame structure some 45 years old. It was built by contractor Robard. The beer tavern and the Texaco station were operated by Vernon Isenberg and his partner Dayle Hall. The hotel was operated by Mrs. Mary (Underwood) Lane. Heinie Kapp stated early this week that his store building would be rebuilt soon.*

*Tuesday George Balsiger was opening up business in the S.P. & S. railway depot which he has leased for the present and telephone lines were strung to the depot Tuesday morning.*

*The big cold storage and packing plant of the Underwood Fruit and Warehouse Co., a short distance west of the business section, and the S.P. & S. railway depot were not endangered.*

From *The Skamania County Pioneer* May 10, 1946:

*Smoldering embers today mark the spot where, until Sunday morning, stood the town of Underwood. Damage totaling over $75,000 resulted from a spark which ignited shingles on the Balsiger general merchandise store, a landmark in the area. Fanned by a stiff west wind, flames quickly spread to adjacent structures and before the last of five fire companies arrived on the scene, almost the whole town was doomed.*

*Sparks ignited one of the two filling stations and for some time, fire fighters feared explosions of gasoline might endanger their lives or kill bystanders. By this time, hundreds of persons lined the highway which passes*

**Fire of May 5, 1946** (continued)

*through Underwood parallel to the river and scores of them were atop the buildings of the Underwood Fruit and Warehouse Co. to prevent the spread of flames in that direction.*

*The Balsiger store, acquired from W. Glover two years ago, was the principal place of business in the town and was widely patronized. The filling station nearest the highway was owned by Frank Hunsaker, of White Salmon, and included a cafe and tavern operated by B.J. Slack. It was reported that both were insured, but not fully.*

*Aside from minor burns and bruises sustained in the rush to evacuate the buildings, there were no casualties. Some 15 persons resided at the 18-room hotel owned and operated by Mary (Underwood) (Olson) Lane. The post office and a meat market and service station operated by Heinie Kapp were totally destroyed. Kapp is a director of the Bank of Stevenson and a long-time resident of the Underwood area. The S.P. & S. railroad station, directly across the highway from the Balsiger store was not destroyed.*

*At regular seasons of the year Underwood is a focal point for Indians from Klickitat county and eastward who sojourn here to replenish their supply of salmon for the winter.*

**Thought to be the old fruit warehouse that survived the 1946 fire.** Photo by Kathy LaMotte

The mercantile building and the Kapp meat market were rebuilt, as well as Hunsaker's garage and gas station. The hotel was not rebuilt. Today the mercantile building is used as a wine tasting facility for Peter and Faye Brehm's White Salmon Vineyards. The meat market building was sold to Harvey Kelchner in the 1960's and is now used for storage by another owner. It is the one story building on the left near the bluff as you travel up Cook-Underwood road.

There is one other building along Highway 14. It is the orange three story residence next to the Mercantile. It is believed to be an old fruit packing house or warehouse that survived the 1946 fire.

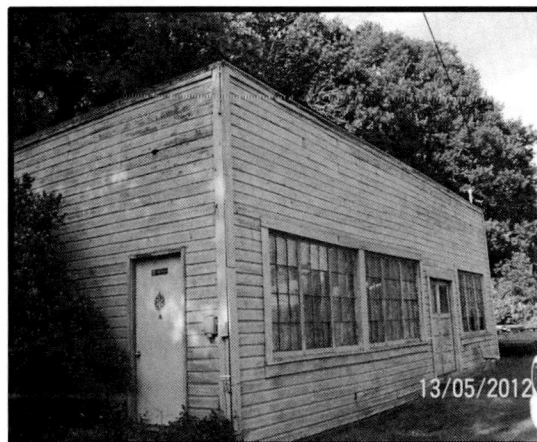

**Kapp meat market building today. Rebuilt as a one-story building after the 1946 fire.**

45

**Fire of May 5, 1946** (continued)

**Balsiger store on the left, Hunsaker service station on the right.**

Photo from Gorge Heritage Museum archives

**Fighting the fire**

Photos from the Bonnie Ternahan collection

**Underwood Fire May 5, 1946**

# Mid-Columbia Town Wiped Out

**UNDERWOOD, WASH.** A thick plume of smoke rises to the sky as flames caused by sparks falling on roof of general store devour small community near White Salmon, Wash., Sunday. This picture of $75,000 fire was taken by ex-Navy Lt. Keith McCoy from vantage point of the Eyrie, White Salmon resort.

From <u>The Enterprise</u> May 10, 1946

# CHAPTER FOUR
# TRANSPORTATION

While the 1896 locks at the Cascades improved travel and shipping for those living in the Underwood area, great strides in the infrastructure occurred in the 1900s. This includes railroads, automobile roads and bridges.

## Transportation: Railroad

The Spokane, Portland and Seattle railroad, also known as the North Bank railroad, was built by James Hill, father-in-law of Sam Hill. Construction of the tracks along the north shore of the Columbia River began in 1905 and was completed in 1908. Workmen were brought from around the world. There were Hindus, Scandinavians, Irish, Chinese and Greeks.

*Skamania County Pioneer* August 27, 1976

The following is a chronology of local railroad history taken from local news accounts:

December 1905 – A number of men are moving rock making ready for the iron horse. Men such as Charlie Thornton worked this winter during the construction of the S.P. & S. railroad between Cook and Underwood. It took the crew a greater part of two years to complete that section, all done by hand labor, even the tunnels.

*Glacier* August 9, 1906 – Residents of Underwood have been anxiously hoping that the railroad company would give them a station or at least a shipping point there. So far there is no indication that it will do so. It is said that the high figure asked for land at Underwood, which is somewhat limited, has decided the railroad company to select Hunsaker's Flat as a shipping point for the country back of it. (Hunsaker's Flat was owned by Jacob Hunsaker, not Daniel Hunsacker, who was no relation.)

September 1906 – Mr. Rock, the blacksmith, and family are new additions to the fish hatchery railroad camp.

July 1907 – Railroad grading is near completion. We will soon watch with eager

eyes for the iron horse with Mr. J.J. Hill's private car.

August 1907 – It appears that the Northbank railroad is planning to place the depot and sidings on the Hunsaker Flat which is two miles below Underwood and difficult to reach by team. This would hamper the large Underwood farming community in shipping their products.

February 1908 – The first passenger train passed over the Northbank road Wednesday containing three coaches with a party of the officials of the railroad. The next Friday the north wing to the east pier of the new railroad bridge across the White Salmon River collapsed. The south wing was also broken. A force of men were working to build something more substantial.

March 1908 – the opening of the railroad through Skamania County was celebrated with an excursion from Portland to Lyle on the newly finished line.

May 1908 – Myron Smith, the Underwood merchant, said that there was a good prospect that Underwood would at least have a platform to load fruit on the North Bank trains and that in fact the train was already stopping to let off passengers at that place. He said it was reported that a platform had been ordered to be built at Underwood and no doubt provisions would be made to load strawberries this year at that place.

The station at Hood, the nearest railroad station at the present, is practically inaccessible to Underwood. There was no road to the place and the only way to get there was to walk down the track for two miles. It lies at the foot of a steep bluff and could not be reached from the top of the mountain above, while along the river there was no wagon road to the place from Underwood.

February 1909 – A.J. Haynes made a flying trip to Stevenson going down on the local in the afternoon and returning on the

## Railroad (continued)

night train. Quite a difference was notice-able. A few months ago it required from 24 to 30 hours to make the round trip and now it could be made in nine hours.

May 1909 – The new railroad depot was to be 62 feet long. The new SP&S time schedule went into effect Sunday. The early train stopped at 4:55 a.m., the local at 9:15 going down river. Returning, the local stopped here at 7:15 p.m. and the other an hour later, so that people could now have several hours in Portland and get back to Underwood before dark.

*Glacier* June 10, 1909 – *The S.P.& S. people moved the mail crane quite a distance west in order to make room for the depot material, which was expected soon.*

*We have already the hinges for the back door on the ground, and if it takes three years to get the hinges, some of the younger people are half inclined to think that they will live to see the building completed.*

July 1909 – Our new railroad depot is already too small to handle the business. After the local pulled out Wednesday night the building was filled to over flowing, while all sorts of freight were piled along the track halfway to the bridge.

May 1911 – F.W. DeHart's saddle pony jumped out of the pasture which was near the railroad and was killed by the fast mail-train.

January 1936 – Postmaster Cordier, of Underwood, was in White Salmon telling about the tunnel cave-in on the railroad. Cordier was worrying about the mail.

**Underwood railway station with 1920's car. Notice the road bridge has a suspension truss overhead, while now it is gone. There is a side rail track, while now there is only one because the train does not stop at Underwood any more.**

Photo from Gorge Heritage Museum archives

**Railroad bridge, but no automobile bridge across the White Salmon River.**
**Built on trestle.**
Gorge Heritage Museum Archives

**Train just east of the White Salmon Bridge.** Otis Trieber Collection Gorge Heritage Museum

D.C. Jesse Burkhardt's book <u>Railroads of the Columbia River Gorge</u> has some interesting photos of building the tracks and tunnels near Underwood. Look on page 50 and 51 of that book.

## Roads and Bridges

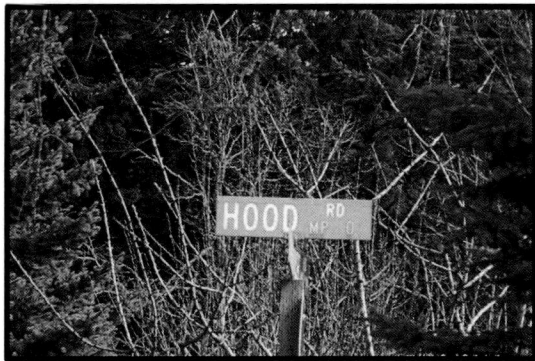

### Hood Road

Many Underwood residents are probably not familiar with a once busy road called Hood Road. Hood Road leads due south off of Schoolhouse Road. After coming out into the clearing, the road traverses down southwesterly, and finishes just behind the Broughton Mill.

According to Cam Thomas, his understanding is that prior to Highway 14, the railroad and Hood Rd. were the only two ways in and out of the mill at Hood. He explained, "Hood" was a flag stop for the railroad. According to Thomas, virtually all the mill workers at the lower mill lived on site. The lower Broughton mill started operations prior to 1923. So we know the road was in place at that time.

Esther Larsen Yarnell recalls, as a child, traveling down the road with horse and buggy, with her mother, in order to visit relatives.

(On a side note): Esther Yarnell was also reminded of a path just west of the cemetery. They frequently used this path down to Mr. Kapp's butcher shop. Her father Aaron Larsen, also used the path for going to and from work at Spring Creek Hatchery.

Hood Road – Sally Newell shared how she used to ride her horse on Hood Road. But she stated that young trees have now sprouted up, closing the upper portion. Her mother-in-law, Betty Wess Newell Boileau, also remembers she used to ride a horse on the road in the 1940's. The road has probably not been used since 1985. Most of the road remains on Broughton property, with the exception of a small portion on the north end being an easement through private property. Cam Thomas stated that Hood Road could be opened again. The lower 1/2 mile is open at this time.

### Husum-Underwood Road

Husum - *Work on the county road between here and the Underwood cutoff is about completed. Under the supervision of Charles Thornton, road supervisor, at an expenditure of only $8,000, the roadbed has been graded for five miles with gravel taken from the hillsides. A remarkable feature of the completion of the highway was that the contour of the road was accomplished without the aid of surveyors, Mr. Thornton using a practical eye for this purpose.*
*The Pioneer - November 9, 1911*

*Underwood heights representatives and ranchers of the White Salmon valley held a road meeting in the Kuhne apple house. An interesting clash has come over the Northwestern Electric highway over the river, up the grade to Underwood heights and then down to the station. Messers. Cash, Love, Packard and others from the heights on the Skamania county side are naturally much interested in the Northwestern's road. That county spent $2200 assisting the company in making the road and building the bridge near the power house site. The Underwood gentlemen now want Klickitat County to re-open the abandoned county road from the Trout Lake road near the old school house to the Northwestern highway near the new bridge, abandoning entirely the present eastside road to Underwood station.*
*The Enterprise, October 11, 1912*

51

**Roads and Bridges** (Continued)

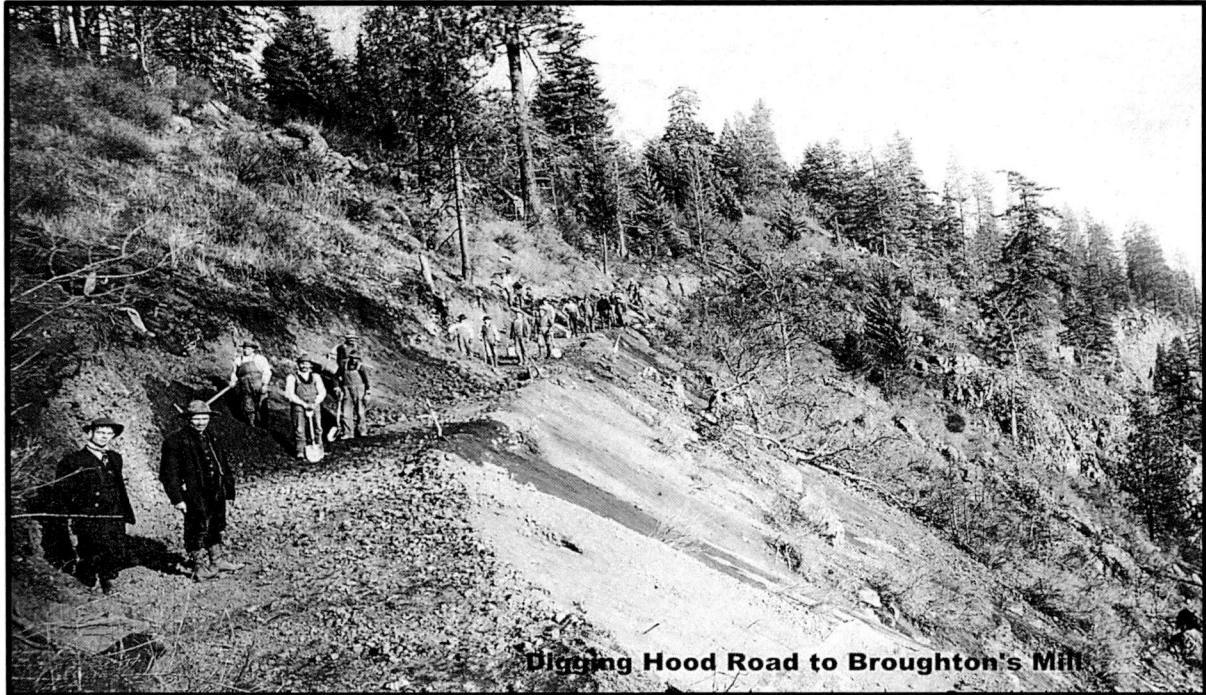

Digging Hood Road to Broughton's Mill

**Dug By Hand!**
Photo courtesy of Gorge Interpretive Center

*There never has been at any time any attention or even a thought on our part of asking the abandonment of the east side road.*

The Enterprise *November 1, 1912-a letter to the editor from Henry K. Love and P.I. Packard of the Good Roads Association.*

**Underwood Mountain Roads**

*William Underwood, the efficient supervisor of the Underwood road district, is having a large crew of men at work and they are putting the county road from Underwood to Chenowith in a splendid condition. It will be leveled nicely and made broader so that our ranchers and those who have contemplated getting automobiles, can have a fine ride on this bluff of the Columbia and enjoy fine scenery.*

Hood River Glacier *May 31, 1909*

The first automobile to visit Underwood appeared in May of 1909. Additional road news of that year was that notice was given that the board of county commissioners of Skamania County will receive sealed bids for the construction of the Mill A-Underwood Road. Ten years later the county had a road cut through what used to be known as Norway, on the northeast side of Underwood Mountain. In 1917 a road was built around the hill to the Henry Love road, giving Mr. Love an ideal road to town.

In April, 1929, Mr. Harvey Kelchner and Mr. Charles Rosenkrantz were busy putting in culverts on the Collins Road.

Many of the roads in Underwood are named for pioneer families. Information about these families is found in the Family History section of this book.

## Roads and Bridges (continued)

### Evergreen Highway/ State Highway 14

*Contractors are preparing for the construction of the Underwood-Hood section of the Evergreen Highway (now State Highway 14), a distance of about two miles. The work calls for the moving of the railroad track back towards the river across from the Underwood store. They also have to cut into the steep rocky hillside north of the fruit warehouse and the making of fills on each side of the crossing over the railroad track just east of Hood which was put in last year.*

*Enterprise February 15, 1935*

March 1937 marked the completion of the Underwood-Cook cut-off of the Evergreen Highway along the Columbia River creating a shorter route for travelers east and west. The closing of the Bonneville dam locks during the remainder of that year, so that the gates, etc. could be installed, was a blow to river traffic. Since the Underwood cut-off was completed, local logging contractors could haul to Beacon Rock where open-river traffic was available to ship to Portland. The haul over Underwood Heights would have been too steep, narrow and curvy to be feasible for truckers.

In the June 16, 1939 *Enterprise* newspaper, the reporter lamented that since the building of the Underwood cut-off along the river, few people now travel the heights road:

*It's worth anybody's time to make the trip again. Just west of the Cummins ranch, from the almost dizzy heights, the view takes in the Columbia River below, the Hood River Valley and Mt. Hood.*

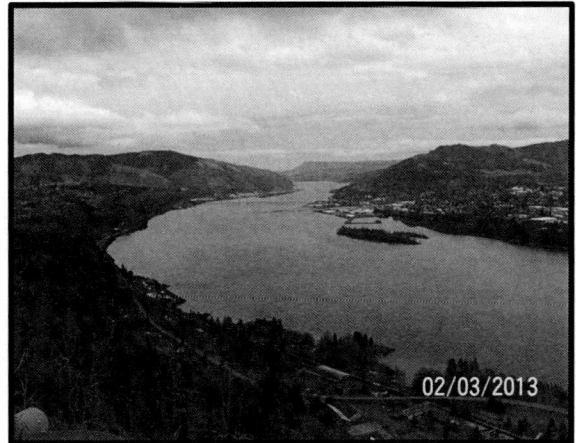

**View looking east from the turn-out on Cook-Underwood Road at Underwood Heights**

In July of 1952 the Underwood Bridge was closed indefinitely to all loads of 10 tons and over. The order was the result of a log truck crash at the bridge due to operating a truck over the legal height. Several vertical suspension beams were cracked and buckled.

**This might be the railroad bridge c. 1907**

Gorge Heritage Museum Archives

**Roads and Bridges** (continued)

**Northwestern Dam  Road and Bridge**

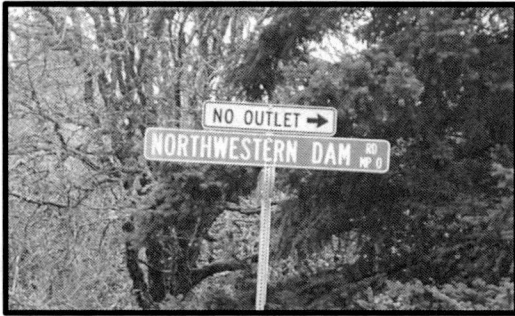

About 8/10 of a mile up Cook-Underwood Road, the first road off to the right is Northwestern Dam Road.

There is a private residence where the road begins, but other than that the road is no longer used for motorized traffic. When the road was created it was intended for travel to link the White Salmon area, and other parts, to Underwood, on the north side of the Columbia River.

Weather and years have taken their toll on the road. The ice storm of 2012 brought down many huge trees, which the county was able to clear.  It is a beautiful walking path that parallels the White Salmon River far below.

**Big White Salmon River down below**

In 1927 a bridge was installed over the Big White Salmon River. This bridge was originally used to span the Wind River at the current location of the Wind River Boat Ramp. The two concrete pillars for the bridge can be seen from Highway 14.

**Pillars used for the Wind River Bridge, moved to the White Salmon River in 1927.**

**Path to the old bridge**

## Northwestern Dam Road and Bridge
(continued)

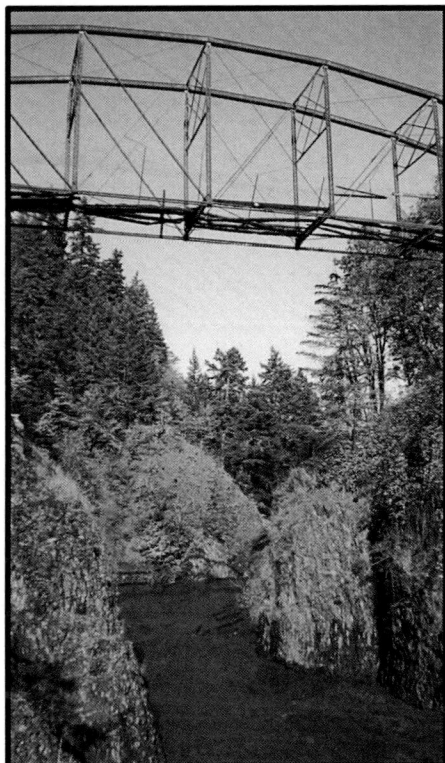

**Remains of the Northwestern Dam Bridge**

It is not clear how the bridge was moved. Most likely it was by boat and then up Underwood Road. The tunnels and that part of Highway 14 were not completed until 1936, so the only alternative would have been transporting up the grade, through Mill A, Willard, and around.

This bridge on Northwestern Dam Road was installed at approximately the same time period as the bridge at the mouth of the Big White Salmon River on Highway 14, with perhaps a difference of a couple of years.

The Northwestern Dam Bridge was used for many years. Some Underwood residents remember it was a necessary alternative when construction or road improvements forced temporary closure on the lower Underwood Road.

In 1976 the bridge was finally closed to motorized traffic. On September 30, 1986 the road was closed to horse traffic, allowing foot traffic only. Then on November 2, 1986 the Sergeant Engineer recommended the bridge be closed for all users. No action was taken for some time.

On July 13th, 1992 the Sergeant Engineer determined the bridge was not structurally sound and once again recommended closure. Finally on June 14, 1993 the bridge was closed to all users. By 1994, the bridge was boarded up and vacated.

Sometime between 2004-2006 the bridge deck was destroyed by fire. The steel frame remains, stretching across the narrow gorge, high above the Big White Salmon River. It still remains a beautiful sight for hikers and river sportsmen.

Research and photos by Kathy LaMotte

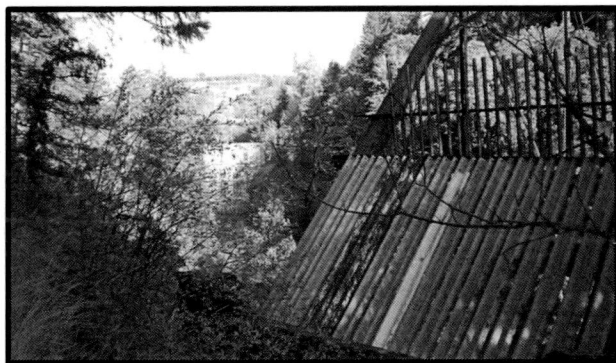

**West end of bridge, now boarded up for safety purposes**

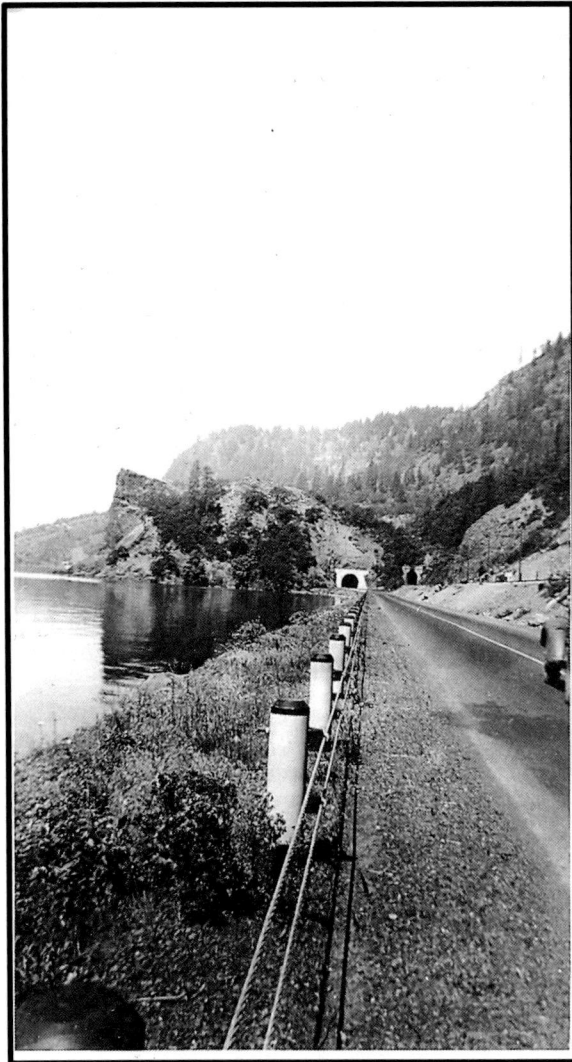

The five road tunnels for years were numbered 1 to 5 going east and 1 to 5 going west, so the far eastern tunnel would be either #1 or # 5, depending on which way you were traveling. Just recently, the numbers have been changed so that they have the same numbers no matter which direction you are going. The far eastern tunnel is #5 and the far western tunnel near Drano Lake is #1

**There are five tunnels, dated 1936, on the state highway between Hood and Drano Lake. The tunnels had to be dug through volcanic basalt that oozed into the river. The five adjoining railroad tunnels were pushed through first to be ready for the running of trains in 1908.**
Photo Gorge Heritage Museum Archives

# CHAPTER FIVE
# COMMUNICATIONS,
# POWER AND WATER

## Telephones

In May of 1905, P.S. Willis of Stevenson put in a telephone line to connect Underwood with White Salmon. This is possibly the first telephone service in Underwood. In June of 1907 the Underwood telephone company had their new line completed as far as Knapp's flat, which is believed to be in the Hood area. However, the Knapps also owned land up the mountain, so the line could have gone in that direction.

In the spring of 1909 the Underwood-Norway Telephone Company, owned by the people of Underwood, installed several new phones and expected to begin work on an extension line into the Little White Salmon country (Chenowith, Mill A, Willard). That summer the local telephone line was incorporated under the name of The Underwood Telephone Company and at a special meeting they elected officers and directors for the next six months. They expected to make a number of improvements in the line and would likely put in a crossing direct to Hood River in the near future, as presently the connection via White Salmon was too expensive.

*The Underwood Telephone Company is about to extend its line through to Chenowith, bringing the people of that neighborhood into communication with the rest of us. With the telephone, rural mail delivery, good roads and automobiles, rural life becomes more attractive.*

*Underwood News section of the* Hood River News *-Sept. 11, 1912*
\*\*\*\*\*\*\*\*\*\*\*\*\*\*\*\*

*In 1974, when moving to Underwood, we were on six party lines. If someone on our line was quite gabby or had lots of children, it made it difficult to use the phone when needed.*

*Thomasina Campbell – Underwood resident*

*We were married and moved here in 1946. We didn't have a phone for a while. I remember it was all party lines for a while. When our first child was coming in 1947, Harley always kept the car parked out front facing downhill ready to go. When the time came, Harley drove up to his brother Lyle's to phone the hospital in Hood River, and let them know we were on our way. We did get a phone sometime after that, but I don't recall that it was a party line.*

*Bonnie Ternahan – Underwood resident*

\*\*\*\*\*\*\*\*\*\*\*\*\*\*\*\*\*\*

*As a kid in Chenowith we had a party line. Our phone was a big wooden phone that hung on the wall. We'd crank the handle and sparks would fly. The telephone operator in White Salmon would come on and connect to the one you wanted to call. We've had a phone here in Underwood now for over fifty years. At first we had a ten party line. It was pretty impossible to try to make a call if others were using their phone. Our ring code might be one long and two short rings. Everyone on our party line knew the codes. So they could just pick up the phone and listen to all conversations. In early years that was with Oregon-Washington Bell.*

*Robert Morby – Underwood Resident*

\*\*\*\*\*\*\*\*\*\*\*\*\*\*\*\*\*\*\*\*\*\*

*There were telephones in Underwood as early as 1905. It was called something like Underwood Telephone Company. It is believed early systems were simply strung through trees running from one house to another.*

*There were a lot of small telephone systems throughout the area at the time. They might be White Salmon Telephone Company, Husum Telephone Company, Underwood T. C. etc. In 1913 many of the smaller systems were*

## Telephones (continued)

*combined and the name was changed to Oregon-Washington Telephone Company.*

*In 1905 Effie Byrkett married Wade Dean. Wade Dean was the main instigator in getting phone lines going from Husum to Trout Lake. The story is that Wade Dean had a stage coach, as did Tunis Wyers. There was competition there. So Dean traded his stagecoach line for the telephone rights in the area. In 1905 Effie and Wade Dean ran the switchboard out of the Carter Hotel in Husum. All calls in the area went through the switchboard at that time. They would take turns at the switchboard.*

*In 1921 Underwood Telephone Company was acquired by Oregon-Washington Telephone Company owned by Wade Dean. It was not a big system at the time. Not all homes had phones.*

*Bob Van Alstine, whose wife Sherry is a granddaughter of the Deans, worked for the telephone company. In the 50s the line was connected along the Broughton flume. Bob helped install the line and would walk the line doing repairs.*

*The telephone company has changed names many times since it was called Underwood Telephone Company. Party lines have long since disappeared and the company now is called Century Link.*

*By Sherry Van Alstine- White Salmon resident*

## Power and Water Come to Underwood

The Public Utility District No. 1 Skamania County, Washington, was created November 14, 1938. Commissioners to serve for the PUD were as follows: Dist. #1 – Clement Akerman, Dist. #2 – J.C. Price, Dist. #3 – Harry J. Card. Harry J. Card was then elected to the office of President of the Commissioners of the PUD District No. 1.

Nov. 14, 1938 – It was the opinion of the board to take steps at once toward the acquisition of the properties of the West Coast Power Company in Skamania County. The secretary was instructed to write to J.D. Ross , Bonneville Administrator, requesting the service of his engineers to make necessary surveys of the property (Skamania County).

July 11, 1941 – Resolution No. 86. A Soil Conservation District has been formed within the corporate limits of Public Utility District No. 1 of Skamania County, known as the Underwood Soil Conservation District. The USCD has requested the aid and assistance of Dist. No 1 in the financing, construction and operation of a domestic water supply system in the area. The establishment of a system for the supplying of water for domestic uses in the Underwood area is necessary and desirable and in the public interest. The PUD agreed to cooperate with the USCD to accomplish this project.

May 16, 1942 – Resolution 110 – It was agreed that the President and Secretary of Commissioners be authorized and directed to sign Assignment by the P P & L (Pacific Power and Light) of S P & S (Spokane, Portland, and Seattle Railway) permits for railway crossings at Hood and Underwood. (*S P & S was completed on north shore of Columbia in 1908, built by James Hill.*) This was an agreement to allow power lines to cross already existing railroad.

*Source: PUD No. 1 and Debbie Hinzman*

## Television Signals From Underwood

**Weak Signal –** Christian Knight
(excerpts *from his article*)

When Olympic swimmer Michael Phelps was butterflying to his fifth gold medal in Athens, the television screen back in Hood River was dead blue, with flickers of formless figures splashing through the water.

In all, an average of 26.7 million Americans per day flipped their channels to NBC during the two weeks of Olympic Games. But much of Hood River, White Salmon, Bingen, Underwood, Odell, and Parkdale simply could not.

Sometime after the Games' first couple of days, something – heat, water, or get this! a porcupine – was interfering with the Ultra High Frequency (UHF) signal that broadcasts Portland's NBC station to the Gorge from Underwood Mountain.

And for that amount of time, the phone at Ralph Smiley's house had been ringing. Ralph Smiley had been vice president or president of Columbia Gorge TV since 1962. In 1962 he attended his first Columbia Gorge TV meeting in the living room of a member's home and as he says, "I opened my big mouth and I've been opening my big mouth ever since. They gave me a big salary: All zeros."

So Smiley headed up to Underwood Mountain, to investigate the source of all those phone calls.

Forty-seven years earlier (in 1957), the late Ted Lehmann plowed a road to the top of Underwood Mountain after nine local "televisionaries" raised enough money - $125 – and received permission from Bingen's SDS Lumber Company to erect a broadcasting tower on a quarter acre of its land. The signal, they believed, would relay Portland's CBS affiliate to the middle of the Gorge. The non-profit organization then hired a 32-year old maintenance man named Bud Chandler, for $100 a month.

By 1960, the tiny translator station was broadcasting four networks throughout the middle Gorge. And it comes almost free. The original cost for the service was $20 per year. Inflation and the increasing cost of

maintenance has forced Smiley to raise the dues. "We charge $30 a year," Smiley says, "While cable TV charges $30 a month."

**Present day tv/cell tower atop Underwood Mtn.**     Photo by Kathy LaMotte

In the early 1990's 1,500 customers supported Columbia Gorge TV with their $30 per year. But that number, in the last decade has dwindled to 200 or so, which has forced Smiley to maintain the signal-sender off about $25,000 in reserves. He knows more people are using the signal than are paying for it.

Smiley parks the SUV on top of the mountain, climbs out and looks up at the huge Washington Department of Transportation communication tower behind him. He then heads down the hill 50 yards, where the red road leads to the Columbia Gorge TV transmitting station.

In the early days, Smiley and Chandler will tell you they'd have to trudge up the mountain in snowshoes whenever the telephones started ringing.

Smiley bends his 84–year old knees to the ground to examine a section of wire with chunks torn out of the insulation.

"Porcupines," he says. "They eat off the ends of the wire's insulation." This, he believes, is what caused the Olympics channel to go out.

At the base of the tower is another source of the problem: a 10 x 10 shack with an uninsulated, tin roof. This is the Translator Building. It houses signal amplifiers for all the stations – UPN, FOX, ABC, NBC, CBS, PBS, OPB, and the Sheriff's radio. Temperatures can reach 107 degrees inside. When this happens, a sensor automatically shuts the translators down to avoid further damage.

Smiley and his fellow board members continued to battle Mother Nature and FCC. They wrote letters for support, while new technology – cable and dish networks – began creeping into their clients' homes. And then, in 1997, the meetings, which started in the upstairs of a local appliance store (Ted Hacket's Appliance), in 1957, ceased altogether.

*Hood River News* – 2004
*Courtesy of Ken Bales and SDS Archives*
\*\*\*\*\*\*\*\*\*\*\*\*\*\*\*\*\*\*\*\*\*\*\*\*\*\*\*

**Power and Water**

Aug. 1, 1942 – Mr. Card moved that the President and Secretary be authorized to sign the switching equipment agreement with the P P & L, for a pole switch on P P & L pole to serve the Underwood lines. Motion was agreed.

Jan. 5, 1945 – Resolution No. 140. Express Building Company, a corporation consisting of Heinrich Kapp and wife Erma, and Carl Kapp, is the owner of certain rights to use water from Little Buck Creek in Skamania County, Washington. The Public Utility District No. 1 was contemplating the establishment of a water system for service of the residents of the community where above water rights were located. It was felt that in order to create the water system, the water rights and land access in question needed to be purchased by the PUD. The Board of Commissioners agreed to make an offer of $3000.00 to Express Building Company in order to purchase the piece of land in question.

Oct. 7, 1946 – Bids on material for the Underwood Water Project were open at 2:00 P.M.

(*The reader may be interested in the price of materials presented in one particular bid.*)

| | |
|---|---:|
| *28,100 lineal ft.4" O.D. Steel Pipe* | *17422.00* |
| *Fittings* | *905.95* |
| *4" valve -8* | *342.40* |
| *4" valves -5* | *214.00* |
| *Corporation Stops* | *63.20* |
| *3/4" Type K Copper tubing – 400 LF* | *94.04* |
| *Iron pipe to Copper connectors -80* | *41.60* |
| *Meters – 40* | *585.20* |
| *Meter Yokes – 40* | *200.00* |
| | *19868.39* |
| *3% sales tax* | *596.05* |
| | *$20464.44* |

Nov. 15, 1946 – the proposed bid from Century Concrete Company was accepted for the construction of two pump houses and of three reservoirs for the Underwood Domestic Water System. One of the reservoirs is for the account of Mr. Harry Card, and will be paid for by Mr. Card.

April 1950, Resolution No. 232. It is wise and equitable to increase the amount of water available to minimum consumers on the Underwood Water Project. *Rates in 1950 were as follows:*
Ist 500 cu. ft. $4.50
Next 500 cu. ft. @30 cents per 100 cu. ft.
Next 1000 cu. ft. @ .25 /100 cu. ft.
All over 2000 cu. ft. @ .15 /100 cu. ft.

April 1950, Resolution No. 233. It appears wise and just to reduce our present Commercial Rate of the Electric Utility. *The rates read as follows:*
Ist 80 KWH used per month @ 3 cents /KWH
Next 180 KWH @ 1.75 /KWH
Next 4740 KWH @ 1.40 /KWH
Next 10000 KWH @ .80 /KWH
Next 50000 KWH @ .50 /KWH
Excess above 65,000 @ .30 /KWH

*All above courtesy of files of PUD No. 1 and Debbie   Hinzman.*

## Power and Water (continued)

*In 1916 some of the fruit growers decided to put in an irrigation system, pumping the water from the White Salmon River by water power wheel up to the first flat. Most of the flume to the pump house was washed away by a flood. The growers decided then to put in an electric pump, the Northwestern Dam and powerhouse being completed (in 1916). But after one year of operation they found that they could not afford the high electric bill, so they decided to take the water from Little Buck Creek by gravity flume. But they made the mistake of not acquiring a right-of-way for their flume from the timber company operating in the upper country at the time. The company was called Norway. When they burned their slash, a good deal of the flume burned up also. That broke up the Irrigation Company.*

*"The History of Skamania County" –*
*Louis Thun - 1959*

\*\*\*\*\*\*\*\*\*\*\*\*\*\*\*\*\*\*\*\*

An article in the September 1, 1922 *Enterprise* reported that orchardist A.J. Haynes on Underwood Heights used O.E. Jensen of Portland to find water by "witching." He dug a well where the "witcher" indicated and got good, cold water at six gallons per minute. For the past twelve years, Mr. Haynes had used cisterns to store water.

*In 1974 the water supply in Underwood was still not too abundant. Six people went to the PUD and explained they needed more water. They were orchard owners. The PUD was pretty good about supplying the orchards first. We were given water but we needed more for our orchards. So we dug a well on up the mountain on our property. It cost $3 every other month for our PUD (power and water) bill.*

*Thomasina Campbell*

A January 12, 1978 news articles from *The Enterprise* told that the source of water for about 50 Underwood Heights households mysteriously dribbled to a halt last week end and then just as mysteriously started up again, but without normal pressure. The main source of Underwood water was Galligan Springs. Water was pumped 1,200 feet up to holding tanks. About 150 households were on the water system. To remedy the situation, other water sources to be considered were Moss Creek near Willard or the Columbia River.

Virginia Wagner Chapman tells about their water supply when her family lived on Scoggins Road in the 1970s. They had a cistern which collected rain water. In the winter the water in the Broughton flume would leak and chunks of ice would form, so she and her husband would go saw off the ice, haul the chunks home and fill the cistern.

\*\*\*\*\*\*\*\*\*\*\*\*\*\*\*\*\*\*\*\*\*\*\*\*

In the late 1990s two new water storage tanks were added to the Underwood water system. SDS donated the land for the tanks, named the "Huber" and the "Connie" tank. Connie Leach was responsible for acquiring a grant to fund the one tank named in her honor. See more information in the Leach family history in part two of this book.

Clyde Leach is currently (June 2013) serving on the Skamania County Public Utility District Board and is the President.

## Northwestern Dam

In December of 1911, The Northwestern Electric Co. began unloading machinery at Underwood, which was moved to the dam site as soon as the repairs on the damaged bridge over the White Salmon were completed. They had almost completed the survey for the power line from the narrows to Camas.

*The Enterprise April 1912:*

*Site No. 3 is now being prospected by the Northwestern Electric Company for its proposed dam on the White Salmon. First the Narrows was selected and a lot of money spent trying to locate the bedrock on the east side of the river. Not finding ideal conditions they moved up to the old bridge back of the Cameron farm and have done considerable sluicing, besides drilling in the bed of the river. In the past few days they have moved up about 1500 feet to "The Jaws," a rock canyon measuring about 70 feet at its base. It is directly back of the Adams tract and where Little Buck Creek tumbles into the river. At this point only a 50-foot dam can be built, says engineer Walsh, while at The Narrows they contemplated a 100 foot dam. Mr. Walsh says all the work is purely exploratory, the company owning too much property to confine itself to just one site. Anyone who will turn in at the school house and follow up the river along a road from The Narrows to "The Jaws" will find it very interesting.*

*The Enterprise June 14, 1912:*

*MEN ON STRIKE AT THE DAM SITE: I.W.W.LEADS 200 MEN IN DEMAND FOR HIGHER WAGES. The men walked off the job demanding an increase of 25 cents to their day's wage of $2.25 for ten hours a day. They also want better accommodations. The men pay the company .75 a day for board. Demands for the additional pay are refused. The I.W.W. put pickets around the dam site, the railroad stations and the ferry landings of White Salmon and Underwood to keep out scabs. The strike fizzled out in a week or two.*

*By June 21, 80 men were back on the job. By August 30, there was a crew of 600 men.*

*The following information is from a Gorge Heritage Museum display :*

The cost of constructing Northwestern Dam was $13,000,000. The powerhouse was named for B.C. Condit, the president of the Northwestern Electric Company. The dam was 125' high. Materials for the entire job were hauled from Underwood by horse or ox teams and motor trucks. Each truck equaled 12 teams. Each team made two trips a day. When weather conditions prevented the use of trucks, the force averaged 80 teams. Labor numbers averaged 900 men. Toward the end of construction, there were 1,500 workers. There were two camps with large mess halls.

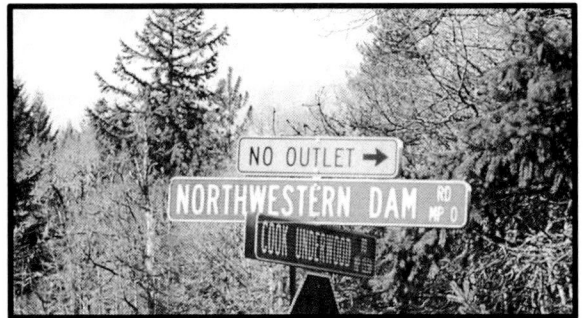

**Now a trail for hikers to the old bridge**

More Dam news from local papers:

September 1912 – the forest fire that has been raging for four days near the dam site is now under control. 150 Greeks from the Stone and Webster camp have been fighting the fire.

October 1912 – there are three distinct operations being conducted by Stone and Webster for the Northwestern Electric on the White Salmon: filling in with concrete, making the way for the 13 foot pipe line, and erecting the power house and excavating for the reservoir. Actual dam construction has now begun with the dumping of the concrete into the bottom of the bared bed.

## Northwestern Dam (continued)

Thousands of feet of lumber are being piled up for use, the lumber being supplied by the Westphal mill a half-mile above the dam. An immense cable carries the lumber and other materials out over the gorge and drops it where needed. The operation of this cable, which is anchored high up on the west bank, 500 feet above the river bed, is one of the interesting sights.

Rock from the quarry on the west bank is carried to a crusher by a scraper operated by the "aeroplane donkey." A stairway of 600 steps leads from the river bed up the face of the bluff to the quarry, outrivaling the well-known Columbia bluff stairway to the town of White Salmon.

November 1912 – 750 men are rushing the work. All hauling of supplies is from Underwood over the new road. The company has erected storage sheds for supplies at Underwood. A couple of Greeks who operated a kind of store quarreled with each other and were ordered off the site by the company. One of them threatened to sue the company for $5000.

January 1913 – 800 men and 76 teams are rushing the work at the dam.

February 1913 – Visitors at the dam were horrified at seeing a man fall a distance of over a hundred feet. While young Laycock, assistant time keeper, was taking pictures he crept out on an overhanging rock, going just a little too far, as he overbalanced and dropped. He was not killed, but several bones were broken, and for a while he was in a dangerous condition.

May 1913 – Northwestern Electric Company is now running the plant. Electrical energy from the turbines is turning machinery in the paper mill at Camas. The project was done in eleven months with a crew that sometimes numbered 1100.

October 1913 – the Washington Industrial Insurance Commission won a hotly contested case today when a memorandum decision was received from Judge Darch, of Klickitat County, holding that a man waiting for his dinner, though at his employer's boarding-house, is not at that time in the course of his employment. The decision denies compensation to Mrs. Kalliopi Hamilthoris, whose husband was killed October 3, 1912, by a rock thrown from a blast on White Salmon River dam work, where Hamilthoris was employed by the Stone and Webster Company.

**The Narrows of the White Salmon River**
Photo from Otis Trieber collection at the Gorge Heritage Museum

**Northwestern Dam** (continued)

c. 2000 – PacifiCorps agreed to remove the dam in six years.

October 2012 – Northwestern Lake was drained in a few hours through a hole bored through the bottom of the dam.

September 2013 - The concrete removal project was completed, causing the White Salmon River to flow freely to the Columbia for the first time in 100 years.

Note: An article about Bill Manly Jr., the former White Salmon postmaster, related that although most people referred to the dam as the 'Condit' dam, it should be called the Northwestern Dam. The powerhouse associated with the dam was named after Mr. Condit. It 'rankled' Mr. Manley to no end when the dam was called Condit, according to his son John Manly. Bill Manley recently passed away at age 92.

*The Enterprise, August 22, 2013*

**below: Northwestern Dam**
Otis Trieber Collection Gorge Heritage Museum

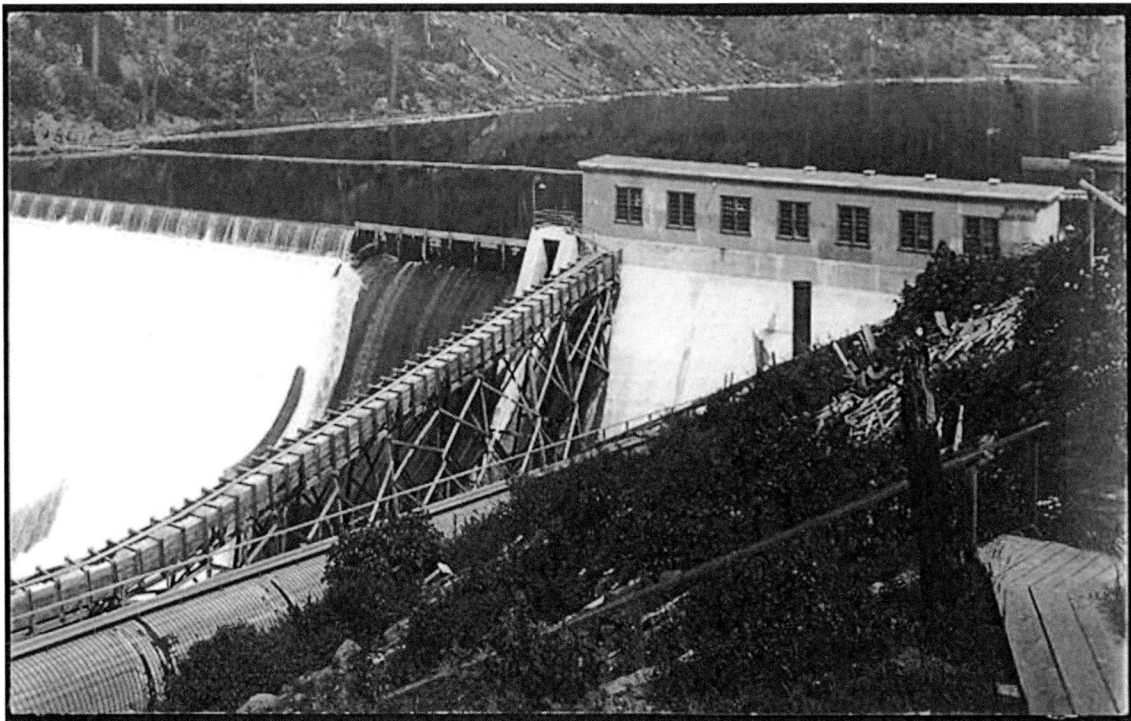

# CHAPTER SIX
# LOGGING

Underwood Mountain is a virtual Douglas fir nursery. Excellent conditions of soil and moisture produce seedlings that are ready to harvest in fifty to seventy years.

A 1901 news journal told this news from Underwood Landing: "Wm. Barr from McIntyre's (lumber) camp informs us that they have been very busy logging and have put in a fine big bridge across the White Salmon just above the old mill site of Cameron. A small portion of the rock dam on the White Salmon River gave way, owing to the recent flood, and delayed floating logs for a few days. We are very sorry for our neighbor Mr. Nicolai. Cameron and Nicolai have a crew of men getting out the timbers to repair the dam."

Louis Thun reported that in the late 1890s Mill B handled logging operations on Chenowith Flat. After that area was logged the company moved over to the west side of the Little White Salmon River on what is now Mill A Flat. By 1907 it was nothing but stump land. Cordwood, which was flumed down to Drano Lake for the steamboats and a shingle mill on Moss Creek furnished most of the employment in the early days.

The *Glacier* of July 1903 reported that, "The Menominee Lumber Company has had a scow and pile driver at the mouth of the White Salmon, driving piling for a log boom."

In 1906 a large mill was built six miles back of Underwood by the Porter Brothers, the contracting firm which was constructing the section of the north bank railroad from Vancouver to Lyle and beyond. They closed the purchase for $30,000 worth of timber in the vicinity of the point where the new mill was located. The lumber was transported from the mill by flume to Hunsaker's flat, a mile and a half below Underwood, where a railroad side track had been built.

In November 1907 the Thornton and Stuart Wood Co. announced it would hereafter be known as the Badger Wood Co. They added reinforcements to their camp,

**Below: Early lumber hauling wagon**
Photo from Otis Treiber collection
Gorge Heritage Museum archives

**Logging** (continued)

putting on thirteen more men and expected to have four teams on the road in a few days. The company expected to put out several thousand cords of wood.

The following are excerpts from various local newspapers regarding logging on Underwood Mountain:

July 1908 – The Buck Creek Lumber Co. is delivering lumber for a new house for Mr. George Sandell.

May 1917 – Hicks sawmill, located on Mrs. Churchill's place, is running full time. It sounds like business to hear the whistle three times a day.

January 1921 – Jake Horne and family moved to Climax Mill, where he will work.

1923 – A small mill was in operation at the present site of the Broughton Lumber Company and was bought out by them in 1923.

April 1924 – Harley Edwards moved his logging outfit to Hick's mill on Underwood Heights. He has a contract to pull logs into the mill this summer. C.W. Berrong, who is logging for R. Waldron at Mill A Flat, near Chenowith, had the misfortune to injure his fine team of horses while yarding logs, one being so badly wounded that its recovery is doubtful.

January 1926 – What has been happening around Underwood in the past few years? A new mill has been built at the Highlands and many improvements have been made at the Hicks and Fagly mill. R. H. Haselton has added a new truck to assist in hauling lumber from both the Hicks and Kee mills. The Climax mill that had been idle for a number of years was rebuilt last summer by Mr. Price and a good business was being done until it was destroyed by fire, which also burned the school house in district 28. Mr. Mickles trucked many logs to the river last summer. Lewis and Edwards were also heavy loggers from this district last summer.

May 1926 – The Porter tract, involving 2500 acres of timber has been taken over by the Washington-Oregon Timber Company for a consideration of about $150,000. This tract was purchased about four years ago by the Express Building Company. The timber will be placed on the Portland market. John Anderson & Co. of Port Angeles and Seattle will take care of the logging operations. Headquarters will be at the camp of the old Climax Mill No 2, which burned last July, and will not be rebuilt. The camp will undergo several changes, including a bathhouse for the men and a garage for their cars.

January 1931 – Hicks Lumber Co. to start a mill at Northwestern Lake. The mill will start sawing in March.

Also in January of 1931, a slide wrecked seven bents of the nine-mile Broughton flume between Willard and Hood. Mr. H.S. Fraley is superintendent of the company.

August 1943 – the Broughton Lumber Co. saw mill at Willard which was damaged by fire last week is being repaired and will be again operating in two weeks according to Wenzel Olson of the company's office at Hood. The Broughton Lumber Co. employs about sixty men at its Willard plant.

September 1943 – Fire Warden Louis Thun, of Underwood, stated that the ban was off on logging and saw mill work in Western Washington.

July 1985 – (from The Skamania County Pioneer)

*Broughton Lumber Company has announced it will suspend operations at the end of the logging season. The decision by the Board of Directors will add 95 full-time employees to the burgeoning ranks of the unemployed in Skamania County. The Broughton flume has been a working historic landmark used to float rough-cut lumber nine miles from Willard to Underwood, and may be the last of its kind in the U.S. General manager Doyle VanDeventer cited the threat of Gorge National Scenic Area legislation and the need to update the mill at Willard as factors considered in the decision to close.*

## Logging (continued)

*The 63-year old operation was started in 1923 by Harold Broughton and Donald Stevenson. As the oldest lumber business in Skamania County, Broughton Lumber has been the largest employer in the east county area and owns 12,073 acres of timber land in the county. The timber holdings will not be sold, according to VanDeventer.*

Stevenson Daubenspeck Stevenson (SDS) Lumber Company owns many acres of forest land on Underwood Mountain. Many residents from Underwood are now or have been employed by the company through the years. In addition to bolstering the economy, SDS has contributed to the area in other ways such as the following from the *Enterprise* March 1991 :

*Despite the snowy frost on Underwood Mountain, Columbia High School's football team planted 5,200 Douglas fir trees to help raise funds for jerseys. SDS Lumber Co., of Bingen, contracted the team to do the job for $1200 as part of the company's reforestation project.*

Thomasina Campbell relates that at one time there was a lumber mill at the north end of McVeigh Road. She believes it hired many Chinese people to work there. Was this the Kee mill mentioned on the previous page?

**Below:**

**Steam Donkey for moving logs**
**Otis Trieber collection**
Gorge Heritage Museum

**Logging** (continued)

**Early logging Operation**
Otis Trieber Collection
Gorge Heritage Museum

## Logging (continued)

**Log booms at the mouth of the White Salmon River.**
Photo from Jack Frederick family collection.

**Log dump on the east bank at the mouth of the White Salmon River.**
Photo from the Jack Frederick family collection.

Article found and re-typed by Jeffrey Elmer

The Mt. Adams Sun, Bingen, WA., December 14, 1961, page 1

**"LIFE" FOLLOWS CANOE TRIP DOWN FLUME**

The holiday issue of Life Magazine is expected to feature a two- page spread of Hal Broughton of Underwood and Miss Barbara Jacobson of Portland shooting the Broughton flume in an aluminum canoe.

The pictures were taken on Sunday, Dec. 3, by Ralph Crane, "Life" cameramen from Los Angeles. Before shooting the pictures, Crane and Hal Broughton walked the flume on the previous Friday.

"Life's" interest in the flume feature was aroused by Roy Kraft, former reporter for Life magazine and now editor of the Skamania County Pioneer.

Craft's career also includes a wartime assignment on the staff of "Stars and Stripes" and post-war publicity agent for Marilyn Monroe and Elvis Presley.

The Broughton flume, built in 1921, is the last long lumber flume in the U. S. It takes lumber about 55 minutes to make the nine mile trip from Willard to Underwood. By frantic bailing, Hal Broughton covers the same distance in 45 minutes.

In order to give "Life" complete photographic coverage, Broughton and Miss Jacobson made several trips down the flume.

Crane's favorite shot was taken at a spot where the flume is 85 feet above the earth.

This photograph is from the December 21 issue of Life magazine.

# CHAPTER SEVEN
# WEATHER

The web site *http://climate.fizber.com* states that Underwood, Washington is a good place to live because of its moderate climate. The average minimum temperature in January is 20$^0$ and the average maximum temperature in August is 80.7$^0$. The average annual precipitation is 40.79 inches. Of course, the temperature and precipitation vary from lower Underwood to the heights at about 1500 feet. Between May and October, Underwood is generally free of frost.

Following is a chronology of weather conditions taken from local news accounts:

December 1884 – The worst blizzard on record to date. The Columbia River froze over in places.

January 1902 - Lots of rain but no snow yet.

January 1903 - Recent heavy snow damaged new orchards, especially so in the upper settlement known as Norway where 90% of trees are damaged and some killed.

August 1903 – *The Hood River Glacier* reported that Amos Underwood's big black ferry boat called "Old Betsy" lies on the sands at Underwood landing with a hole in her side. During the high wind last week, the breakers dashed the ferry onto the beach and it landed on a lost anchor.

January 1904 – the snow melted with sun and rain.

February 1905 – Four above zero.

August 1905 – A little rain would be much appreciated here. A severe windstorm blew several large trees to the ground, damaging fences of J.C. Clarkson and R.D. Cameron and several of C.E. Larsen's fruit trees.

Winter 1905-1906 – Charles Thornton remembered this as the mildest winter weather he ever experienced. Not one part of an inch of snow fell.

April 1909 – High winds wrecked the wood chute at Hood.

November 1917 - TERRIFIC WIND
The *Bailey Gatzert* on her up trip, was thrown on a sand bar near Underwood and stayed there until night when she was pulled off by the Steamer *Dalles City*. This was one of the heaviest wind storms ever experienced in this section.

January 1918 – High water has done considerable damage in this vicinity, having washed out part of the Underwood Irrigation Company's flume on the White Salmon River, and driftwood has made the White Salmon River Bridge impassible.

1919 – Louis Thun reported that the freeze, which started the end of November and lasted to the 18$^{th}$ of December with a temperature of -18 on the flat and -24 up on the heights, killed many apple trees, causing growers to plant winter pears instead.

Late November 1921 – Heavy snow caved in the roofs of the Underwood mercantile, the chapel on the flats, the dance pavilion at Shipherd Springs in Carson and many barns and buildings. There was no train service on the North Bank for nine days.

February 1923 – William Lane drove up from Underwood Tuesday afternoon during the blizzard. It took him one and one-half hours to make it to White Salmon. There were two feet of snow. Back on Underwood heights there are seven feet of snow.

June 1931 – Heavy rain storms damaged orchards on Underwood heights. The R.G. Moore orchard had a gully 40 feet wide and five to six feet deep cut through its center by a sudden river of water and mud that developed. Trees at the upper level were toppled over with all their roots exposed, while at the lower section of the orchard, mud and silt covered the trunks to four and five feet above ground level. On the George Reinland farm many outbuildings were filled with mud that washed down the hillside and much of the rich top soil was

**Weather** (continued)

carried away from the orchard. K.W. Kramer, H.V. Rominger and F.R. Frazer also suffered heavy damage.

January 1969 – A storm brought icy tentacles to highway tunnels that had to be batted down by highway crews.

For years Paul E. Newell was the weather recorder for Underwood, reporting to the *Skamania County Pioneer.* Here are some of his weather observations for Underwood:

December 1, 1917 – temperature extreme of -27 $^0$ F.

February 1919 – Hardest winter weather on tree fruits in the Underwood-White Salmon area; day temperature averaged 65$^0$ F. above and dropped to 2$^0$ F. at night during the entire month.

May 31, 1924 – high temperature extreme of 117$^0$.

December 26, 1924 – temperature dropped 58 degrees F. in one-hour period between 3:00 and 4:00 p.m.

1942 – Driest year on Underwood Heights, 19.45" of precipitation.

November 14, 1955 – temperatures dropped extremely rapidly, a 30 degree F. drop from between 4:00 and 5:00 p.m. with a total drop of 50 degrees F. in the 24 hour period (42$^0$ to -6$^0$ F.).

1960 – wettest year on Underwood Heights, 64.15" of precipitation.

Mr. Newell's average annual rainfall records in inches:

Underwood ..... ................46
Compared to:
Portland/Vancouver ...........46
Cascade Locks/Stevenson..92
White Salmon...................36
The Dalles .....................12

Reported in McCoy, The Mount Adams Country

**Columbia River frozen over, ice breaker trail in middle. (winter 1949-50)** Photos from Gordon Baker family collection.

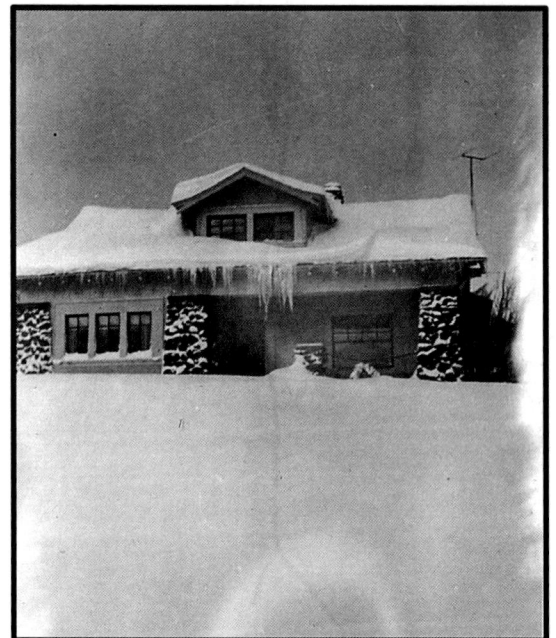

**Gordon Baker house in winter 1949**

# CHAPTER EIGHT
# UNDERWOOD FLATS

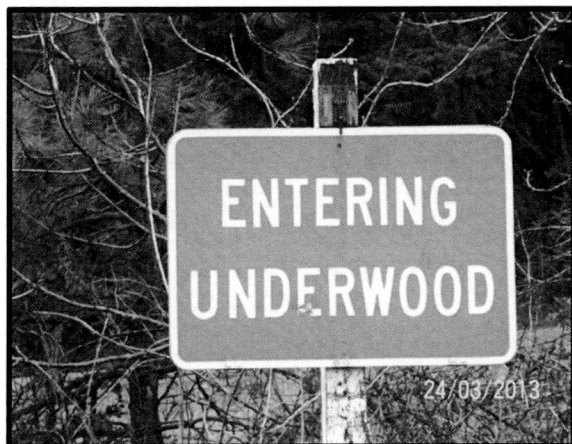

Sign up the Cook Underwood Road. When did "Underwood" change from the riverside to the flats? After the fire destroyed the town in 1946? When the Post Office moved to the flats in 1996?

## Chris-Zada Cemetery

The Underwood Chris-Zada Cemetery located on Cooper Road is named after two young friends, Christina Dark and Zada Larsen. They both died in 1901 of an illness, probably diphtheria. The land for the cemetery was donated by Edward Underwood, grandfather of Christina Dark. There are about 370 persons interred at the cemetery. Ralph Brown, who grew up in Underwood, has compiled a book of obituaries for nearly all those in the cemetery, plus some family members who are buried elsewhere but were connected to this area. Many of the obituaries contain valuable history of the Underwood area.

In November 1906, Mrs. Amos Underwood (Ellen) was buried in the new cemetery, the Indians of the Shaker faith performing the services.

It was Mrs. Underwood's last request to exhume the bodies of her two sons (Jefferson and John) from the family burying ground on the old homestead, buried over twenty years ago, and place them in a coffin by her side. This was faithfully carried out.

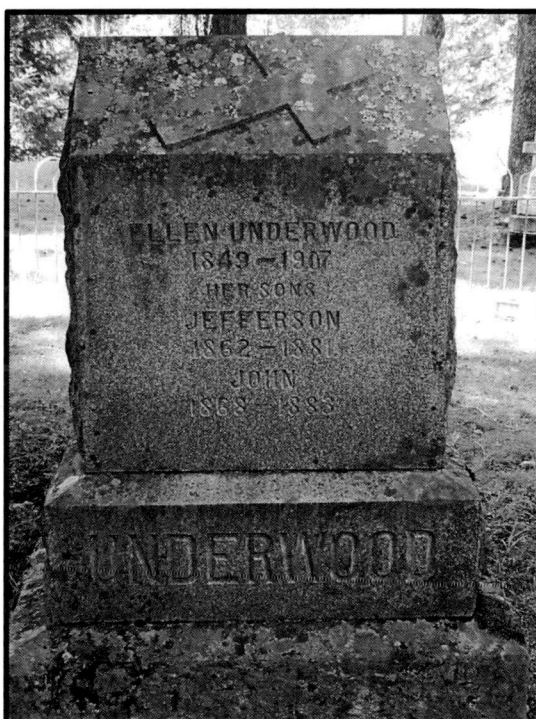

Ellen's tombstone     Photo by Ralph Brown

In August 1907 the newly organized Underwood Improvement Club fenced the cemetery. L. Comini, proprietor of The Dalles Marble and Granite works, came to take orders for monuments. Several sales were reported.

In October 1907 Mr. DeHart placed a nice tombstone at the grave of Grandpa (Moses)Thornton for the Thornton brothers.

In June 1928 the Underwood Uplift Club, a women's organization, gave a dance at the school house. Proceeds were used for improving the cemetery grounds.

## Chris-Zada Cemetery (continued)

In the July 6, 1978 <u>Enterprise</u> article praising Martha Lehmann for her volunteer work in the Chris Zada Cemetery in Underwood, Martha said she had received some donations to help pay cemetery clean-up expenses, but admitted a lot came from her own pocket. She hired workers who were employed at her orchard to do the heavy work like brush removal and mowing. Her parents, Louis and Emily Thun were buried in the cemetery. She said she couldn't stand to see the grounds go to pot. It had gotten to the point where she couldn't even find the markers. The weeds were a foot high. Martha would go to the cemetery every other day to water the plants that people from out of town brought because she couldn't stand to see them die. There being no running water at the cemetery, she would haul milk cartons full of water in her Jeep.

She started the project of making signs for all the unmarked graves. She located about 50 unmarked plots from an old map of the cemetery and she got metal frames from the funeral home to write in the names and dates. Martha got help at times from Reno Ziegler, Fred W. Frazer, Rose Larsen Shepeard and Doyle Pearson.

Memorial Day found Martha carrying water for the fresh plants and also putting extra flowers on those graves not decorated.

*************************

## The Chapel

Louis Thun wrote that in 1916 the Union Chapel Association built a log church on School House Road in Underwood Flats. Land was given by Mrs. E.C. Goddard for a building site. Mr. Thun was off one year because the Oregonian of March 28, 1915 announced the dedication of the newly built chapel. An account in *The Pioneer* of March 17, 1915 describes the new chapel:

*The new building, designed by E.M. Cummins has been completed under his direction, assisted by the building committee, M.S. Smith, R.H. Haselton, G.A. Cooper, A.J. Haynes, H.W. Hamlin, P.I. Packard and by many other people. The main building is thirty by forty feet with twelve-foot posts. The vestibule is eight by twelve feet and the porch over the driveway, ten by twelve. The building is of logs, which stand on end. These logs have the bark left on them. The foundation is of logs laid horizontally on a rock base. The chapel stands among native trees and near it is a spring of running water. Inside, the walls are finished with a wainscoting five feet high and burlap.*

Before that there was mention in a local paper of Sunday School classes being held in 1901 in the Underwood school house, probably a one-room building on Underwood family land. In 1907 a Congregational church was to be built in the near future. Was this the church built in 1916? After visiting pastors provided spiritual help, in 1909 Rev. H.C. Lowden became a permanent pastor. In 1912 the Congregational Church was still in existence, meeting in the school building perhaps.

In December of 1916 there was an annual bazaar and chicken pie lunch held at the chapel. It was said to be a social and gastronomical success. People came in sleighs from Husum and as far as six miles from the surrounding hills and had a good lunch and a fine visit, as well as securing Christmas presents, home-cooked food and candy. The net receipts were over $95.

In late November, 1921, a snow and sleet storm broke down the roof and the chapel was never rebuilt. Services were then held in the new school.

In 1928 Rev. Kendall of Yakima became pastor of the community church of Underwood, presumably meeting in the school building.

**Item located by Jeffrey Elmer**

The Sunday Oregonian, Portland, OR., July 25, 1915, section 1, Included the following photographs and illustration.

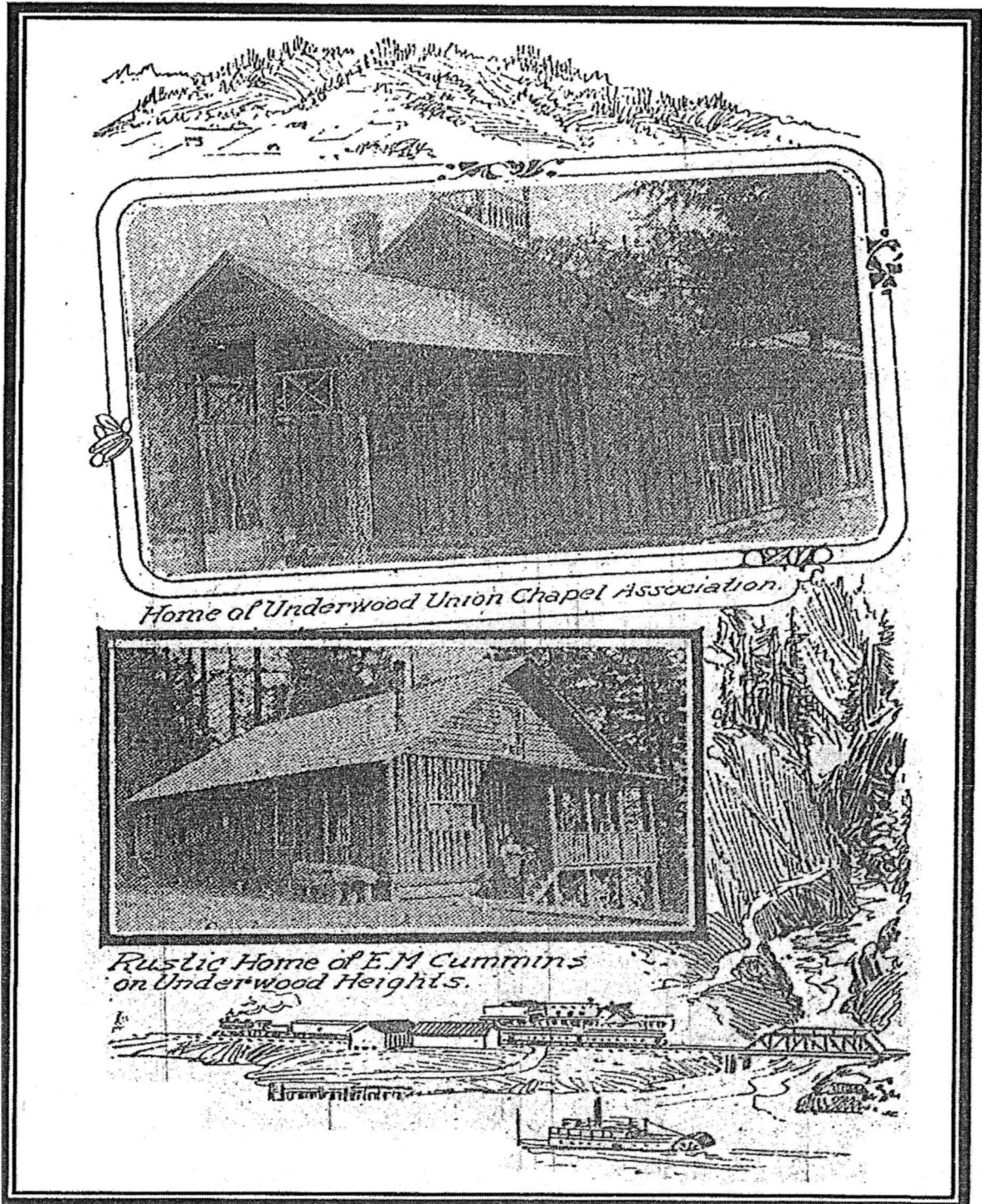

Home of Underwood Union Chapel Association.

Rustic Home of E. M. Cummins on Underwood Heights.

## Schools

The first mention of a school in Underwood that we found was an interview with Mary V. Lane, daughter of Amos and Ellen Underwood, in the *Hood River News* of May 20, 1938. She was recalling her life before the turn of the century. She said that for a time her father hired his own teacher for three months of the year. The Underwoods kept the teacher in their home and used their front room for a school room. Friends sent their children to attend this school in the Underwood home.

Louis Thun told that the first public Underwood school was in a small one-room building built by the Grange. It was soon after taken over by the school district. It was in existence in 1901 according to a *Weekly Journal* newspaper account that Sunday School was held at the Underwood school house. It is thought that the log building was located on property on the corner of Larsen Road and Cook Underwood Road.

*The Skamania County Pioneer* of October 9, 1902 relates that Miss Agnes Moore was again working at the Underwood School.

The following pupils were mentioned: Fannie Haynes, Elnora Larsen, Catherine Kellendonk, Lizzie Kellendonk, Aaron Larsen, Olaf Larsen, Bennie Cline, and Rose Luthy. Perhaps some of them are the unidentified students in the photo below.

Following are Underwood school highlights from local newspaper accounts, most of the early ones from the *Hood River Glacier:*

April 1903 - Prof. Cromwell is the teacher. There will be a school recess during berry harvest.

August 1903 - Miss Phoebe L. Moore of Carson is the teacher. There are 36 children of school age in the district and the school house has a seating capacity for 26.

October 1903 - The school director is A.J. Haynes. Miss Agnes Moore will be the new school instructor.

**Below: Underwood school students with teacher Agnes Moore c. 1903.**
Photo courtesy of Gorge Interpretive Center

## Schools (continued)

January 1904 - Improvements in the Underwood school include a nice greenboard, new erasers and two framed pictures. 100% attendance last month- Fannie Haynes, Elnora Larsen, Olaf Larsen, Aaron Larsen, Phoebe Lyons, Etta Lyons, Hazel Lyons, Maggie Cline and Bennie Cline.

March 1904 - Parents are having trouble getting children to school because of an unusual amount of snow. Mr. Luthy has taken his children either on horseback or in the sleigh to and from school. The reporter thought, "Really the schoolhouse should be moved a little nearer the center of the district."

August 1905 - Underwood school to commence October 2, with C.H. Cromwell as teacher. The district voted a $1000 bond to build a new 42' X 30' school house. There are 30 to 40 pupils in the area.

October 1905 - Mr. Cromwell has purchased the old school house. Mr. Haynes, Mr. Rosencrans and Mr. Luthy have begun the erection of our new schoolhouse. The board purchased an acre of land from E.C. Goddard for the site and he in turn gave the money back to enlarge the school library.

November 1905 - Mr. Luthy left Monday for Portland to buy new seats and supplies for the new schoolhouse.

March 1906 - The bell was installed in the Underwood school belfry.

August 1906 - Mr. Kollock signed a contract to teach here. He will receive the largest salary paid any teacher in the county for a school of nine grades. Eighth grade pupils receiving diplomas were Kate Kellendonk, Nora Larsen, Fanny Haynes, Phillip Finley and Fred Luthy.

September 29, 1906 - School begins Monday. The ninth grade will be added and a new blackboard installed. Professor Kollock comes well recommended, having been principal over sixteen teachers, but on account of failing health is unable to take charge of a large school. Underwood people are indeed fortunate in securing so able an instructor.

March 1907 - Mr. Hamilton, the teacher, and his family lately moved on to his place here.

June 1907 - Mr. Brown, the railroad contractor, expects to finish his grading on this side of the White Salmon River soon. The log school (the building that Mr. Cromwell purchased in 1905 ?) will be left until the Porter Brothers finish their logging.

November 1907 - Mr. Kollock, who has been teaching here temporarily, has been relieved by Mr. Mason, a young man from Idaho.

August 1908 - School begins August 31, with C.H. Cromwell as teacher.

November 1908 - Mr. and Mrs. Bristol and baby, of Seattle, arrived Thursday. Mr. Bristol is to take charge of the school. Mrs. Bristol is a talented musician and Underwood is glad to give them a hearty welcome.

August 1912 - School starts September 3rd with Professor Hedrick as principal and Miss Harold as primary teacher.

## Schools (continued)

87-160-243

New Underwood School   from Gorge Heritage Museum archives

**This school was built in 1905. The bell on the front porch was installed in the school belfry in March of 1906. A new school was built in 1917 and this building was intended to be moved to the new property and used as a gym.**

Thomasina Campbell recalls hearing about an early school up in the Auspland Road area.

January 1912 - A.R. Hedrick was principal of the school and upper grades teacher. A parent-teacher association committee was composed of A.R. Hedrick, Mrs. R.H. Hazelton and Louis Thun.

The McGuffey series of graded primary readers was widely used in American schools from the mid - 19th century until the 1930s, when the Dick and Jane series was published. These were probably used at the Underwood school to teach reading.

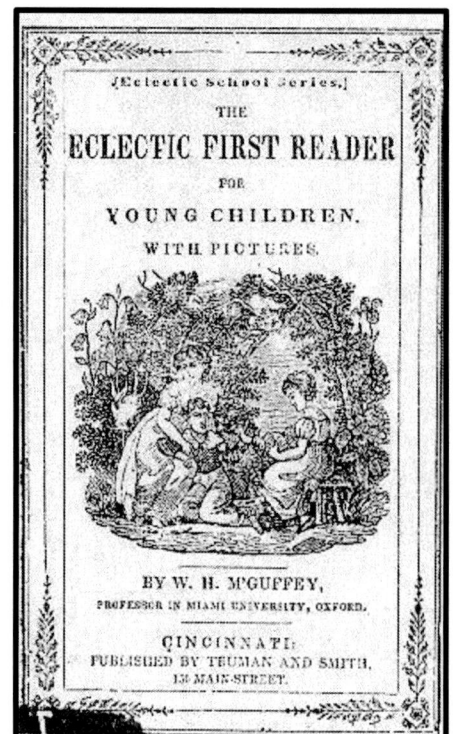

[Eclectic School Series.]

THE
ECLECTIC FIRST READER
FOR
YOUNG CHILDREN.
WITH PICTURES.

BY W. H. M'GUFFEY,
PROFESSOR IN MIAMI UNIVERSITY, OXFORD.

CINCINNATI:
PUBLISHED BY TRUMAN AND SMITH,
150 MAIN-STREET.

**Schools** (continued)

c.1912 Underwood schoolhouse on corner of Cook Underwood Road and School-house Road.

1st row left to right: ? Carson, Henry Kapp, Frances Walther, ?Carson, Fred DeHart, Clyde Veach, Alfred DeHart, Carl Kapp, Curtis DeHart.

2nd row left to right: Mae Lusk, Betty Kapp, Violet Walther, Isabel Haynes, Dorothy Cash, Katie Walther, Margaret Lake?, George Walther, Dale Lusk, Lewis Larsen

3rd row left to right: Amos Larsen, John Collins, Ellis Collins, Roland Cash, Wiley Veach, teacher Miss Harold, Principal Hedrick, Charlie DeHart.

Photo from Gorge Interpretive Center
Museum in Stevenson

## Schools (continued)

March 1916 - Keen interest is being taken in the Parent-Teacher Association lately organized in Underwood. The question as to whether or not the school board should be authorized to purchase five acres of land for school grounds was voted upon by the people of Underwood at the regular school election, and carried by an overwhelming majority.

September 1917 - Mrs. Frances Caswell Hanna of North Yakima is the new principal and Miss Carolyn Kraft of Seattle returns as primary teacher. Mrs. Cora Tichnor Jones of Vancouver is in charge of the school at Hood.

November 1917 - The teachers enjoyed a treat of bear meat, compliments of the Lusk family. The fine **new school building** was occupied November 12. The Mission style frame building is 47' X 68' with a concrete foundation. There are three classrooms, a domestic science laboratory, two dressing rooms and a furnace room with a wide hall extending through the building. Between two of the classrooms are accordion doors which can be turned back to form a commodious assembly hall. The building has sanitary plumbing. It is the plan to move the old building onto the grounds for a gymnasium and manual training work.

February 1918 - Owing to the dampness of the Chapel, it was found desirable to move the piano to the school house. The accordion doors were thrown back and a dance was held to raise money to purchase the piano. Music was provided by Mr. Keyes of Bingen, Louis Thun, Mrs. Frances Caswell Hanna and Charles Davidson. (When the White Salmon School District acquired the Underwood school in about 1946, the piano was taken to White Salmon, causing bad feelings on the part of some Underwood residents.)

March 1918 - Mrs. Cora Tichnor Jones is the teacher at the Hood school. Underwood school is one of the first in the district to have a Junior Red Cross auxiliary. A flag honoring those who are serving in the military is hung in the school with a star for each of the following: Arnold Barton, Roy Beals, Fred Brock, James Calkins, James Chib, Roland Cash, Ellis Collins, Arthur Collins, Claude Davidson, Samuel Hanna, Frank Hogue, Henry Husky, Foster Irwin, Delmar Judy, Harvey Kelchner, Roy Lyons, Raymond Moore, Walter McNutt, Walter Nichaus, Joe Pitt, Allan Porter, Ben Tubbs, Bert Tubbs, Elmer Tubbs, Wylie Veach and Haley Witheronx.

The Underwood school teachers are Mrs. F.C. Hanna and Miss Carolyn Craft.

November 1918 - The enforced vacation (from the flu epidemic?) cancelled the Halloween and Thanksgiving programs. By Christmas, fundraisers were held to meet the pledge to the War Work Fund.

The board of directors purchased the first set of International Encyclopedias. Henry Love and his mother Mrs. Patsy Love gave the school library a set of Dickens and several other volumes of first class fiction as well as a beautiful room picture, a Holland scene.

The Lusk family has moved to Moro, Oregon. School boys Lee, Clarence and Ollie will be missed. The 6th grade pupils Julia Kapp, Frances Walther and Carl Kapp, having done extra work, will be permitted to continue their reading work with the 7th grade.

June 1922 - Those graduating from 8th grade are Marguerite Cole, Naomi Hunter and Louise Walther.

August 1922: J.B. Dickover, a contractor of Underwood, will work on alterations to the present school building. It will be raised up and a full story added underneath. The cost will be $5,410.

## Schools (continued)

**Underwood School and Gym 1928. Originally one story, elevated in 1922.**
Photo courtesy Lester L. Davis, a student there from third grade to eighth grade.

## More School news from local papers:

August 1928 - Mr. and Mrs. Earl Mansfield arrived in Underwood and have taken up their residence in the teacher's cottage. Mr. Mansfield is the new principal of our school and Mrs. Mansfield will teach the primary grades. Our school building has been repainted outside and in and presents a very neat appearance.

January 1929 - Mr. and Mrs. Mansfield are the teachers.

February 1931 - The new Underwood school gym is almost finished. The lights are all put in and half the floor is laid. The school children can hardly wait until it is finished.

March 1931 - the primary teacher is Mrs. Ingham. The upper grades elected new officers to take care of the room. They are Charles Kramer, Cleo Larsen, Frances Frazer, Ivan Larsen and Esther Larsen. There was a basketball tournament. Underwood beat Carson and Stevenson.

March 1931 - Mr. Howard Ericson was elected to succeed Mr. R.H. Haselton as school director. Sadly, also In 1931 Native American Bessie Quiemps (also spelled Quaempts) of Underwood wrote the Yakama agency "to report the trouble of my little boy in school. The teacher beat him on the head and face in a fit of temper." (Fisher, p. 144)

June 1933 - Eight pupils from Underwood School eighth grade received diplomas. They are Fred Berrong, Frances Frazer, Charles Kramer, Ivan Larsen, Bessie Schwinge, James Severs, Josephine Wess, and George Woosley.

March 1937 - School board elections resulted in Harry Card being chosen to replace Cliff Cordier, retiring member.

March 1941 - Fred Frazer and Clifford Cordier, of Underwood, were elected to the directorship of the Underwood School district for a three year term of office.

September 1941 - Mrs. Mac Daniels will be cook for the WPA hot lunch program again this year. The school gymnasium is open to the Underwood community for roller skating every Friday night. This is attended by both children and adults. New student body officers are Virginia Wess, Jeanne Ericson and Ray Gustafson.

December 1941 - "The Life of Stephen Foster," a play written by the Underwood grade school, was performed by Ralph Gustafson, Jeanne Ericson, Dorothy Thun, Betty Ann Wess, Patsy Leep, Patsy Durfee, Carlie Kapp and Mary Boyer.

January 1942 - New student body officers are Ray Gustafson, Andy Reinland and Dorothy Thun.

## Schools (continued)

**More school news from local papers:**

February 1942 - The Primary room presented a play "A Day at the Post Office," a story of defense savings stamps. The school children also presented a skit, "The First Aider Rescues the Bombed," at a community supper sponsored by the women doing Red Cross sewing. A Washington's birthday assembly featured "My Visit to Washington's Home at Mt. Vernon," by Mrs. Pendleton, "The Life of Washington," by David Ohnemus and a poem, "Washington" by Ralph Gustafson.

March 1942 - Reno Ziegler and Martha Lehmann were elected school directors in the Underwood district.

May 1943 - Miss Marian Clarke, who taught in the primary grades at Underwood for two years, is engaged to Staff Sergeant Martin Headman whose mother is Mrs. Irving Emstrum of White Salmon.

*Pioneer* November 1948: at a meeting in the Community House one person said,

*"We were taken into the White Salmon school district a couple of years ago and right now we are trying to find a way to get out of it."*

*Mt. Adams Sun* July 2, 1964 :
UNDERWOOD SCHOOL DISTRICT ASKS INDEPENDENCE FROM WHITE SALMON

*An Underwood committee headed by Howard Ericson met with the White Salmon School Board and petitioned for release from the White Salmon Valley consolidated school district 405-17 as soon as possible.*

A vote of 62 Underwood residents had overwhelmingly asked for the transfer of their students to Mill A District 31 in Skamania County. If approved, the transfer would mean the withdrawal of about 114 students from the White Salmon school system, thirty of these in high school.

June 1967 - At a White Salmon Board of Education meeting Ted Kolbaba Discussed the Underwood School land and the lease agreement to be made with the Skamania County Commissioners. A lease would be drawn up for fifty years. If the land is abandoned, the Board has the option to give a 60 day notice that the lease would terminate unless the Commissioners revived the activities being held on the property. Also the school has the option of serving notice to cancel the lease if the district needed the land for school building purposes. The property is to be used for community projects. The commissioners would have the authority to use the buildings or raze the buildings as they determine. The motion passed to accept the resolution.

July 1972 - New wiring at Underwood Recreation Center has been completed by Sohler Electric Company.

January 1974 - There will be no skating until further notice due to remodeling at the recreation center.

**Spring 1919 two-room Underwood Schoolhouse.**
**Helen Thun – back row to the right.**
**Bertha Schweitzer – back row beside Helen.**
**Haselton twins Hannah and Elizabeth – middle row clear to the left (with hair bows).**
**Angeline Walther – middle row in front of Helen.**
**Emil (last name?) middle row, scratching his ear.**

Photo from the Hannah Haselton May collection

**Underwood School c. 1920**          Photo from the Jayne Allen collection

**Front row left to right :  Katherine Wess, Rosa Kapp, Maria Kapp, (?,?,?) Berniece Schwinge we think, (?,?,?,?,?,) Alice Rine**

**Row  2:  Amel Schwinge, Max Kapp, John Wess, (?,?,?, - girl with hands on two in front of her ), Hannah Haselton, ?,?, Helen Thun, (?)**

**Row 3 : 7 unknowns, including boy on the left, slightly in front.**

**Row 4 in back :  (?), Julia Kapp. (?,?)**

Oct. 1924 - Underwood, Wash.

**Underwood School October 1924**

**Emma Christensen and her sister, teachers.**
**Hannah Haselton, in the photo,   recognizes  only  Alice  Rine,  Helen  Thun,**
**Elizabeth Haselton,  Angeline Walther,    Bertha Schweitzer    and**
**maybe a Wendland girl.**

Underwood School primary room 1936/'37

Photo from Gorge Heritage Museum archives

Front row left to right: (?) Edward Bradley, Addie Auspland, (?) Eddie Grove, Fred Abrams, Robert Morby, Johnny Quimpts, Robert Cordier

Middle row: Carlie Kapp, Patsy Miller, Cecile Newell, Frank Abrams, Dorothy Thun, Charlie Kramer, Betty Wess, (?) Stultz, (?), Jeanne Ericson

Back row: Henry Godfrey, (?), Stultz, (?), Raymond Bradley, Verne Newell, Gilbert Bradley, Andre Auspland, (?), Shirley Morby, John Kock, Mary Ann Miller, Joey Mae Collins, Patsy Leep. Teacher in back is Lavelle Swetman.

Grades in this photo ran from 1st to 8th. Robert Morby, front row, was in second grade. Note the model A Ford in the background. After some years of use the large schoolhouse walls began to spread from the weight of snow in the winter. So sometime in the 1950s Leroy and Reno Ziegler overhauled the roof structure. They inserted steel rods that ran the length of the building. This halted any additional spread or droop to the roof.

*Information given by Robert Morby*

**Schools** (continued)

Margaret Hearn Shaddox
Third Row, Second from right

**Underwood School Upper Grades**
    **1936-37**
**Last row left to right - #4 is a Kock boy**
**Front row - #6 is Harry Abrams**

Photo from Gorge Heritage Museum archives

**Schools** (continued)

According to the *Mt. Adams Sun* of April 14, 1944, there was a vote to unite the Underwood and White Salmon high school districts. In Underwood the tally was 14 <u>yes</u> and 11 <u>no</u> out of 400 voters. There was a complaint that the polls closed before people got off work.

The Underwood school was closed about 1945, the students being bussed to White Salmon. Ted Balsiger, chair of a council meeting in the 60's noted that the minutes of the meeting when Underwood joined with White Salmon clearly stated that a grade school would be maintained at Underwood as soon as teachers were available. The *Sun* article of October 18, 1962 went on to say that a vote the previous week to withdraw from the White Salmon district was 21 <u>yes</u> and 3 <u>no</u>. This vote was apparently taken because Skamania County had federal timber funds that could build a school in Underwood. However, they could not use the funds to build if Underwood was affiliated with an out-of-county district. At that time, 125 Underwood children were involved.

The main building was torn down in 1961 because the upkeep was too difficult for the White Salmon Valley School District. When they sold it, Paul Tate got the bid and tore it down, selling the material for scrap. Dan Tate, son of Paul, remembers he was fourteen years old at the time of the teardown. He calculated the year to be 1961.

Many in the community fought to keep the gym as a community meeting place. The gym, built in 1931, still exists as a community hall.

Schools also existed in the nearby communities of Hood, Climax and Chenowith. See Chapter 10.

\*\*\*\*\*\*\*\*\*\*\*\*\*\*\*\*\*\*\*\*\*\*\*\*\*\*\*\*\*\*

## Underwood Fire Department

**Underwood Fire Hall**

Prior to 1972 fires that occurred in the immediate Underwood community were aided by the county road crew, with what tools and service they had available. Additional help was often brought in from the White Salmon, Bingen, and even Hood River volunteer fire departments.

In 1972 there was a big bluff fire started near the railroad. After many groups came to assist in extinguishing the fire it was decided that Underwood needed its own fire department. Lyle Ternahan was county commissioner at the time. He appointed Ray Moore, Doyle VanDeventer, and Clark Ziegler as the first fire commissioners.

*Original building housing the UFD*

A building was found near the corner of School House Road and Cook Underwood Road that was suitable to house the newly formed Underwood Fire Department. The structure belonged to the White Salmon Valley School District. It was originally the

## Underwood Fire Department (Continued)

bus garage for the school that once sat on the same property. All that stands today of that school is the old gym, which is now a recreation/meeting center. So, originally Skamania County leased the building from WSVSD, which then turned around and leased it to the community of Underwood. Soon however, Skamania County bought the building from the WSVSD and continued to rent it to the fire department for a very minimal amount annually.

The first fire truck the newly formed organization acquired was an American LeFrance, donated by Underwood resident George Baker. George Baker also took on the duties as the first fire chief for the organization. Some of the early volunteers for the original department included Clark Ziegler, George Baker, Don Thomas, Don Morby, and Verne Newell. We apologize for those names that have been unintentionally omitted.

The Underwood volunteers usually average about 12 members at a time.

It was eventually apparent that the UFD was outgrowing its original facilities in the bus garage. In 1995 the department agreed to give up their meeting hall space to be converted into the US Post Office. More trucks and equipment were added to the department over the years and they were badly in need of more space.

Bob Allen owned the piece of property directly across the road, or east of the fire hall. Previous owners before Mr. Allen had been the Sooter Family. The property sits on the corner of Cook Underwood Road and School House Road, the address being 13002 Cook Underwood Road. In 2004 Mr. Allen agreed to sell the property at cost. This purchase was made possible through funds the fire department had saved over the years. After the purchase there was money left over to set aside to start the new building.

**2008 Groundbreaking – left- Jim Bryant, Nuala the mascot, Albert Grove, Eric Ziegler (Fire Chief), Nathan Ziegler, Jerry Grove, Chris Gardner, John Hardham (Fire Commissioner), Steve Nance, and Howard Anderson.**

In 2008 groundbreaking for the new building took place. Some of those present for this exciting event are shown in photo above. A county levy was passed allowing funds to be added to existing funds, and construction of the new hall was underway.

On February 12, 2009 a license was granted for opening the new building. The building was finished and paid for thanks to taxpayer funds.

*Photo by John Hardham*

**Underwood Bluff Fire -  9-21-2007**

## Underwood Fire Department (Continued)

Throughout the years, along with their efforts in putting down local fires, the fire department has given help with medical emergencies and traffic accidents, as well as lending assistance to adjacent towns and communities upon request.

*Photo by John Hardham*
**Standing in front of new fire hall are, left – Steve Nance, Jerry Grove, Todd Mera, Jeremy Morley, and Gus Combs.**

Those currently serving as Fire Commissioners are: Jerry Grove, John Hardham, and Rich Potter.

Since the onset of the Underwood Fire Department in 1972 eight men have given their time as Fire Chief. They are as follows; George Baker, Erman Bryan, Robert Morby, Jim Schwinge, Scott Allen, Dan Collins, Tim Newell, and Eric Ziegler.

The beautiful building, well-kept trucks and equipment, as well as the countless volunteers that serve or have served as members are a source of pride to the community.

**References: Clark Ziegler, Eric Ziegler, Tim Newell, John Hardham, UFD webpage.**

# CHAPTER NINE
# LATER BUSINESS ESTABLISHMENTS

## The Partridge Inn

Established in 1973, the Partridge Inn on Cook Underwood road was the accomplishment of Nora and Murray (Mack) McNab. The building was designed as a home, one-half of which housed a restaurant to accommodate 50 guests. Soon after opening, Mack McNab died. Nora later remarried Jacque (Moe) Moyse, who helped her run the restaurant until they retired in 1982. Nora and Mack's son, Pete McNab continued the Partridge Inn business until 1989. (Sadly, we presently have no restaurant of any sort in Underwood.)

A 1987 book by Lucille Bowling Carloftis titled Favorite Recipes from a Treasury of Country Inns and Lodges states,

*"Guests enjoy the warmth of the restaurant that features delightful dishes served family-style by owner Chef Peter McNab. The menu includes traditional Cornish Game Hen barbequed with a zesty sauce, Steaks, Country Style Ribs, Chicken Tarragon, Thermidor Del Mar, Shrimp and Scallops Saute', all topped off with delicious deserts."*

**Columbia Gorge from the Partridge Inn**
by Gretta Chandler

The Cobblestone Cookbook by Nora McNab contains one of her favorite recipes:

**Cobblestone Coffee Cake (Nora McNab)**
Blend :
　2 1/2 c. flour
　½ t. salt
　¾ c. brown sugar
　¾ c. white sugar
Add:
　¾ c. butter – crumble with fingers or pastry blender. Take out 2/3 of these crumbs, set aside for topping.
Sprinkle over crumbs in mixing bowl and continue to mix:
　1 T. baking powder
　1 t. cinnamon
　½ t. nutmeg

Beat together:
　2 eggs
　1 c. milk
　1 t. vanilla
Add to cake. Mix only until blended.
　Spread in baking pan, sprinkle with crumbs. Bake at 350° about 30 min. or until lightly browned and done in the middle.

## Grapes and Wine

Underwood Mountain lies within the Columbia Valley American Viticulture Area. A Columbia Gorge Wine Map brochure states:

*"Our marine-influenced climate where it rains 40 inches a year is ideal for cool weather-loving varietals like Pinot Noir, Gewurztraminer, Chardonnay, Pinot Gris, and Riesling."*

In recent years, vineyards have been replacing orchards and even fir trees on the mountain. There are two wine tasting opportunities: **Aniche Cellars** on Little Buck Creek Road is owned and operated by Todd Mera and Rachel Horn. The **White Salmon Vineyard** owned and operated by Peter and Faye Brehm offers tastings in the old town mercantile building along state highway 14.

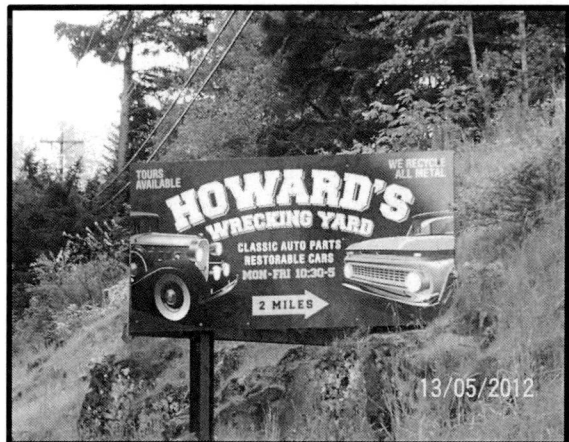

## Underwood Alpacas

Rita and Dale White started raising alpacas on their acreage on Cook Underwood Road in 2004. The herd has grown to thirty five, with three babies on the way. Sadly, Rita passed away in 2012. Dale is carrying on with the alpaca gift shop at their place. The public is welcome to stop by to visit with the gentle alpacas during open hours.

## Howard's Wrecking Yard

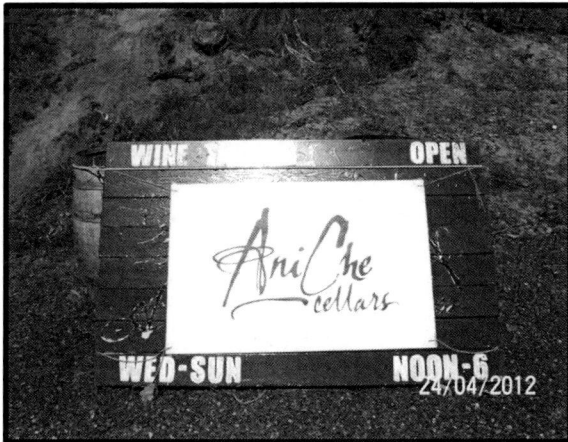

Jim Howard has run this car parts yard for many years. It is located near the power lines where they cross Laycock-Kelchner Road. Classic car buffs can take a tour of the wrecking yard to look for restoration parts.

# CHAPTER TEN
# OTHER COMMUNITIES ON
# UNDERWOOD MOUNTAIN

## Norway

In September 1904, a Hood River *Glacier* newspaper representative visited the Underwood area and gave this report:

*The Norway settlement is on the upper part of the Underwood district. It is a community of hardy pioneers, mostly Norwegians. Here is found the log cabins with puncheon floors and homemade furniture, industrious housewives and healthy-looking children. The land is all taken and homesteads are located even up and over the mountain as far as Chenowith. There is much comparatively level land in the Norway settlement. The soil is rich and seems to be the same depth of 15 feet or more, with no rocks. A heavy growth of fir timber makes clearing slow work, but the settlers have made wonderful progress in clearing their farms.*

*The valuable saw timber of this settlement should be an inducement for the location of a big saw mill. Plenty of water can be taken from Buck Creek to flume lumber to the Columbia, and a good wagon road from here to the river would make hauling the lumber easy. Portable saw mills would pay.*

*P.I. Sather's place is the first upon entering the settlement. He is three miles from Underwood landing by road, and three-quarters of a mile from the White Salmon River. He homesteaded 160 acres, but has sold 10 acres to Thomas Anderson, a newcomer from Minnesota, who has cleared the land and will make it a garden spot of a home.*

*K.S. Knutson has a homestead of 160 acres adjoining Mr. Sather on the north. David Satre has 80 acres of a homestead adjoining Mr. Sather on the west. He has a clearing of ten acres, keeps several cows, and Mrs. Satre makes an excellent brand of butter. Charles Knutson's homestead adjoins that of Mr. Satre of which H.A. Tawney of Hood River bought 10 acres.*

*Next comes N.M. Munch, a progressive young man who is improving his homestead and carving out a desirable home for himself and his family. Isreal Ziegler, who purchased C.D. Moore's homestead, is building a dwelling house and will continue the work of clearing begun by Mr. Moore. Mr. Ziegler is the nephew of Sam Ziegler of White Salmon, a young man from Pennsylvania, industrious and of sturdy character, and we predict his homestead will some day show how they do things in Pennsylvania, where the best farms in the union are found.*

*Ole Tenold has a claim adjoining Mr. Munch on which he resides with his family and is making improvements. Other settlers here are Gilbert Knutson, Simon Knutson, Mr. Jackson, Mr. Seeley, Mr. Dixon and Mrs. J.E. Churchill.*

## Chenowith

A logging operation was started on Chenowith Flat, sitting above Drano Lake. When all the trees were cut, the loggers moved to the west side of the Little White Salmon River, and called it Mill A, which by 1907 was also logged off.

James Morby homesteaded here in 1893. Some time before 1917, Rosa and Emil Walther donated one acre to be used for the original school in Chenowith. A Mr. King was a teacher there at one time. Besides his children and the Walthers' children, there were some Morhouse students at the school. (See Walther in the Family History Section.) One of their sons, Adolph, lived in Chenowith until he died in 1969.

An April 1928 *Pioneer* article said that Dr. Zenner of White Salmon was called to Chenowith to see the infant daughter of Mr. and Mrs. Jas. Morby. She had been a very sick babe, but they were glad to report her much better. Other Chenowith people mentioned in this time frame: L.L. Thomas, Herbert Williams, Edwards, P.A. Nederhood, Walter Kock, Harold Betts, and F.A. Fisher.

**Chenowith** (continued)

*From Skamania County History  Vo.l. I*
By Carl Nielsen :

*A flume was constructed on the east side of the Little White Salmon River to carry cordwood. (circa 1889) It ran across the Chenowith Flat, and down a steep incline into Drano Lake. The cordwood was loaded on boats and barges and hauled to The Dalles to fuel steamboats for the long upriver run through timberless country where no fuel could be obtained. It was also sold in the growing city of The Dalles as the major source of fuel."*

*It is said that 300 men were working in the cordwood camps of Chenowith flat. The pay was $1.00 a cord and a skilled and steady worker could cut as high as two cords a day.*

The Morby family settled in Chenowith. Moroni Morby, born in 1853 in England, immigrated to Washington about 1894 and died in 1902. He was buried at the Chenowith cemetery. His wife Harriet then married Willard Young in 1903. Willard was another pioneer of the Chenowith area. Mildred Morby, granddaughter of Moroni and Harriet Morby, graduated from Chenowith grammar school in 1920. Mildred White, who married Jack Morby in 1938, taught school at Chenowith Flat before her marriage. Jack was another grandchild of Moroni and Harriet Morby.

Charles Walter Morby another descendent, wrote a book about life in the Little White Salmon area. Born in Chenowith in 1918, he went on to become an engineer who built launch pads at Cape Canaveral and designed two of the ten minute-man missiles.

Robert Morby, son of James, grandson of Maroni, believes that Chenowith got its name because that is where Chief Chenowith and the Indians used to stop on their way down from the huckleberry fields, on their way to the Columbia River. They would camp on the flat. Mr. Morby remembers the Indians stopping and camping when he was a kid. They often had with them Indians who had died along the way. They would take their dead and place them on a rock that is still there in the Columbia River, by the first tunnel at the east end of Drano Lake. Before the Bonneville Dam, the river was way down.

There is no sign of the Chenowith School now except a broken wooden fence and a short rock wall. When the school closed, Washington State University bought the property to build an outdoor school to teach students how to live off the land. But that didn't happen. Remnants of the old flume can be seen at the end of Chenowith Road. The cemetery was vandalized in the 1970s and all but two headstones thrown over the cliff. The stone markers of Moroni Morby and Delbert Tubbs are the only two left. The Chenowith cemetery is now difficult to locate, there being no sign to indicate the location.

**Chenowith Mill  1905**
**Photo from *Pioneer* Newspaper**
**The photo is titled "Mill A," but other sources call the Chenowith area "Mill B"**

## Cook's Landing

Because Cook is at the end of Cook-Underwood Road, we will make mention of it here. It is actually on the west side of the Little White Salmon River and not part of Underwood Mountain. In the early days of white settlement it was a boat landing on the 1894 homestead of Charles A. Cook and Johan, his wife. According to BLM records, Mr. Cook was granted title to his 160 acre claim in 1896. The property was later sold to a man named Gerlinger and in 1908 sold to a Mr. O.A. Perry who had a store there. He also started to build a hotel in Cook's Landing which was finished by Nancy Wallace. At one time there also was a confectionary store, a post office, a railway station and a garage with a dance hall above.

*Source: Skamania County History, Vol. 1, 2^nd edition*

## Climax

The Climax area on Underwood Mountain at one time was so populated that it had its own news column in the *Skamania County Pioneer*. The community had a lumber mill and a school on the northeast side of the mountain. Here are some news articles regarding Climax:

October 1923 – There will be a Halloween party at the old Climax mill cook house (*On the corner of the present Laycock-Kelchner Road and Little Buck Creek Road*) on October 31, given by the Underwood Christian Endeavor. Apples, cider and doughnuts will be served.

January 1926 – The old Climax mill that had been idle for a number of years was rebuilt last summer by Mr. Price and a good business was being done until it was destroyed by fire, which also burned the Climax school house in District 28 (*On the present Little Buck Creek Road north of Laycock-Kelchner road.*) The school has been replaced with a new one much better than the one destroyed.

January 1928 – The community of Climax got news that Mrs. Thomas Anderson had died in Portland. Her husband, had died in June 1920. They were among the early settlers, living on a ten-acre tract.

February 1928 – People mentioned in *Pioneer* Climax News section: Walter and Norton Judd, Miss Jessie Estey and Miss Kathryn Glesner. There were weather problems that winter; Snow was 20 inches deep on the level. The Climax road was blocked by a Buick car whose owner went away and left it in the middle of the road. There is only one way traffic in this locality and when a car stops all the rest of the traffic is stalled. With the assistance of several others the stalled car was backed down the hill and out of the way. No owner appeared to claim the car and it was left on the side of the road.

The I.R. Ziegler family of six children grew up on their Climax homestead in the north part of Little Buck Creek Road. Reno, the eldest son wrote this piece for the February 28, 1928 *Pioneer*:

### Story of My 4-H Sheep Club Work

*I became a sheep club member because I wanted to take up some kind of livestock work. I am interested in sheep and chose them because I thought it would pay to raise them. I have four ewes and five lambs. I bought my ewes from Mr. Pyate who is a sheep raiser. I took a liking to his sheep because they were big and good looking. I earned the money to pay for them by working for my dad on the ranch. I feed my ewes and lambs enough feed to keep them in good shape. I did not sell any of my sheep this year. The market lambs we kept for our own use. My breeding ewes averaged around 11 pounds of wool each which I sold for 35½ c per pound. I exhibited my sheep at the Skamania County Fair, having three different entries in Club work. One buck, one ewe and a pair of ewe lambs.*

*I got first prize on each entry which amounted to considerable. I did not spend much time on my sheep because my flock is small. I hoped to induce other boys to go into Club work, but most of them said, "No," and thought it no use. I plan to enroll in Club work next year for I am very much interested in sheep.*

*I think sheep will pay on our ranch because they help to build up the soil and furnish meat for home use. My sheep netted me a profit of $61.25.*

> RENO ZIEGLER, Age 15
> Little Buck Creek Ranch
> Underwood, Washington

More *Pioneer* news articles:

March 1928 – People from Climax mentioned: C. Herman, Pete Doherty and Harvey Kelchner.

April 1928 – Miss Carrie Fournier of Everett, who taught at the Climax school three years ago spent the Easter holiday with the I.R. Ziegler family and her friend Miss Estey.

The community of Climax enjoyed the Easter egg hunt Sunday afternoon and everyone seemed to catch the spirit of youth once more when they found hidden baskets.

June 1928 – C. Rosenkranz and family and H.D. Kelchner and family spent Sunday with Mr. and Mrs. Fred Bueche of Underwood. The cool weather has somewhat checked the berry crop which has been coming on nicely. No damage has been done. The Climax camp is again awakened by the mill whistle. Mamie and Reno Ziegler, members of the 4-H Club spent the week at Pullman at the Club Camp.

July 1928 – Mrs. A.S. Rosenberger and Miss Eva Rosenberger of Soudeton, PA, mother and sister of Mrs. I.R. Ziegler, arrived Saturday and will remain until the middle of August.

September 1928 – School started in District 28 with Mrs. E. Phebus of Richfield as teacher. The first rain since the 4th of July fell on Tuesday. A. Townley has recovered from his accident of a few weeks ago. He received a cut in the head from an ax.

January 1929 – Climax had two feet of snow when the old year passed out. Since then it has rained and the snow has settled considerably.

*****************************

The school in the Climax area of Underwood was on Little Buck Creek Road. The Climax School District No. 28 was organized June 22, 1918 and it was dissolved and annexed to District No. 17, Underwood, March 1, 1944. The I.R. Ziegler children attended this school before it closed.

The school building no longer exists, nor does the Climax lumber mill, nor the I.R. Ziegler homestead, nor any of the houses. Edmond and Mary Laycock lived in a house with a magnificent circular staircase north of the Zieglers. Their house is gone. A lively community has been mostly taken over by the determined Douglas fir trees. Nearly the only remnant left is a stone wall and some metal left from the Climax Mill at the end of Laycock-Kelchner Road. (Note the misspelling of Laycock on the county road sign.)

**Photo of the stone wall and metal from Climax Mill**

**Climax** (continued)

**Climax School  Jessie Konopski teacher**
Photo courtesy of Eva Ziegler Frazer collection
at the Gorge Heritage Museum

**1929 Climax School - Teacher Beulah Phebus – Myrtle and Esther Ziegler are in the photo.**
Photo courtesy of Eva Ziegler Frazer collection
at the Gorge Heritage Museum

**Climax School -  Eva Ziegler middle front.**
Photo courtesy of Eva Ziegler Frazer collection
at the Gorge Heritage Museum

Eva Frazer recalls the names of these teachers who served the one-room Climax School:  Carrie Bertz, Lavelle Swetman (married John Wess), Jessie Konopski Mrs. Hewitt, Mrs. Boyce and Beulah Phebus. The teachers lived in a room attached to the school building or sometimes stayed with the I.R.Zieglers.

## Sooville

There are some early Underwood news references to a community of settlers from Iowa:

June 1909 - An engineer from Cape Horn has been busy laying off the F.M. Seeley tract of 100 acres along the river. It has been sold to a group of people from Sioux City, Iowa. E.M. Cummins and son have decided to locate here.

July 1909 – the Sioux City colony is having some slashing done at "Sooville." When cleaned up this will be one of the finest tracts on the north bank of the Columbia. Frank B. Hogg closed a deal for ten acres of the Seeley place and Earl Cummins, of Sioux City, bought another ten acres.

May, 1910 – Earl Cummins and W.G. Detwiller arrived here with their families and will make their homes with the Sioux City colony where they each own land.

## Hood

The *Skamania County Pioneer* of September 7, 1916 gives an account of a proposed school at Hood, a lumber mill town west of lower Underwood. At a Parent-Teacher Association meeting, Mr. Rine, in behalf of the Underwood school board, presented a petition from the people of Hood in regard to establishing a school there. The Hood people had granted the sum of $500 to provide for eight months of school. Mr. Rine and Mrs. Leta Haselton had gone from Underwood to Hood to locate a suitable school room, and while there, learned that only two pupils would attend the school. Since then it had been learned that only one student would attend a Hood school. Mr. Lowden, who advocated for the advantages of a larger school, offered a motion to support the decision of the Underwood School Board, which was seconded by Mr. Chas. Walther, and was carried unanimously.

In the information given by Doug Ohnemus in the Family History Section, he states that there was a school house in Hood near the railroad tracks. So at some point, the Hood people must have prevailed on the question of a school. There is also mention in the news that Cora Tichnor Jones was the teacher at Hood School in 1917 and 1918.There was also a train depot in Hood.

The Broughton Lumber mill was started at Hood in 1923, employing many Underwood residents. Some families lived near the mill in the town of Hood. The mill ceased operating in 1986.

**Broughton Mill in operation**
Photo from Gordon Baker collection

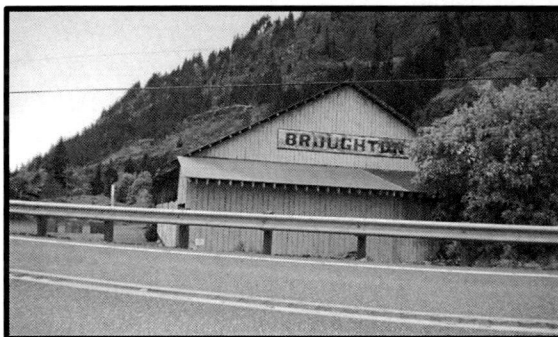

**Presently used for storage**
Photo by Kathy LaMotte

# CHAPTER ELEVEN
# MILITARY NEWS

There are about 30 military veterans buried at Underwood Chris-Zada Cemetery. The earliest veteran is Amos Underwood, who served in the Indian wars of the 1850s. Then there are two Civil War veterans who later lived and died in Underwood; Nicholas Barton and Dr. James A Smith, a dentist from Ohio.

World War I found Harvey Kelchner serving in watery trenches so long that forever after he had a fungal infection on his legs. Elmer "Mick" Sooter served in France with a horse-drawn artillery outfit.

The following local news accounts were related to World War II and the Viet Nam war:

April 1939 – Eugene K. Berrong and Elmer A. Larsen, both of Underwood, enlisted in the United States Marine Corps on the same day, May 12, 1938, after having graduated from Columbia Union high school together. They recently participated in fleet maneuvers, going twice through the Panama Canal and visiting Haiti, Cuba and Columbia.

February 1942 – Several letters have been received from Eugene Berrong, who is in Samoa. He says that he is fine and that the weather is very hot there at the present time.

March 13 1942 *Mt. Adams Sun*– In an essay against discrimination in the military, Rev. H.V. Rominger, of Underwood, states that his father and grandfather had been slave owners in North Carolina.

*A Negro mess boy on the battleship Arizona, amid the rain of Japanese bombs, rushed to the bridge and manned a machine gun until the ammunition was exhausted. The Negro press and the Society for the Advancement of Colored People have asked Secretary Knox and President Roosevelt to reveal the name of this Negro boy. They have refused and remain silent, though they did on demand give the name of the white Marine, Joseph L. Lockhart, who at the listening-station detected the approach of the Japanese bombing planes and whose warning was disregarded by his superior officer. Why this miserable race snobbery and discrimination? On the score of heroism and alertness this Negro boy avowedly ranks higher than Admiral Kimmel and Gen. Short, and who have now been permitted to retire on a pension of $6000 a year! Their court marshal has been postponed until after the war when the people will have forgotten and no trial will ever take place. The name of the Negro mess boy cannot be given, for he has no place in the Navy except in a menial position. No wonder the Negroes are growing bitter and have no enthusiasm to sweat, bleed and die in this war to establish the four freedoms for men everywhere when they are denied those blessings in their home democracy. "Jimcrowism" discriminates against the Negro in the army and navy, in transportation, in residence districts, even in churches and religion, while in eight states ten million Negroes are not allowed to approach the voting booth.*

June 1943 – Mr. and Mrs. Charles Berrong, of Underwood, have three sons serving in three branches of our armed forces. Charles Berrong enlisted in the Seabees, Sergeant Eugene K. Berrong enlisted in the Marines long before Pearl Harbor, and P.F.C. Lloyd Berrong is in the Air Corps. (Another son, Frederick, enlisted in the infantry and was killed July 25, 1944 in Normandy. He is buried there.)

**Fred Berrong High School Senior photo 1937.**
From yearbook collection, Gorge Heritage Museum

**Military News** (continued)

Additional local news items:

May 1945 – Sergeant William H. Simmons, Underwood, has been awarded a Presidential Citation with Oak Leaf cluster. News of the high honor has just reached his sister, Mrs. Lewis A. Larsen, Underwood, and it came from action when his squadron landed in France and started toward Germany. Sergeant Simmons has been in the armed forces overseas about 16 months. The Citation recited his part in the service of keeping planes gassed and in the air, a factor which had considerable to do with the success of the rapid advance of American soldiers across France.

June 1945 – Underwood is the first Skamania county precinct to scale the top in the sale of Series E bonds in the Mighty Seventh war loan drive. The report came from Mrs. Ruby Sooter, chairwoman in the precinct.

September 1952 – Private Charles L. Roshone, son of Mr. Ed I. Roshone of Underwood, Washington, is now enrolled in the Anti-aircraft and Guided Missiles Branch of the Artillery School at Fort Bliss, Texas. He will spend eight weeks studying in an anti-aircraft artillery mechanic course.

October 1966 – Private Gerald O. Hore, 22, son of Mr. and Mrs. Jim Hore, Underwood, Wash., completed reconnaissance training Sept. 30 at the Army Armor Center, Ft. Knox, Ky. He received eight weeks of training in the methods of scouting and patrolling, with the emphasis on the operation of Army jeeps on rugged terrain. Instruction was also given in camouflage techniques, concealment in natural terrain and handling of weapons.

February 1968 – Cam Thomas, son of Mr. and Mrs. Don Thomas of Hood, Wash., was recently awarded the Bronze Star Medal for the outstanding job he did while stationed with the 15th Support Brigade, Chu Lai, Republic of Viet Nam.

January 1969 – Lance Corporal Tim Estey arrived at the home of his parents, the Howard Esteys for a 20 day leave following a year of duty in Vietnam. Joining the family for Christmas week were Tony from Ellensburg, the Charles Esteys, Portland, the Bob Esteys, Dan Esteys, and Jim Esteys and the Merlin Yarnells, and Tom Estey, California.

January 1971 – Sp/5 John Halver left from McCord AFB for a year of duty in Vietnam. He had been teaching at Ft. Belvoir, VA, engineering school and was home since before Thanksgiving before going to Viet Nam.

March 1971 – Jerry Fincher arrived home from a tour of duty in Thailand with the Air Force. After a month leave, he will be stationed in Germany.

April 1973 – Visiting Mr. and Mrs. E.R. Sooter were his nephew, Mr. and Mrs. Walter Sooter, Umatilla, and his brother, David Sooter a POW recently returned from Viet Nam.

**Cam Thomas, Sp/ 5 Army**

# CHAPTER TWELVE
# SPORTS AND SOCIAL ACTIVITIES

**Sports**

From various local news articles:

May 1905 - Quite a number of Underwood baseball fans attended the game at Hood River Sunday.

May 1908 - A local baseball association has been formed. The second defeat of the season came at Husum. A basket social and dance given at Smith's Hall for the benefit of the club netted $55.50. The baseball boys are very busy preparing a new ball ground on Uncle Amos Underwood's land.

July 1908 - Underwood won a game 11-10 over Bingen. As the Underwood boys lined up for the 11 a.m. train in their bright new uniforms, they certainly looked like winners. .

Feb.1909 - B.W. Pollard was at the Underwood ball grounds with his two teams, putting the finishing touch by disking and dragging. He was assisted by Will Underwood.

April 1909 - The Hood River baseball team played the Underwood nine. The score was 2 to 4 in favor of Underwood.

**Below:**

**Underwood Baseball team – 1908**
Photo courtesy of Gorge Interpretive Center at Stevenson, Washington
Can anyone identify them?

**Sports** (continued)

Boxing was a popular sport. This match was to raise money to build a gym, which was completed in 1931.

# Smoker!

A Card of fast, clever and thrilling fights will be run off in the

# Underwood Auditorium

UNDERWOOD, WASHINGTON

# Friday Night, Feb. 7

Some of the Bouts already arranged are:

Isaac (Kid) Berrong — Dave (Shiek) Dewey

Andy (Pug) Rineland — Chuck (Tuffy) Berrong

Eugene (Cauliflower) Kramer—
John (Happy) Wess

Teddy (K.O.) Everett — Fred (Shires) Berrong

## And the Feature Bout
**WESS VAN CARNOP (175)**

vs.

**FRED MOORE (175)**

These boys have fought in rings throughout the state and both pack plenty of mean wallops!

A wrestling match will be staged between two contestants who will be named at the smoker. Anyone wishing to try for this match ($5 to the winner) enter name and weight with G. E. Mansfield—Phone 982— by Wednesday, February 5. The judges will pick two who are in the same class, weight and experience to go on Friday night.

Proceeds are to go toward the building of a gymnasium in Underwood. Don't forget the date and place. Admission 25c, 35c and 50c.

From *The Enterprise* January 31, 1930

February 1983 – Lenny Schalk of Underwood pressed 245 pounds during a lift-a-thon fund-raiser at Columbia High School.

Windsurfing and kite boarding have become a major sport in the Underwood area. The Columbia River Gorge is known worldwide for its summer west winds of 15-30 knots. The state park at the Spring Creek Fish Hatchery attracts hundreds of visitors a year. The site is known as "The Hatch." Just west of The Hatch is Swell City, attracting expert wind riders.

Rafting and kayaking are popular sports on the White Salmon River, bordering Underwood Mountain from its mouth up to what used to be Northwestern Lake. Running the falls at Husum is great fun for the courageous.

**Zoller's raft trip on the White Salmon River**

Fishing is another river sport at the mouth of the White Salmon. Salmon, steelhead (an ocean-going trout) and an occasional sturgeon are caught in season by sport fishers. The Cascades River Fisher Indians have a fish camp at the mouth of the White Salmon River, as they have had for thousands of years.

## Social Activities

It wasn't all hard work in the early years. People made time for fun, as recorded in local papers:

June, 1905 – Amos Underwood will open his new barroom on the morning of July 4. Ed (Underwood) will mix gin fizzes, high balls and cocktails. Fine gasoline light fixtures have been installed in the bar.

June 1907 – Miss Elma Luthy and Clifford Robards married at the home of her parents Mr. and Mrs. Luthy. An elegant luncheon was served and the couple caught the train for an extended tour of the coast. Mr. Robards, with his father and brother, built our first store (*The Mercantile*) and sold to the present owners, Smith and Clark.

A 4th of July celebration is planned at Mr. Goddard's park. There will be sack races, potato races, three-legged races and fat men's races. Also a sledge throwing contest and wood sawing and nailing exhibitions. There will be a literary and musical program and an ample feast.

July 1907 – Mr. and Mrs. Cash, Mr. and Mrs. Haynes and children leave today for a fishing trip on the Little White Salmon River.

The young people gave a very enjoyable party at the home of Miss Millie Barton for her 16th birthday.

July 1908 – Miss Florence Evelyn, daughter of Mr. and Mrs. Hamilton of Underwood married Mr. Clarence Welden of Husum. The ceremony was performed by Rev. J.L. Hershner at the residence of the bride's parents. A reception was given in the evening. The rooms were tastefully decorated with flowers and Oregon grape and the grounds were illuminated with Chinese lanterns. The occasion proved to be one of the more pleasant events of the season.

More local news items:

July 1908 - A gala union picnic given by the Underwood and Stevenson Sunday Schools. People came by the steamer *George W. Simons* and by train. Lunch was served in Goddard Grove. A game of baseball between Underwood and Stevenson teams was won by the visitors.

November 1912 – The Underwood Union Chapel association has inaugurated a series of entertainments for the winter months. The first of these was given in the Riverview Orchards, A.J. Haynes apple warehouse. The young folks pulled off a very clever vaudeville show, clearing a tidy sum of money. The next attraction is to be a musical.

February 1922 – A fancy dress masquerade Valentine party and dance was held at the Underwood school.

A surprise party was given at the Adams' home in honor of Mr. Adam's birthday. The evening was spent in dancing and playing games.

A birthday surprise party was held for Louis Thun with games, cards and dancing.

January –1923 – A dance will be held in the Larsen Hall at Underwood this Saturday evening. Music from Hood River will be provided.

January 1937 – the Mt. Adams Ski club will ski on the Card ranch on Underwood Heights next Sunday. I.W. Donaldson reports that everybody is welcome to the ski run and that there is plenty of snow and that there are runs for both beginners and advanced skiers. There is a cabin where heat will be provided for those who come to watch. This is an ideal place and skiing can be enjoyed there all winter. It is along the main highway and easy to reach, four miles above Underwood.

March 1938 – A group of Underwood folks enjoyed a week of clam digging at Long Beach: Mr. and Mrs. J.B. Christiansen, Mr. and Mrs. Kenneth Holmes, and Mr. and Mrs. Amel Schwinge.

August 1951 – Mr. and Mrs. Jim Anthon of Underwood Heights, were hosts to the Rusty Squares square dancers after they enjoyed an evening of dancing at the old Underwood school gym.

December 1960 – Teenagers are invited to attend a dance from 8:30 to 12:30 p.m. at the Underwood gym.

# CHAPTER THIRTEEN
# ORGANIZATIONS

## Grange

The Underwood Grange was organized in 1905. The Big White Salmon River Grange No. 160 held its 1st entertainment Saturday May 20 of that year. The picnic and dance inaugurated the new hall near the Underwood school house. Nearly 50 farmers joined the Grange. The first officers were C.H. Cromwell, C.D. Moore, Mike Thornton, W.A. Orser, and Bert Veach.

In September of 1917 the third and fourth degree was conferred on Miss Edna Weberg and Graham Chandler at the Grange meeting. Ice cream was served to all and a very pleasant social time held.

In 1936 the Underwood Grange was reorganized and became No.1073. Officers were: Harry Card, E.W. Dieterich, Herbert Miller, Mrs. Rose Larsen, Earl Harrah, Olaf Larsen, Mrs. Martin Koch, John Koch, Harvey Kelchner, Mrs. J.W. Shipley, Mrs. John Wess, Mrs. Inez Swetman, Mrs. Margaret Card, and Earl Cummins. The Grange was still in existence in 1939, holding its regular meetings at the school house. Members elected to attend the state grange meeting were Mr. O. Larsen and Mr. Harvey Kelchner.

## Underwood Improvement Club

In August of 1907, W.F. Cash was chosen as president of the newly organized Improvement Club. P.I. Packard was chosen as secretary, and M.S. Smith, treasurer. Meetings were to be held every two weeks at Smith and Clark's hall above the store. The first project was improvement of the cemetery in the way of fencing. In 1911 Mr. Henry Love was selected to be on the "managing committee" of the Underwood Improvement Club. Plans were to secure a good road from the bridge to the rail station.

## Ladies Aid

In May 1912, over forty people attended the "Old Times" quilt exhibition given by the Ladies Aid at Mrs. Hendrick's home. It was a great success and $16.50 was raised. There were 54 different quilts exhibited, representing ten different states. Among those most admired were a handmade bed spread made in 1849 and a piece of a blanket 140 years old. The candy table presided over by Miss Cooper and Miss Brooks won its share of attention and also its share of the profits. The next month the Ladies Aid held a business meeting at Mrs. E.R. Cobb's.

## Literary Society

A 1922 local paper noted that the next meeting of the Underwood Literary Society would be held in the school house on Friday evening Feb. 3. The following were among those who would appear on the program: Miss Katherine Walther, song; Miss Bertha Schweitzer, reading; John McNutt, reading; Debate question: Should the Japanese be admitted as citizens of the United States? Negative: L.A. Johns and Mr. Ames; Affirmative: H.V. Rominger and W. Marsh. Refreshments would be served.

In June of 1928 the annual meeting of the Underwood Literary Society was held at the school house. The following officers were elected: President, R.H. Haselton; Vice President, Louis Thun; Sec.-Treasurer, M.S. Smith; Sergeant-at-arms, Zed Porter.

## Women's Club

This organization began in 1913. In January of 1916 the Women's Club meeting was attended by Mrs. R. Meiggs, Mrs. H.J. Friedrich, Mrs. Smith, Mrs. Packard, Mrs. Hussey, and Mrs. Mann. In June of 1922 the Underwood Women's Club met in regular session at the beautiful new home of Mrs. Jim Haynes. Mrs. M.S. Smith had charge of the program, the subject of which was Henry Van Dyke.

## Organizations (continued)

In June of 1933 the Underwood Women's Club celebrated its 20th anniversary. These members were in charge of the reunion garden party at the home of Mrs. Herb Williams: Mrs. C.W. Gibbs, Mrs. J. W. Shipley, Mrs. J.E. Slade, Mrs. M.S. Smith, Mrs. Roy Anthon, Mrs. Ray Moore, Mrs. Arthur Atkinson, Mrs. Richard Bates, Mrs. Howard Ericson, and Mrs. Selby Leep.

The group was still going strong in the 1970s. In January of 1974 the Women's Club met at the Jane Halver home. Special speakers were exchange students from Arapongos, Brazil, Sueli Crena and Vladimir Sousa.

At the May 1975 Women's Club meeting these officers were elected: Dora Perry, Betty Collins, Mary Ziegler, Dora Crego, and Betty Baker. Jane Halver presented a very interesting program on her recent trip to Hungary. The February 1976 meeting of the Women's Club was held at the Partridge Inn on Underwood Heights.

**August 1985 – Four members of the Underwood Women's Club, Margaret DeWilde, Pat Colton, Vivian Nichols and Rose Shepeard show the quilt they helped make for their club's benefit. A drawing for the quilt will be held during Huckleberry Festival in Bingen.**

## Underwood Uplift Club

June 1928 – This women's organization gave a dance at the school house, the proceeds of which were used for improving the cemetery grounds.

## 4-H

Officially organized nationally in 1924, the youth group emphasized "Head, Heart, Hands and Health." There has been a 4-H group of some kind in Underwood for many years. In 1928 Reno Ziegler had a 4-H sheep project. In February 1933 there was a 4-H benefit dance in the Underwood gymnasium. Music was by Cecil Rowland's orchestra. The cost was 50 cents and included refreshments.

A 4-H achievement program was held at the Underwood school in November of 1937. Mildred Davis, president of the girl's 4-H Club opened the meeting. Mr. Harry Card spoke about the merits and value of 4-H Club work and then a play was given under the direction of Mrs. Ford and Mrs. Moore. Mrs. Balsiger and Mr. Cordier were given pins for leading the clubs.

Quite a large crowd turned out for the dance sponsored by the 4-H Club in March, 1939. In February 1942 the girl's 4-H club elected these officers: Carlie Kapp, Mary Boyer, Betty Ann Wess and Dorothy Thun.

An April 1973 news article noted that the Green Mt. Ghost Riders, newly formed 4-H Club had elected the following officers: Brenda Ziegler, Karl Elliott, Deborah Halver, and Jackie Barnedt. The adult 4-H leaders were Connie Lehmann and Myra Schwinge with Bonnie Baker as Junior Leader. The group planned to build a horse arena at Underwood Rec Center, as a civic project for community use.

In 1982 these members of the Underwood Small Animals 4-H Club went home with awards from the Mid-Columbia Rabbit Show: Eron Ensminger, Tama Demchuk, Duane Roland, Amy Demchuk, Becky Holtman, and Michele Leek. The leader was Jodi Ensminger.

**Organizations** (continued)

In July 1980, the Underwood Tailwaggers Dog 4-H Club geared up for the Skamania County Fair in August. They were involved in dog obedience classes and dog showing.

## Homemakers Club

*Mt. Adams Sun* December 29, 1960 :

When the Underwood Homemakers held its recent election of officers, they elected Mrs. Lyle Ternahan president. Mrs. Ternahan was absent with a cold. Nevertheless she accepted with the following verse:

*When you have a friend at home in bed,*
*With a running nose and a cold in the head,*
*There is one thing to do, I'm very sure,*
*And that is to let her know you're thinking of*
*    her.*
*Now don't send flowers 'cause they will wilt*
*    and die,*
*Nor a gushy card that might make her cry,*
*Do something different, make it an EVENT!*
*Be a bunch of stinkers and elect her president.*

## Boy Scouts

In the 1950s Wilma Brown had a troop of Cub Scouts. They met at her home and went to monthly meetings with the White Salmon Cubs. In November 1961 Hal Broughton took his Scouts for a hike to Camp Baldwin near Dufur, OR. The same year, Jane Halver received a 10 year pin for her services as a Girl Scout leader. In October 1962, three Underwood young men achieved the Eagle Scout award; John Halver the 4th, Howard Ostroski, and Dick Lehmann. In May 1968 the Underwood Boy Scout troop No. 709 held its first major court of Honor of the year at the Underwood gym.

## Community Club

March 1931 – A large crowd attending the Underwood Community Club met in the school house. They set a price of 50 cents to attend the minstrel show and 50 cents if you wanted to dance afterwards.

## Underwood Community Council

This organization was formed in the 1970s and attained non-profit status in 1982. At first it was known as the Community Club, possibly a continuation of the previous group mentioned. Club members paid $2.00 a year in order to pay the electric bill on the community center. Roller skating parties helped raise money. A community Halloween party was also a fund raiser.

The Underwood Community Council continues to meet monthly to this date. The purpose of the Underwood Community Council is to give voice to the community in its dealings with government (county, state and federal) and other entities (business, non-profits, etc.). The Council is held in the Underwood Community Building, which was the old school gym on Schoolhouse Road. Managed by Skamania County at the present, a community park center is on the surrounding property, including a tennis court, a basketball court, a ball field, a horse arena, a covered picnic area with tables and barbecue pits and a playground equipment area for children. A gazebo to enhance the park center was built in the summer of 1993.

A hasty perusal of the council minutes since 1988 shows the following people have served as Underwood Community Council presidents: Dave Compton, Judith Allen, Linda Saunders, Paul M. Newell, Lonnie Rogers, Ed LaMotte, Linda Hardham, Sally Newell and Keith Fredrickson. Others involved were Ted Lehmann, Lyle Ternahan, Carole Ziegler, Mary Ziegler, Helen Paulus and Thomasina Campbell. For a number of years the council published a newsletter called "The Underwood View." At the present time, communication is conducted through email and a web site. Monthly community meetings are held on the third Thursday at 6:30.

**Organizations** (continued)

In the year 2000 the Marjorie Miller Family, under the direction of Bob Miller, donated $2000 to be spent on improvements in the Underwood community. A plaque was designed to honor individuals from the community. Monies left over were used to help fund the construction of the barbecue pit.

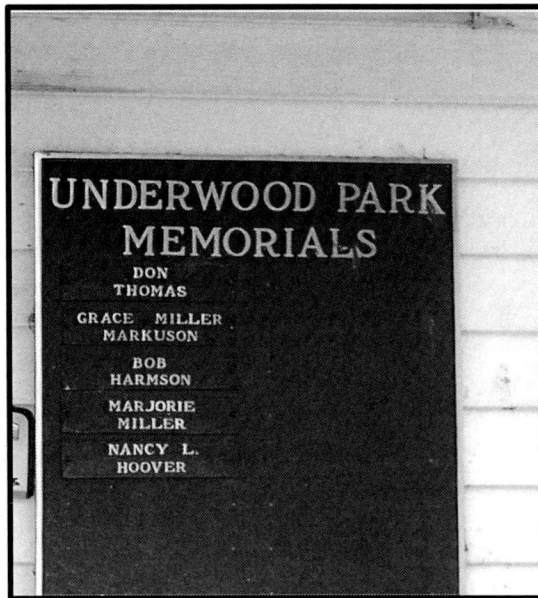

Those honored are Don Thomas, Grace Miller Markuson, Bob Harmson, Marjorie Miller, and Nancy L. Hoover

At some point the teacher's house on the school property became a caretaker's house. In 1972 Mrs. Phare was the center's caretaker. Also in that same year a rummage sale was held by the Underwood Community Club. Mrs. Phare retired from this position in 1981.

In 1984 Mike and Jackie Tiffany became the new caretakers of the Underwood Community Center, replacing Mrs. Phare, who retired from that position when a fire gutted the caretaker's home three years earlier. Since that time the Underwood Community Council organized remodeling projects on the home with members of the community getting together to do the work.

The caretaker's home sits on the corner of Schoolhouse Road and Cook-Underwood Road, next to the post office building.

As caretakers of the Community Center, the Tiffanys arranged for renting of the skating rink, gym, kitchen, meeting room and outside grounds. They also cleaned the building and mowed the lawn in return for free rent in the caretaker's house. The council sponsored a spaghetti feed fundraiser for upkeep expenses on the center, such as refinishing the rink floor and painting the building.

In May of 1984 the rumor that the Underwood post office might close was discussed at the Underwood Community Council meeting. Wilma McCarthy, postal officer-in-charge, feared that the 225 route customers would receive their mail in Bingen, but the 60 mail box customers would still probably receive their mail in Underwood. John D. Wyatt, senior postal inspector from Portland visited the facility and declared the post office building at the bottom of the hill was substandard.

The Underwood Community Council June Jamboree of 1984 raised money to refurbish the Community Center and build an outside picnic shelter. There was a slow pitch softball tournament, a beer garden, a dessert sale and a Father's Day pancake breakfast.

In July 1989 Jackie Tiffany announced that she was leaving. She and her husband Mike were moving to Port Angeles, where he had a job diving for sea cucumbers. The new caretaker was Nancy Hoover. The Community Center now had a new outdoor covered patio/picnic area, thanks to SDS and Broughton's for donating the lumber. The Don Thomas memorial basketball court was almost finished in that year.

In 1996 Skamania County purchased the Underwood Recreation Center property from the White Salmon Valley School District. Thomasina Campbell recalls the price was $240,000.

The Community Council is presently involved in a community garden project,

**Organizations** (continued)

headed by Caroline Elliott. A pot luck picnic is held each fall and desserts are raffled to raise funds for community projects.

## Skamania County Weed Board

In March 1975 Ted Lehmann, Underwood, was elected to the countywide weed board. The immediate goal was to control tansy ragwort, star thistle, blue lupine and Scotch broom.

## Underwood Conservation District

This group was organized in 1940 to assist local farmers in solving agriculture problems. Although the office has moved to White Salmon, this organization originated in Underwood in 1940. It was established by local Underwood orchardists and farmers who saw the need for natural resource assistance to maintain the viability of their operations. The major objectives of the Underwood Soil Conservation District, as it was originally called, were to control erosion, maintain and /or increase soil fertility, readjust farming systems, develop and conserve adequate water supply, control weeds and control rodents.

In February 1941 the second meeting of the USCD was held in the Underwood school. Harry Card was chair of the board of supervisors. Trevor Steele, district conservationist, discussed land use capability.

The Underwood Conservation District was organized as a legal sub-division of the State of Washington, governed by local people, to identify and help private land owners solve their conservation problems. The office of UCD supervisors includes such Underwoodlians as Earl J. Cummins, Olaf Larsen, Howard Ericson, Harry J.Card, R.G. Moore, L.W. Ternahan, Clark Ziegler and Jim Ziegler. The Underwood Conservation District has expanded to encompass all of Skamania County and the western third of Klickitat County. The objectives have expanded to include fire mitigation and the spring native shrub and tree sale.

Thank you to current manager Tova Tillinghast for the information. Tova has been manager since 2007. The office now has five full-time employees and one part time forester. The Underwood Conservation District website is: www.ucdwa.org

**Below:**
**Painting by Hood River Artist Jerry Pickard**
**Looking east from Underwood heights.**
From the Gordon Baker family collection

# PART TWO: FAMILY HISTORIES

## Map of Underwood Roads

From Map of Skamania County

Many of the Underwood roads were named for early local settlers. In the following pages you will learn their histories. A 1934 map of land owners can be found at HistoricMapWorks.com. You can zoom in to get a better view than what we can print here.

# PART TWO

# FAMILY HISTORIES

Not all of the families that inhabited Underwood Mountain through the years are found in this history. Some of the early settlers were mentioned in old news accounts. Some of the current inhabitants were interviewed. Others can be found in the Underwood, Washington Cemetery Obituaries book by Ralph Brown. Even so, many have been missed, but the following reports and memoirs represent a cross-section of the Underwood population. For some of the families, all we have found is a brief local newspaper report. We have included those to place them here at a certain time.

In the 1900 census report, the population of Underwood was 130. The movoto.com web site gave the recent population of Underwood zip code area 98651 as 457 females and 548 males, totaling 1005.

Many of the early settlers lived elsewhere, but came in the summers to tend their orchards, which they called ranches. This was understandable due to the snow conditions in the winter on the mountain and the lack of developed roads or automobiles in this area before 1910.

*******************

### Airsman, Claude

Born 1879 in Missouri, in 1911 he acquired a 120 acre homestead on Underwood Mountain. He worked for Broughton Lumber Company at Hood. He was gored to death by his bull in 1938.

### Amos, I.N.

In 1909 the family expected to spend most of their summer here and were enlarging their summer camp at the ranch.

### Anderson, Thomas and Christine

Born in Norway, they were among the early settlers and lived on a ten acre orchard tract in the Climax area north of Underwood. Thomas died in 1920 and

Christine died in 1928. At the time of her death, survivors included a son Arthur Anderson of Portland and a daughter Mrs. E.J. Buehler of Osage, Iowa. A May 1917 news article noted that Tom Anderson was busy spraying his orchard. Mr. Anderson was one of Underwood's successful orchardists.

### Asbury, George and Edna

George was born in Colorado in 1875 and died in 1930 in Underwood. At that time their children were all living in Underwood: Alma Newell, Viola Faubion, Ava, Verne, Irwin, Lawrence, Virgil, Ronald, Ralph and Lyle. Son Lawrence was a World War II Navy veteran and worked in the woods for SDS Lumber Company. Daughter Alma was married to Paul Newell and was an Underwood resident for 34 years. Daughter Ava married Pete Grove and was an Underwood resident for 46 years.

### Ashley

Ashley Drive, off Kollack-Knapp Road, was named for a doctor from Seattle.

### Ausplund, Aundre

In September 1928, the *Pioneer* reported, "Mr. Ausplund is all smiles again. Mrs. Ausplund returned from Portland bringing a fine baby boy. Aundre figures that by the time the pear orchard, which he recently set out, comes into bearing he will need a few extra pickers."

Ausplund Road connects to the far west end of Kollack-Knapp. Mr. Ausplund had a big orchard there, Triple A Orchard. It was eventually sold to Mt. Adams Orchard.

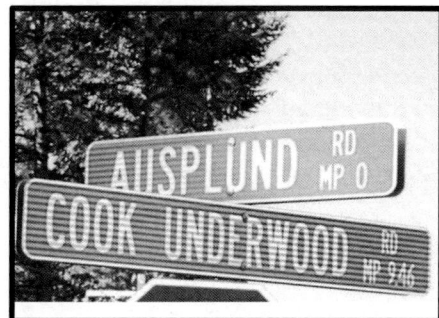

## Baker, George and Elva

*The Mt. Adams Sun,* September 1, 1955 edition had an article on the Bakers titled WATER TRANSFORMS WORTHLESS LAND INTO SPECTACULAR ACRES FOR BAKERS. The article mentions that George Baker married Elva Schwinge in 1942 and they lived on the bluff above Old Town Underwood. The land originally belonged to Mary Underwood Olsen Lane, who inherited it from her ancestors, (probably her father Amos Underwood.) She sold the waterless volcanic rock shelf to Elva's mother, Mrs. Hazel (*Sturtevant*) Schwinge Christiansen. George and Elva bought it from her and obtained priceless water from the Underwood heights PUD water district. "Without water the place wouldn't be worth five cents," George says. He was planting their 31 acres in pasture and alfalfa. The Bakers had a herd of whiteface cattle, a horse, chickens, about 50 turkeys and seven or eight parakeets.

The news article goes on to describe the finely detailed pumice block house and the magnificent lawn and gardens. Elva even planted rock gardens on the tall stone pinnacles that lean out from the bluff on their property.

The Bakers opened the Automotive and Industrial Supply store in Bingen in the late 1940s. Elva passed away at age 81 in 1999.

A *Pioneer* May 1973 item mentioned that Mr. George Baker returned from a tour which took him to Ireland, Turkey, Greece and the Black Sea.

## Baker, Gordon and Betty

They were married in April of 1929 and moved from Locke Hill to Underwood in 1942. (Laurie says 1945.) They moved to the Shipley ranch which had been purchased by Harry Card who was a gentleman farmer. Mr. Baker acted as ranch manager. The Gordon Bakers raised four sons: David (born 1930), Gerald (1935), Dick (1937) and Laurie (1945). They all

graduated from White Salmon High School and graduated from college.

At the passing of Gordon and Betty, the Shipley/Baker place was sold to Paul and Pier Huber in the 1980s. It is now a beautiful vineyard.

By David and Virginia Baker and Laurie Baker

Gordon Baker orchard. Photo from the Gordon Baker family collection.

Gordon Baker house. Photo from Gordon Baker family collection.

## Barney, Elmo and Nancy.
*(As told by Nancy Barney)*

Elmo and I (Nancy) Barney moved to Underwood in 1968. We arrived on our daughter Marion's 10th birthday. My elderly mother moved with us as well as our dog and canary. Our oldest son Tim, stayed behind in California, as he was in college. Other family members included Barbara, a junior in high school, and Brian, in 8th grade.

**Our view of Mt. Hood**

We moved to Underwood because Elmo took over the position as manager of Spring Creek NFH. Elmo was born in Aurora, IL, in 1920. He served in the US Marine Corps from 1942 to 1945, in the South Pacific. We were married in Newport, RI, in 1945. Elmo started school at the University of IL in the fall of 1946. I was born in South Bend, IN in 1925. We moved to Aurora, IL after my father's death in 1928. Years later Elmo and Nancy met in an ice cream parlor, through a mutual friend.

When Elmo graduated from college jobs were scarce in wildlife. But he managed to get a job at Creston Hatchery in Montana.

Elmo and I had been introduced to Underwood in the fall of 1956. We were living in Montana at the time. Elmo was asked by Harlan Johnson, at the Little White Salmon National Fish Hatchery at Cook, to come out for several weeks to help with spawning. We both fell in love with the Gorge, even though we were very fond of the Flathead Valley of Montana.

So in 1968 Elmo arrived in Underwood first. A decision had to be made on where to live. The hatchery residence normally used for the manager was not going to be large enough for our family. Another couple graciously switched homes and we moved in to a larger home and yard to accommodate our family.

The next decision was about school. Benny Cox, a former employee, had sent his daughter to Stevenson. The children in the other three nearby hatcheries all were going to Stevenson. We were approached by both Stevenson and White Salmon Districts. The Strunk's daughter went to White Salmon and they were very happy with the grade school. Since our two older ones, Barbara and Brian, didn't want to spend so much time on the bus, we opted for White Salmon also. It was the right decision because the kids from Upper Underwood all went to White Salmon, so ours made friends fairly quickly.

**Our front yard in 1981, and pet Annie**

## Barney, Elmo and Nancy (continued)

We both truly loved our time at Spring Creek, though we did find it somewhat difficult to get acquainted. There was a bit of Skamania vs. Klickitat County at the time. Officially the hatchery was in Skamania, but we were more connected to White Salmon because of school choice and the fact that our church was in Bingen. We used White Salmon doctors, shopping, etc. We knew several people from the other hatcheries when we moved there, which made it nice.

I started volunteering at Skyline Hospital shortly after we moved there. I joined the guild. Our main fund raiser was the chicken barbecue at the Huckleberry Festival. We had a lot of support from Dick Crothers who owned the grocery store in White Salmon. Five of us started a lobby gift shop at Skyline. After several years we got weary and it eventually closed.

I was also active in the Lutheran Church in Bingen. Most involvement was with a Lutheran Home for mentally handicapped located in Cornelius, OR.

In the late 70's and early 80's I was appointed to the Washington Columbia Gorge Commission.

The Broughton Mill was always a good neighbor to the hatchery. Even to the point that our dog Casi, was more or less welcome there-- as evidenced in the picture I'm including. Casi did worry Don Thomas because of the heavy equipment moving around. But the men working there were partly to blame -- they fed him while they were on their lunch hour -- and Casi could tell time!!

**Casi at Broughton Mill**

**Ray Chambers pokes lumber headed for the resaw into a roller lined chute after a 55 minute flume ride. At right, Chambers' companion intently eyes a tiny minnow darting up and down the channel.**
*The Enterprise* – May 17, 1979

A delightful elderly gentleman, Captain Treiber, lived down the road from us, in the group of homes and businesses near the mouth of the White Salmon. Elmo got well acquainted with him. The kids and I did also, but Elmo spent more time with him as Cap liked to visit the hatchery. He was a retired commercial ship captain. One of his claims to fame was that he took the very first shipment of cattle to Alaska, landing them at Seward. It was part of the government's settling the valley east of Anchorage.

> *Elmo took over the position as manager of Spring Creek National Fish Hatchery.*

114

## Barney, Elmo and Nancy (continued)

**Our home in 1979 or 1980, 72 inches of snow in 72 hours.**

We loved our time there in Underwood. If we hadn't both been adventuresome, chances are we'd have retired there. We left Underwood in 1985. Elmo had spent 34 years as a manager and biologist for the US Fish and Wildlife Service. From there we were asked to go to Alaska, for two years while he worked at the hatchery at Metlakatla. We made several more interesting moves before finally establishing our lives in Battleground, WA. Three of our four children have settled in the area as well.

We lost Elmo in February of 2010. He was 89. We had been married 64 years.

> *Broughton's Mill was always a good neighbor to the Fish Hatchery.*
> *Nancy Barney*

### Bauerle
A 1953 *Mt. Adams Sun* advertisement said that the 145 acre Bauerle estate was for sale. It had spring water and a 4 bedroom house with a basement. It was located off Love Road in Underwood.

### Beebe, Gerald
In 1908 he purchased the Luthy place. Mr. Beebe made some extensive alterations and improvements to his home, as well as clearing up more land. In 1909 he was a partner with Henry Love in Bear Springs Ranch. In 1912 his half-interest in Bear Springs Ranch 2 ½ miles Northwest of Underwood was sold to Calvin Phillips of Tacoma. H.K. Love was the owner of the other half interest. Mr. Phillips was Mr. Love's uncle.

### Berrong, Charles and Edna
Charles was born in 1888 in Georgia, married Edna Swanson in 1908 and moved to Underwood in 1925. He died in 1952, leaving his wife and six children: Charles and Ike of Portland, Mrs. Herb (Lois) Sellsted, Willard, Eugene and Earl of Underwood and Lloyd of Mississippi. Son Fred had died in World War II in a battle at Normandy.

### Boersig, Fred and Josephine
Mrs. Boersig spent the winter of 1917/18 in Portland. The 1934 Plat Map of Underwood shows that Mrs. Josephine Boersig owned land to the east of Love Hill, also known as Green Mountain.

### Bolle, Henry and Elsie
He was manager of the fish hatchery for many years, beginning in 1908. Elsie spent her early years at the home of her Underwood pioneer parents, Christian and Mary Larsen.

## Brehm, Peter and Faye

The Brehms are owners of White Salmon Vineyard and operate a wine tasting room in the historic Underwood Mercantile building. In 1990 they purchased the Paul Newell, Sr. acreage on Newell Road and transformed an aging pear orchard into a 20-acre vineyard.

Originally from Connecticut, Peter earned a degree in business and worked a few years before entering law school in San Francisco. Being exposed to the wine country of the area, he became engaged in home winemaking. He soon turned his focus from the law to the lore of the grape. He and Faye opened a wine and beer-making retail business where they sold supplies and fresh grapes from the now famous vineyards of Napa and Sonoma to home winemakers. Peter was also instrumental in legalizing home beer making in California.

Peter soon developed the process of freezing and shipping wine grapes. In 1988, he began buying and distributing these grapes around North America and signed a contract to sell the grapes from a vineyard in Underwood Heights. The grapes were processed in Gresham and Bingen and were sold nationally.

Faye Brehm, after raising their two children, retired as an administrator in the architectural field, and now runs the White Salmon Vineyard Tasting Room in the old Underwood Post Office housed in the Old Town Underwood Mercantile building at the foot of Cook-Underwood road at State Highway 14.

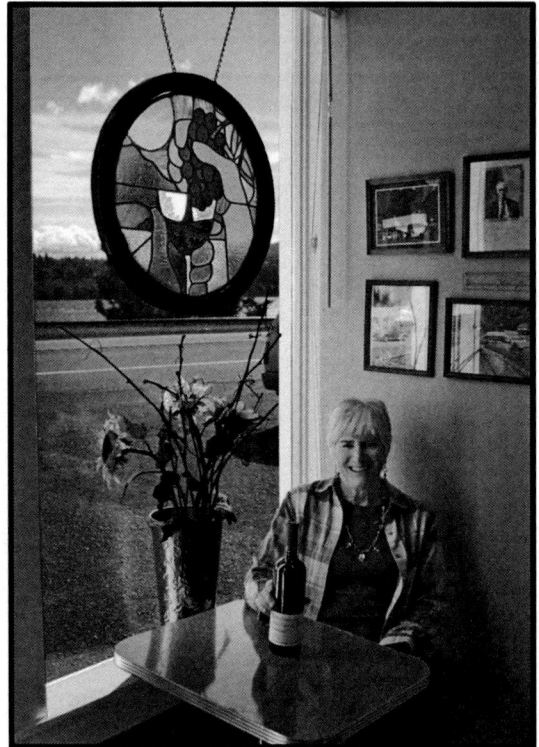

**Faye Brehm at the "Merc"**

## Brown, Kermit and Wilma.
(*As told by Wilma Brown*)

We moved to Underwood in January of 1944. We bought our place from a woman named Cordier.

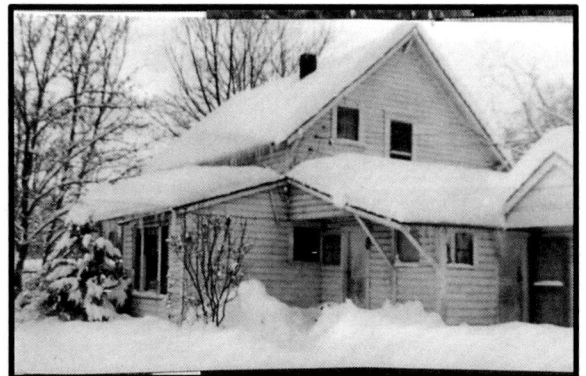

**Brown Family Home – Corner of Cook/ Underwood Rd. and Orchard Lane. Photo from Brown family collection.**

## Brown, Kermit and Wilma (continued)

Kermit Brown was born in Warwick, ND on October 16th, during the flu epidemic in 1918. I was born in Harlow, ND 6 days later on October 22. We were married in 1940 on the 18th of October, so he could be older than I on our certificate. It was important to me that the man be older than his wife. Our son Ralph was born in 1943; Beverly, 1945; Kathy, 1946; Judy, 1950; Barbara, 1953; and Kerma, 1957.

Other than Ralph, our family was all born when we lived in the house on the corner of Orchard Lane and Cook/ Underwood Road. (*It is a green farm-house today.*) We had 3 acres, short platted it and sold the home place and the 2nd acre. We kept the 3rd acre and moved into a manufactured home there in 1978.

**The Kermit Elmo Brown Family in 1955**
Left to Right: Beverly, Judy, Wilma, Ralph, Barbara, Kermit, Kathy
Missing: Kerma b 1957

The post office was by the railroad tracks and we could even go down on Sunday mornings and get mail. The Underwood Mercantile was being rebuilt in 1946 after the fire. I cooked meals for the carpenters at the time. Ralph and Beverly were small and I was pregnant with Kathy. I couldn't finish out the cooking for them because Beverly was getting to be too much of a handful and Ralph was not old enough to be much help.   When

the building was finished George Balsiger was able to re-stock his store with new appliances. We bought the first electric stove he got in. Before that I cooked on a wood stove.

Left to Right Statnding: Beverly, Kathy, Ralph, Judy
Left to Right Sitting: Wilma, Kerma, Barbara, Kermit
The Kermit Brown Family in 1965

We came to Washington because Kermit had asthma and the doctor told him that if he wanted to live long, we had to get out of North Dakota. We had other relatives in Bingen at the time. All our kids went through school in White Salmon.

My husband Kermit worked first as an engineer at the Underwood Fruit Ware-house in Underwood. Can't remember how long, but it was rather hard as there were 3 shifts, and they had 1 week on days, 1 week swing, and 1 week graveyard. It would have been much better to have a longer time on each. Later he worked at Broughton's as a timber faller. Later he had his own logging company, and was on his own until he bought a second-hand store. That was in the early 1970's and the store was in White Salmon.  We moved the store to

## Brown, Kermit and Wilma (continued)

Bingen after a couple of years. We had part of the big building that is now Insitu. Kermit retired from there in 1983.

I never worked out in earlier years, but I sold door-to-door for seven years. I was an Avon dealer and also sold for a few other companies. I sold greeting cards for a company, and also children's books for another company. I think I quit in about 1959.

In 1962 I bought out the Walters Variety Store in White Salmon. That was sort of a spur-of-the-moment thing. Heamans in White Salmon had a mercantile and also a yardage section. I sewed a lot and needed some interfacing. I went into Heamans and asked for interfacing. They didn't have any. I walked across the street to the variety store. When she asked if she could help I said, "I am so mad. I have to go to Hood River just for some interfacing. I think I will start a fabric store in this town." She said, "Why don't you buy me out and put some in here?"

I went home and asked my husband and he said O.K. So that's what I did. I opened the store July 1, 1962. In 1964 we moved across the street into the Hunsaker Building. That was where Donna Ervin had a restaurant later. I stayed there until 1974 when I closed out the store. By that time I was selling and repairing sewing machines. Kermit had his second-hand store down the street. When he moved to Bingen I sold out and moved my sewing machine business into his store. I stayed there until 1983, then moved to the building that became a photo shop, until I retired in 1984. I then moved the repair business to our home in Underwood. If you ask people about Brown's Variety and Brown's Bargains they will remember.

There have been several times that the Cook/Underwood Road has been repaired. I remember one time we had to use the Dam Road to get to White Salmon.

When Ralph was six years old he fell out of my car one day and hit his head. He

was unconscious for six days, then five more days that he could respond but was not quite alert. Later the community had a dance and donated the money to us. Everyone had such a good time that a community club was organized. We ended up with a Sunday School homemakers' group, and roller skating every Friday night which I helped with every week. We also had regular dances which led to a square dance group. Later Boy Scouts and 4-H groups were formed. I had a Boy Scout group. One of my scouts was Ralph, of course, Jimmie Schwinge, and others that I can't remember. I also worked as advisor to a girls group who were learning to sew.

There were several large families in lower Underwood. The other mothers and I decided the children needed to have an Easter egg hunt, to be held at our place. We bought wrapped candy and charged each child 10 cents to hunt. We planned three age groups. Some of the families involved were the Tates, Finks, Zieglers, Newells, Ellsons, and Balsigers. This worked well for several years. Then I bought a store in White Salmon and Margaret Oliver and I organized an Easter egg hunt there. Merchants donated prizes which the kids could receive when they discovered a slip with the merchant's name in their eggs. I bought all the candy from my sources for the variety store. I also helped organize the first Huckleberry Festival. Those were busy but fun times.

Once in a while in the winter the school would declare a snow day due to bad weather. My good friend Teresa Ziegler, myself, and a couple others would call up one another and say, "What do you have for leftovers?" We'd all congregate in one home. We'd put meals together for lunch, the kids would all play, and we ladies would play cards.

I still play a lot of cards to this day. I mainly enjoy playing hearts, pinochle, whist, and of course solitaire. Although it is hard to find many to play whist. And it is

118

**Brown, Kermit and Wilma** (continued)

sometimes hard to find enough people to play any cards at all. But it is such a good past time.

I am not sure when the Underwood School was torn down. I know we got a sheet of blackboard and lined a wall in our upstairs with it.

We were very, very busy.

**Wilma and Kermit Brown**
**Photo from the Brown family collection**

**Wilma Brown – August, 2008**

Mrs. Brown, now 94, still has their place on Orchard Lane. She spends part of each year in California with her daughter Kathy Layman. Her husband Kermit Elmo Brown died in 2000 at the age of 81.

************************

*Additions to Wilma Brown's story – shared by son Ralph Brown:*

Our house was on the west corner of Orchard Lane, then on the east corner was Ted Balsiger, then just east of his house was the Reed house. Great people.

In June of 1950, I made a fatal decision. My mother was taking a bunch of us 7 and 8 year olds to a Bible School in White Salmon. We just got through picking up the last kids and somehow, I was standing in the backseat behind my mother who was driving. (The seat was full of Avon products.) The door did not get completely shut, so, I was going to do what dad always did and that was open the door and slam it shut. The car was going down Cook/Underwood Road, not too far from where Robert Morby now lives. The car my parents owned had suicide doors in the rear, so when I opened the door to slam it shut, the speed of the air jerked me out and I lit on my head fracturing it in five places.

In those days there were no air-lift facilities. My dad was in the crummy coming down the hill from working at Broughton's that evening. He knew something was wrong as there was a cloud hanging over our home. The ambulance, called by Harry Card and Gordon Baker, took me to the Hood River Hospital and then, because of a landslide on the Oregon side, travelled the Washington highway to Portland. Police escorted us over the bridge at Vancouver. We arrived at Providence Hospital, where I stayed for the next 13 days, most of the time unconscious, and not expected to survive.

**Brown, Kermit and Wilma** (continued)

Now here is the sad part of the story. It was that very morning that mom and dad sat at the breakfast table and decided that was the day that mom was going to stop by the Dr. office and pay off their balance of what was owed and then they were in a position to save $100 per month. Well, they did have insurance on me, but since I was not operated on, the insurance did not pay up. So my parents canceled the insurance policy. In the next few years we kids had hospital stays because of appendicitis, and other ailments. So because of a decision I made, my parents spent a good number of years getting out of debt and my body was damaged in ways that technology in 1950 could not see. My first indication that there was an eyesight problem was when I could see two cars instead of one in our neighbors', the Reeds', yard. Technology in 2012 has been able to see other head and brain damage, but it seems like even with the damage caused by a 20 mile an hour head bump on the pavement, sufficient healing took place to allow a decent career.

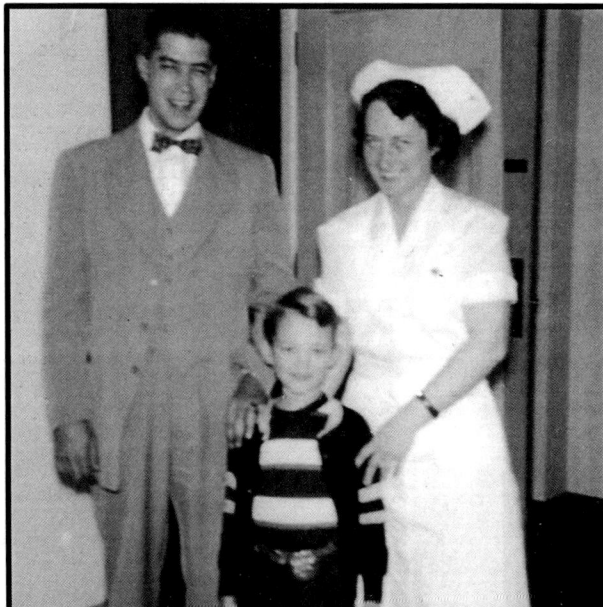

**Ralph Brown at Providence Hospital, Portland, Oregon - June 1950**

I remember before this time that we kids would play around the old school house which was still standing. We would go inside where all the books were. I wish now we had taken some for historical value, but did not.

Our house was on the route for migrant workers heading to the Thun orchard. They would stop at our house and cut the grass with a scythe, and then my mom would feed them.

I used to baby-sit for Dr. and Mrs Halver on up the hill.

When I fell out of the car, the community rallied behind my folks. They got together at the gymnasium and had a fund raiser for my parents as their insurance did not cover my hospital stay. To my understanding this event brought the community together and then there began community dances, skating parties, etc.

Mom has one sister and two brothers left. She has coordinated all of her class reunions in North Dakota for the past 15 years. There were only five classmates left a couple of years ago.

\*\*\*\*\*\*\*\*\*\*\*\*\*\*\*\*\*\*\*\*\*\*\*\*\*

*(A daughter, Beverly Brown Martin, added the following)*

I remember one time the road was closed and we had to use the Dam Road in 1964. I remember having Sunday School in the old school building. I also remember going over to use the bathroom in the old school when we were roller skating. It was a neat old building. For some reason I remember the main floor and the kitchen with the wood stove. But I don't know when it was torn down.

\*\*\*\*\*\*\*\*\*\*\*\*\*\*\*

*(Additions shared by daughter Kathy Brown Layman)*

When I was very young I would slip on over to the cemetery. It was only about a quarter mile from our home. I remember feeling so bad that many of the grave stones did not have flowers. Right after

## Brown, Kermit and Wilma (continued)

Memorial Day there would be lots of flowers on graves. I would take a flower or two from other graves and put them on the graves that did not have any. It made me feel good.

I remember Mrs. Moteki who lived down the road past us at the corner of Orchard Lane. She and her husband lived in a very tiny place in the peach orchard. Mrs. Moteki loved children. On Halloween we would go to her house. She would have prepared all these small, brown bags. Inside each bag were dozens of tiny little, fancy cookies she had made. We did not speak Mrs. Moteki's language, nor did she speak ours, but we were able to communicate, and it was wonderful.

*(Note: Mrs. Hatsu Moteki died in 1980. Her husband Makoto Moteki died in 1960. See Underwood, Washington Cemetery Obituary book)*

I usually accompany my mom to North Dakota each summer for her class reunion, which mom usually helps plan. The last time there were about five graduates and 15 attending (spouses and grown children). We all had a good time.

A final comment: Wilma and Kathy traveled by car to a family get together in North Dakota the end of June, 2013. When Ralph called to see if they had arrived, he was informed that they could not talk on the phone as they were already involved in a card game of Whist.

From *The Enterprise* April 2, 1987 – *"Kermit Brown has invented the Brush Breaker, a heavy-duty weed eater made from a chain saw blade and two round-cut, center bored metal plates held together by two bolts."* He later received a patent for his invention.

## Bueche, Frederick and Bertha

Frederick was born in 1866 in Germany. He married Bertha Hall who was born in 1866 in Wisconsin. They lived for 28 years in Underwood. Mr. Bueche was a miner. He died in 1937, Bertha in 1961.

## Bueche, Herman

He emigrated from Germany in 1883 along with his brother Frederick. A 1907 news item said that Herman Bueche came up last week to visit friends. He had been spending several months in the mines in southern Oregon that he had an interest in. He was Skamania County engineer for two terms, being elected in 1914. He was also a mining engineer in later life. He died in 1927 and is buried in the cemetery in Underwood.

## Cameron, R.D.

He came to the area in 1883 and settled on 640 acres in 1889. He was in the saw mill business for several years with George Nicolai. In 1896 Ann Cameron obtained 160 acres and Colin Cameron, 80 acres. A news note in 1909: " R.D. Cameron was quite badly injured last week by getting into a mix up with a bull which he was attempting to lead while riding a horse. The bull bolted down the hill and threw the horse over onto Mr. Cameron, who was badly hurt around the head and chest, several ribs being broken."

## Campbell, Donald and Thomasina
(As told to Kathy LaMotte)

The Campbells, Donald and Thomasina, came to Underwood in 1974. They first started looking for a farm to buy in the San Francisco area. When that search wasn't successful they then turned their thoughts to perhaps settling in the Hood River Valley. But after several trips back and forth from Florida, Don heard about a piece of property off the west end of Kollock-Knapp Road that was owned by Bill and Russ McVeigh. They convinced the brothers to sell and soon the 80 acres belonged to the Campbells.

Thomasina Campbell was born in Burlington, NC, and Don was born in Cleveland, OH. How they met was work related. After marriage they lived for many years in Boca Raton, FL, where they

## Campbell, Donald and Thomasina
(continued)

owned an orchid business and a scuba diving shop. Thomasina had one daughter, Carol, who is deceased, and together Don and Thomasina have two children. Dale lives in Wilsonville, and Nanette lives in Vancouver. While living in Florida, Don was a fire officer for 25 years.

**Donald Campbell**

As a young man Don enlisted in the Navy. He spent his naval career on submarines. He was honorably discharged from the Navy. Then the Korean War began in 1950 and Don was drafted into the Army. He was sent to Germany, which is where he spent the duration of the Korean Crisis.

When the Campbells took over the property on Underwood Hill much of it was covered in orchards. There were some apple trees standing at the time. Thomasina recalls one beautiful variety of apple was called winter banana. The apple trees have nearly all been cut down and the farm was soon raising only pears. The trees were all pretty old when they first started working their orchard. Don went through and planted new trees in between all the old, and when they had

grown to substantial size to produce, the old trees were cut down.

The Campbells were living in the original farmhouse, a beautiful red structure dating back to the late 1800's. In about 1978 Don began building a new house on the property. This large brown home sits somewhat southeast of the old home. Doing all the work themselves, building the home was a long process. They moved into their new home in 1980. The old home still stands up behind.

The Campbells' twin granddaughters came to live with them in 1979 and were a close part of their family and of the community for many years.

**Thomasina Campbell**

Over the years both Donald and Thomasina have been very active in the Republican Party. Thomasina has been precinct chair since 1974.

They have always held an interest in the Underwood Community Center. For many years Thomasina was secretary of the Underwood Community Council. As explained by Thomasina, the Underwood School became a part of the White Salmon Valley School District during WWII. The district could not afford to have a teacher in the small district. But over the years the community felt it was important

## Campbell, Donald and Thomasina
(continued)

to keep an active community center. They would have fund raisers to pay for electricity and repairs. A caretaker would live in the small house on the corner of School House Rd. and Cook/Underwood Rd. In the late 70's the house burned. Mrs. Phare was living there as caretaker at the time. Many of the community felt it was important to rebuild the home and also to keep the community center open. Rebuilding began. Plumbing and electrical work was donated, funds for supplies were raised, and labor was all donated by local residents. During this time, ladies of the community, Carole Ziegler, Thomasina Campbell, and others, would take turns going down, unlocking and re-locking the center morning and night in order that it could be used. After the home was rebuilt Jackie and Mike Tiffany moved in as caretakers. Later, Nancy Morby lived there as caretaker for 15 years.

**Donald K. Campbell**

On May, 2011 Donald K. Campbell passed away after being ill for some time. The Campbells had been married for 59 years. Thomasina still lives in the home they built and keeps in constant contact with family and many friends.

A couple of historical inserts as told by Mrs. Campbell are as follows: On the east side of their property is McVeigh Rd., which leads on up into Underwood Mountain. At one time there was a lumber mill on that road. The mill employed many Chinese workers. Near the west side of their property is Ausplund Road. At one time, she was told, there was a school house on that road.

## Card, Harry J. and Margaret
*Enterprise* Feb. 15, 1935 – **Harry Card buys Herbert Ziegler Place on Underwood Heights**

*C.H. Estes, local realtor, reports the sale of the Herbert M. Ziegler (son of Samuel Ziegler of White Salmon) orchard on Underwood Heights to Harry J. Card of the Mountain Brook district. The orchard ranch consists of 40 acres, highly improved, 25 acres with bearing pear and apple trees. A beautiful residence is on the place, overlooking the Columbia River and the Hood River Valley. This is one of the finest properties of this section. The Cards will occupy their new home right away. Mr. Card is director of the Production Credit Corporation for Klickitat and Skamania counties.*

Mr. Card bought an additional 145 acres on Underwood Mountain in 1936. He previously owned property in the Mountain Brook area. He had come from the Denver area where his family owned manufacturing facilities, the Card Iron Works. The land in the Underwood ranch operation consisted of four main properties and was used for fruit, hay, wheat, and Black Angus cattle. At that time water for household use was pumped from School House Road up to a holding tank on the Shipley/Baker place. The crops were raised dry land. Water for spraying was trucked by tank from the Broughton flume. In 1943 Mr. Card harvested 3,810 boxes of fruit. He put in agriculture practices of thinning out half the trees, spraying, pruning and using cover crops. Harvest increased to 10,000 boxes of fruit in 1948.

**Card, Harry and Margaret** (continued)

In 1951 he bought the Jim Haynes place. The same year Harry Card of Columbia Crest Farms was Skamania Co. Cattleman of the year. Harry helped organize the Underwood Conservation District and was chair for six years. He was one of the first contour strip crop farmers in the northwest. The Card home, perched 1000 feet on the bluff above the Columbia River, commanded one of the world's most spectacular views. Mr. and Mrs. Card had a son John.

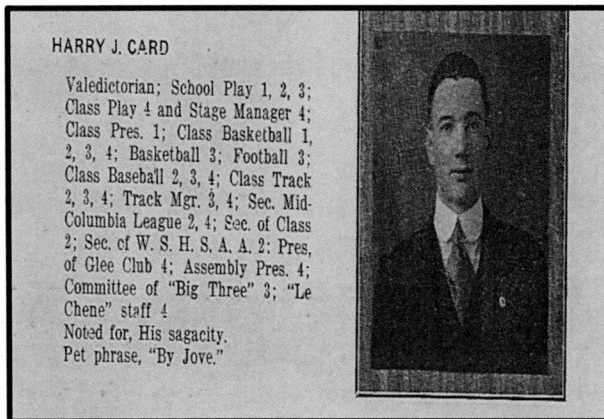

HARRY J. CARD

Valedictorian; School Play 1, 2, 3; Class Play 4 and Stage Manager 4; Class Pres. 1; Class Basketball 1, 2, 3, 4; Basketball 3; Football 3; Class Baseball 2, 3, 4; Class Track 2, 3, 4; Track Mgr. 3, 4; Sec. Mid-Columbia League 2, 4; Sec. of Class 2; Sec. of W. S. H. S. A. A. 2; Pres. of Glee Club 4; Assembly Pres. 4; Committee of "Big Three" 3; "Le Chene" staff 4
Noted for, His sagacity.
Pet phrase, "By Jove."

**1919 Senior Class in White Salmon**

**Margaret Card at Bird Creek Meadows**
Photo from Gordon Baker family collection.

**Carstens, Wm.**

In August 1911 he purchased the blacksmith shop at Underwood and moved there from Stevenson. It was reported that he was doing well in his new location and that he now had Grandpa Pugh with him and both men are kept very busy in this shop.

**Cash W.F.**

In 1907 he purchased 40 acres of garden land from Mr. Kellendonk. The greater part of this land was under irrigation. A January 1915 news note said that the holiday was a very merry one at the home of Mr. and Mrs. Cash. A delicious dinner was served. The rooms were artistically decorated with Christmas greens and beautiful wreaths of holly. Among the guests were Mr. and Mrs. H.A. Hussey. In September 1917 Roland Cash (a son?) left for the Presidio in California. He had volunteered and would train as a motor truck driver. The Cash family must have moved away from Underwood because a news item in October of 1923 said that Mr. Cash of the Multnomah Hotel in Portland was in Underwood superintending the harvesting of his apples. And in August of 1928, Mr. and Mrs. Cash of Rhododendron Inn were in Underwood looking after the fruit on their ranch.

**Chevalier, Raymond and Elnora**
Interviewed and Written by: Darla Johnston

For 28 years Raymond (originally from St. Cloud, Minnesota) and his wife, Elnora (1936-2008) lived in housing provided by Broughton's Lumber Company in Willard, Washington. Rent was paid once a month. The company store was on the site and Harold Broughton ran it. The nice thing about the store was that workers could get draws when their money was in "short supply." As the only mechanic, Ray's job was to take care of all equipment. Because of the random breakdown he did not have a regular shift because he was available 24 hours/7days a week. Hours were kept by Ray and turned in every week. There was an air of satisfaction that the company never had any reason to question the hours submitted for pay.

Broughton's had quite an operation. Logs that were 26 to 28 inches in diameter by 4 feet long were floated down the flume in Willard from the mill into a lake at the bottom of Underwood Mountain to Hood, Washington. From there the logs were sold to steam boats.

One day sparks from a burner at the mill landed in saw dust in back of Raymond's home. The well was almost dry so there was not enough water to extinguish the flames and his home was completely destroyed. Broughton's built another home for Raymond one mile away at his current address in Underwood flats. Eventually Raymond purchased the house. He worked for the mill for 38 years.

Reminiscing about the past, he remembers his current home was built in an orchard. By the 1970's Raymond and Elnora had been married for 50 plus years and had been blessed with three sons. Eugene is not married and works as a Fiber Optics Linesman for Bill & Melinda Gates. Billy is a mechanic for a bus company in Portland while his son Ray is a baker at Costco in Portland. A sadness is felt as Raymond tells about having to endure another devastation of a fire recently in his Underwood home.

Raymond's growing up years were in St. Cloud, Minnesota. As to his descent he states his blood lines come from Mexican, Irish, and French. Proudly, Raymond relays that his great grandfather was a horseman for Napoleon's Army and that he has many relatives in Paris. Other notable relatives include an aunt (a banker) on his mother's side who lived in Waterloo, Iowa, but was originally from Scot-

land. She had the mishap of being aboard the Titanic. One other connection to fame is that "Seattle" was named after a family member.

Ray Chevalier served with the 37th Infantry from 1940 to 1945. Two of these five years he was stationed in the Pacific Theatre in the Aleutian Islands as Tech Sergeant with G2 army intelligence. While he states he was not particularly fond of living so long on such a small, isolated island, the beautiful "dance" of the colors in the sky from the Northern Lights and the moon reflection on the water at Kodiak Island were and are unforgettable and still vivid in his mind. The fox holes that he lived in at Dutch Harbor when Pearl Harbor was bombed were not among his best memories. However, he feels very proud of his military career. A quote from Ed LaMotte: "Ray has hundreds of stories about his experiences. One story involved Japanese on Kodiak Island. It was discovered the Japanese were using diapers hung on a clothesline to signal their submarines off shore with information about American fleet movements."

Seeing Mrs. (Eleanor) Roosevelt as she toured the Aleutian Islands on the General Tide Ship was exciting and a once in a life-time experience. Raymond, who was expecting to see a very refined lady, was "taken back" to see she was a very plain and "homely" in appearance. He was also surprised to hear her directness of speech as he was expecting the First Lady to be soft spoken, refined, and sophisticated. In spite of the contradictions of his expectations for the President's wife, seeing her in person would be something he would talk about for the rest of his life.

Upon returning to the States, Raymond spent some time near Hot Springs, Arkansas, guarding German POW's. Raymond has been a member of the American Legion Post 87 for 62 years and has lived in the Underwood area for

**Chevalier, Raymond** (continued)

approximately 62 year also. He is currently living at the Veterans' Home in The Dalles, OR.

> **Ray Chevalier served with the 37ᵗʰ infantry from 1940-1945.**

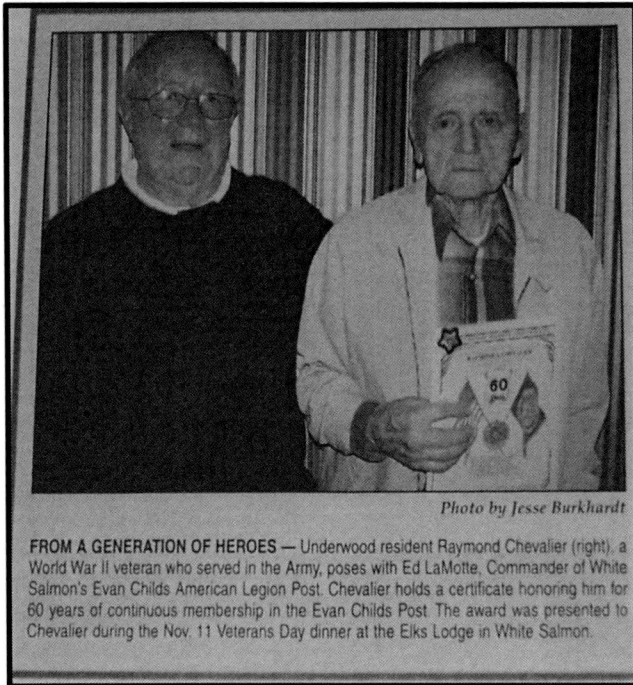

*Photo by Jesse Burkhardt*

FROM A GENERATION OF HEROES — Underwood resident Raymond Chevalier (right), a World War II veteran who served in the Army, poses with Ed LaMotte, Commander of White Salmon's Evan Childs American Legion Post. Chevalier holds a certificate honoring him for 60 years of continuous membership in the Evan Childs Post. The award was presented to Chevalier during the Nov. 11 Veterans Day dinner at the Elks Lodge in White Salmon.

**Underwood resident Raymond Chevalier (right) a World War II veteran who served in the Army, poses with Ed LaMotte, Commander of White Salmon's Evan Childs American Legion Post. Chevalier holds a certificate honoring him for 60 years of continuous membership in the Evan Childs Post. The award was presented to Chevalier during the Nov. 11 Veterans' Day dinner at the Elks Lodge in White Salmon.**

*The Enterprise*, November 19, 2009

**Clark, C.S.**

A neighbor of H.A. Hussey, he owned a ten acre orchard and berry farm in 1913. Mr. Clark previously had been the chief cook at the Hotel Potter, one of California's most fashionable hotels.

**Clarkson, John C.**

In 1893 he owned 40 acres in Underwood. In 1904 he had six acres in strawberries and orchard.

**Claridge, Joseph and Mable**

Mable Ellis Claridge died in 1936 and Joseph in 1944. In 1940, Joseph remarried to Mary Gale Snipes. Joseph and Mable are buried at Chris-Zada cemetery as are some of their children-Shirl, baby Myrtella, Melverda Lamoreaux and Valore Burles.

**Cochran, Thomas and Joanne**

(As told to Kathy LaMotte)

The Cochrans have lived here since 1988. They moved to the area from Eugene, OR, in 1985 and rented in Hood River for three years before buying their place on Hale Drive in Underwood. Tom had taken a job as Timberlands Manager with Co Ply in Stevenson, which was his profession.

Both of the Cochrans were born in Council Bluff, Iowa. Joanne in 1924, and Tom in 1927. They both attended Iowa State College. Joanne earned a degree in Home Economics. Tom graduated in 1952 with a degree in Forestry.

In 1952 they moved to Orting, WA where Tom was employed by a private forest industry. They then moved to Eugene, OR, in 1959 and bought a 28 acre tree farm, while Tom worked in the same profession. This is where they raised their four children. While in Eugene Joanne taught kindergarten. The kids were all active in 4-H. Joanne was leader of the beef club.

The Cochrans' family, all grown adults now, live in fairly close proximity to

## Cochran, Thomas and Joanne (cont.)

their parents. The oldest daughter, Patricia, and husband Del, live in Banks, OR. Their son, Dale, and wife Carol, live in Burns, OR, and their youngest daughter, Carol, and husband Al, now live in Lyle, WA. Their daughter Nancy recently passed away. They have nine grandchildren, and six great grandchildren, part of whom live on the Warm Springs Reservation.

The Cochrans have always kept busy with various hobbies. For many years Tom flew planes, owning five, the latter two being Stearman bi-planes, which he kept in Hood River. He enjoyed painting, using water colors, and was a collector of antique guns. He was an avid golfer for many years.

Joanne has always kept active. She is an avid quilter and has belonged to a quilting group for many years. She does all kinds of sewing, loves to garden and read. She too is an accomplished painter, flower scenes being one of her specialties.

The Cochrans enjoyed the companionship of their three pet Welch Corgis over the years, the first being Duffy. After Duffy came Wally and now a corgi puppy named Max.

Tom was in the military, serving in the US Coast Guard. His travels were in the North Atlantic during WWII. He was in Times Square to celebrate VJ Day (Victory over Japan) in September of 1945.

The Cochrans bought their place in 1988 from John and Carmen Rosenburger. They recalled theirs was the only house on their side of the street on Hale Drive at the time. Since then, at least nine homes have been built in the Hale/Ashley Drive neighborhood. With shrubs and trees constantly maturing they appreciated what view they had of Mt. Hood and the Hood River Valley.

**Thomas and Joanne Cochran**

**Thomas Cochran passed away November 8, 2012.**

## George W. and Harriet E. Collins

George and Harriet Collins were emigrants from Pennsylvania. George Washington Collins was born in Dixon, Tennessee, on June 10, 1870. His parents were James Shaffer Collins and Mary Eliza Johnston Collins. Harriet Emma Marshall Collins was the daughter of Ellis Lee Marshall and Mary Margaret Zimmerman. Harriet was born on April 23, 1874 in Franklin Square, Columbia County, Ohio.

**Collins, George and Harriett** (continued)

George Collins spent his early life in Dixon, TN. At the age of five he moved with his family to Lawrence County, PA. He attended Normal School, and then taught in Lawrence County, PA, and later in Franklin Square, Ohio. George met Harriet while they were both teaching in Volant, PA. They were married on April 12, 1894.

George Collins was not only a teacher, but also a carpenter. He worked on building a church in Volant, PA, where his wife's family, the Marshalls, came from. So he had the skills to build the family homestead in Underwood.

The Collins' would eventually have 13 children. Three children would die as infants. The rest of the family is as follows:
1. John M. Collins – born in 1895, in PA, died in The Dalles, OR in 1953. Was married to Eudocia (Angel) Pointer.
2. James Ellis Collins – born in 1896, Lancaster, PA, died in 1986, Bainbridge Island, WA.
3. Arthur James Collins – born in 1897 in PA and died in 1971, in Portland, OR. Was married to Jewel Dowdy.
4. Florence M. Collins Lilligard – born in 1899 in PA, and died in 1991 in Marion County, OR. Was married to Granville Lilligard.
5. Sarah E. Collins Bachus – born in 1902 in Volant, PA and died in 1986, in Orting, WA., husband Lester Bachus.
6. Lorna June Collins Ranslam – born in 1905 in PA, died in 1987 in Portland, OR, married Ed Ranslam.
7. Edith Emma Collins Dallas – born in 1907 in Volant, PA and died in 1999 in White Salmon, husband James Dallas.
8. Dr. George W. Collins – born in Underwood, WA in 1913. He became a physician, courtesy of the Army during and after WWII. He died in Pleasanton, CA in 1996.
9. Rev. William Robert Collins – born in

1915 in Underwood, WA. He died in 2012, in El Paso, TX at the age of 96. He married Edith Zouria McMahon.
10. Esther Elizabeth Collins Allaway – born in 1918 in Underwood, WA. She died in 2004, married Carlton Allaway.

**Photo: July 4, 1925**
**Back Row: Sara Collins Backus, Florence Collins Lillegard, Granville Lillegard, William Collins "Uncle Billy" brother of George W. Collins, Harriet Marshall Collins, Aunt Lucy Collins, Art Collins holding Toni Collins, Aunt Jane, Mrs. Lillegard, Jenne Collins wife of Hiram, Uncle Hiram Collins brother of George W. Collins.**
**Front Row: George W. Collins husband of Harriet, Lester Backus, June Collins Ranslam, Edith Collins Dallas, Esther Collins Allaway, George Collins Jr., Laurie Backus (Lester's brother), William Collins.**

The Collins family moved to Underwood from Pennsylvania in 1909. Their three youngest children were born in Underwood. Mr. George Collins and their two oldest sons traveled out west to Underwood first, probably transporting as much of the family's goods as possible. Mrs. Collins and the rest of the family followed later by train. The Collins' homesteaded 80 acres on top of Underwood Mountain. They homesteaded later than most, so there was not much land to choose from, except high up on the mountain. With help from the family, Mr. Collins first built a barn, then built a house, dug a well, and planted apple trees. There the family remained for about 19 years.

The children attended grade school in Underwood, and later many of them attended high school in White Salmon. Part of the time the three oldest girls, Florence, Sarah, and June (Lorna) boarded with families in White Salmon, as the family felt it was too far to travel back and forth from Underwood to White Salmon each day for school.

**Harriet and George Collins standing alongside young apple tree on property in Underwood.**

In 1928 financial struggle hit the Collins family. Due to reasons connected with the depression the family was unable to keep up with the taxes on their property. They sold their homestead and moved to White Salmon. There Mr. Collins continued to farm for others and also con-

tinued his trade as a carpenter. By then many of the older children were married or off to college. The Collins first lived in a home in White Salmon. This burned down. Daughter June, mother of Phyllis Hollingsworth, bought land one mile north of White Salmon for her parents. At about the same time George, with the help of sons Bill and George Jr., was hired to tear down the old Colburn Hotel. George Collins acquired much of the wainscoting and other materials from the hotel and used these in the building of their new family home north of White Salmon.

Mr. Collins' health began to fail in 1931. He passed away April 10, 1937 in White Salmon.

Mrs. Collins continued to live in White Salmon. She worked for local fruit packing companies into her 60s. She passed away July 21, 1950. At the time of her death they had 55 grandchildren and 13 great-grandchildren.

Both George and Harriet Collins as well as Edith Collins Dallas are buried in White Salmon.

*****************

The following is taken from interview with June Collins Ranslam by her niece Helen Woodings many years ago:

June, born June 1, 1905, was five years old when the family moved west. The train ride was long and she was always thirsty. When the conductor noticed how often she ran to the drinking fountain, he told her to sit there with the boys, all afternoon.

*Aunt Anna and Uncle Charlie also came west with us. We arrived in Underwood in October. It was dark. Dad was waiting. We walked up the hill to Hamilton's and slept on the floor. The next day we walked on up the hill to the Homestead.*

The house was framed and roofed but not ready. They had left a nice house in Volant, PA. The neighbors helped put the house together.

**Collins, George and Harriett** (continued)

It was a long walk up to the homestead, and three miles down to the school. She started school when she was five, but only attended when the weather was good.

*The horse broke trail by dragging a log, to Underwood Heights. When the sawmill went in, Dad built the new school at the mill site. The new school, only one mile away, was through the woods.*

When June's brother Jim Ellis went to WWI she rode the pony Ginger to the bluff to get the mail. Often a sister went along with her on the horse.

The Homestead lacked water. Her dad had to build another cistern. The family used a round, hand operated washing machine. Older sister Florence boiled the water for washing. Everyone felt happy to have enough water to wash with. Everything was hard work, from laundry to the orchard, the thinning and picking of apples, and the picking of strawberries. Strawberry picking paid at first, until the nutrients from the volcanic soil was depleted. When they plowed the orchard, one would drive the horses, and one would handle the plow.

Brothers Jim Ellis and Art (Arthur) were in the service. John Jr. was teaching school.

In the fall, the girls packed fruit at the Underwood packing house. They stayed out of school six weeks, since this was their only spending money. When they sewed for the Red Cross, they wore Bloomerette Bottoms, called Farmerettes.

June spent her freshman year of high school at Washougal, as did some of her brothers. Her last three years of high school were in White Salmon. June worked for room and board, living with a family in W.S. while going to school. She spent a half year living with her sister Sara, while Sara taught school.

On the college level, she spent one semester at San Jose, CA, then at the Normal School in Ellensburg for one semester, and worked for her room and board.

The orchard did not produce for years, and times were hard on the large family. Father George would take a couple children along at a time to Oroville, CA. Here they would work packing oranges or canning olives. Once when June and Sara were working in CA, Sara got sick and had to have her thyroid removed. The doctor said it was because there were not enough minerals in the cistern water.

Later, after Sara was married and living on Chenowith Road, mother Harriet and the three youngest children went to stay with her while father George took some of the older girls back to work in California.

June did not get married until she was 27, and her health was not good. June and a girlfriend worked together in a restaurant in The Dalles, OR three to four years. She met Ed Ranslam while working in the restaurant.

The Crash and Depression came, and June went back to White Salmon to pack apples, and lived with her folks, now in White Salmon.

Today there are 40 plus grandchildren of George and Harriet still living, mostly in Washington and Oregon. There are grandchildren and great-grandchildren with the surnames of Allaway, Dallas and Lillegard still living in Skamania and Klickitat counties.

*The Enterprise*
*Family Tree Maker*
*Phyllis Hollingsworth – granddaughter of George and Harriet*
*Helen Woodings – niece of June Collins*

**Collins, John and Mary**

Both were born in England and immigrated to Chicago, where they married in 1893. They moved to Underwood in 1931. Children surviving at the time of Mary's death in 1954 were Rhoda, Clara, Elsie, and Phoebe. Elsie Collins Boyer was the mother of Mary Boyer Ziegler, married to Leroy Ziegler.

## Cooper, George A.

As early as 1907 Mr. Cooper had a ranch in Underwood, presumably in the vicinity of Cooper Road. In 1908 he planted one of the first commercial orchards, with strawberries between the rows. He did not live here. A news item of 1909 said that Mr. Cooper, his wife and daughter came up from Portland to see how their ranch had stood the winter. They expected to spend most of the summer here. In 1917 George Cooper sold ten acres of his ranch to F. A. Schwinge, who had assisted Mr. Cooper in the management of the property for two years. In May of 1918 the ranch residence of G.A. Cooper was entirely destroyed by fire. With the exception of the piano and a few small articles nothing could be saved. The fire spread to the adjoining timber and was put out with difficulty.

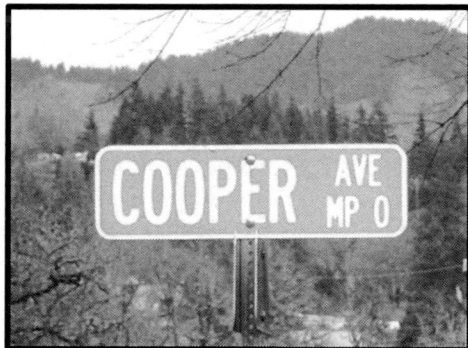

**Avenue named for Cooper family**

## Cordier, Clifford W. and Aurelia

In 1928 the Underwood post master Mr. Cordier underwent surgery for appendicitis in a Portland hospital. He returned and resumed his duties in the office. He was the postmaster from 1927 until 1943. An *Oregonian* article of February 1932 said that C.W. Cordier, World War I veteran, resident of Underwood, Wash. for many years, had been taken to the Veterans' hospital in Portland, a victim of sleeping sickness. Mr. Cordier had been a Sergeant in the 162nd Infantry, 42nd Division during WWI. He was a member of both the American Legion and the Veterans of Foreign Wars. In March of 1939 the news reported that C.W. Cordier lost a valuable cow. The Cordiers had a son Robert. Clifford died in 1943 and is buried in White Salmon.

## Corlie, Glenn Cooper

Born 1880 in Wisconsin, Glen Corlie came to Underwood about 1906. In 1912 Mr. Bellew of the Musical Academy of Chicago, visited G.C. Corlie and entertained at a party given by Miss Ruth Vinton. Mr. Bellew, a college chum of Mr. Corlie, spent the summer here with him. Glenn was an electrical engineer by trade. He was employed by the Apple Growers Association in Hood River, Oregon for 14 years. He moved back to Underwood in 1938 and lived there until he died in 1947.

## Counts, George and Suzie
By Karen Newell

George Counts was born in Madison County, Missouri in 1855 to Adroniram Counts and Olivia M. Stevenson. There he met Suzie Tabitha Pirtle. Suzie was born February 8, 1866 in Fredericktown, Missouri to William Henry Pirtle and Eliza Jane Wilson. George and Suzie were married in Missouri on November 1, 1885.

George and Suzie had six daughters; Lolita (my great grandmother), Lillian, Maggie, Jessie, Nannie and Myra.

George and Suzie came west traveling by way of California, Oregon, then settling in Washington. They lived in Lucas, Washington before settling in Underwood, Washington. George purchased 60 acres of property adjacent to Broughton Lumber Company, once known as Hood Station. There they raised strawberries and asparagus. They also grew alfalfa and had a large vegetable garden. Their bountiful yield of strawberries and asparagus was sent to Portland on the train, which began serving the area in 1908. They also had farm animals. The five Counts girls would work hard and often complain that there were no brothers to share the work.

## Counts, George and Suzie (continued)

William J. Hopper who was born in Tennessee, traveled his way west to find a better life, met my great grandmother Lolita Counts. They had one daughter Alameda. William and Lolita divorced and she remarried George Johnson. Together they had three daughters and five sons. Four are still surviving today. They settled in Underwood until their death.

Alameda Hopper married Cecil Everett Combs in September 1924. Cecil and his family came west from Missouri in 1909. Cecil was born in March, 1904 to Mary Florina Copley and Samuel Thomas Combs. Cecil and Alameda had two daughters, Beverly Irene (my mother) born in April, 1926, and Verna May was born in May, 1928. She met Charles "Harvey" Mansfield and together they raised three daughters, Dianna, Anetta and Lori. They attended grade school in Underwood, later moving to Stevenson, Washington.

Beverly married Richard Keith Morley in August of 1943 and had five children: Richard Jr., Teresa, Donald, Karen and Robbin. Karen married Timothy Newell, an Underwood native, and together they reside in Underwood. They have two children, Matthew and Jilyn. Matthew Michael Newell is married to Lisa Meece Newell. They have two children Addison and McKenna. Jilyn continues to live in Underwood, Washington with her husband Jeremy Wood. They have three children, Karter, Karlie, and Abigail Wood.

## Creighton, Reginier and Mildred

Dr. Creighton was an optometrist in the Bingen-White Salmon area from 1946-1969. He was born in 1905 in Spokane, Washington. The family owned acreage on the Underwood heights used for hay farming. Their children were Jim and Jeanne.

## Cromwell, C.H. and Sadie

In 1904 he acquired 120 Underwood acres and had an orchard of Newtown apple trees. Professor C.H. Cromwell was a prominent farmer and educator in the area. He taught at the Underwood school in 1903 and 1905. When a new school house was built in 1905, Mr. Cromwell purchased the old school house. Mr. Cromwell's ranch was near the edge of the hill overlooking the White Salmon River. At one time he was the master of the Underwood Grange. He was a County Commissioner in 1908. His father-in-law was William Orser.

## Dark, John

He came to live on the Underwood Mountain area in 1888, building the first known log cabin in the Little White Salmon valley. He married Grace Underwood, daughter of Ed and Isabelle Underwood. Their daughter Christina Dark died as a youngster and is part of the namesake of the Underwood Chris-Zada cemetery.

John Dark was an explorer and gold miner in the Mt. Adams vicinity. The Dark Divide, Dark Creek, Dark Mountain and Dark Meadows are named for him.

A news item In August of 1898 said that Mr. John Dark was seriously injured when his wood hauling wagon upset. He lay unconscious several hours. When he came to, he managed to mount a horse and ride home. His right hip was injured and he had a gash in the groin. He died in 1944 and is buried in the Underwood family plot.

## Darting, Albert

*Pioneer* February 7, 1911 –

*Albert Darting of Underwood met with a painful accident last week by having an indelible pencil forced into the muscles of his right wrist. He suffered excruciating pain for several days and finally had to have an operation performed. The lead, or whatever the inside of the indelible pencil is made of, poisoned the flesh and also caused blood poisoning. Mr. Darting had so far recovered Saturday night as to be able to attend the Odd Fellows district meeting in White Salmon with his hand in a sling. He reported at supper all right and the way he put food into his mouth with his left hand was quite remarkable.*

### Davidson, Derward

Born in 1874 in Nebraska, he settled here in 1900. In 1906 he purchased 40 acres and planted mainly peaches. In 1911 an advertisement in the *Pioneer* states: "A.D. Davidson / Underwood, Wash./ Piano tuning, Action repairing, Organ cleaning and repairing. Graduate of Niles Bragaret School of Piano Tuning, Battle Creek, Michigan. Your patronage solicited."

### Davis, Garnett and Linn

They married in 1918. Garnett died in 1941, having lived in Underwood for 16 years, leaving Linn and their children, Lester, Charlie, Leonard and Mildred. Linn died at age 84 in 1964.

### Debo, Henry C.

Henry in 1905 owned 80 acres one mile down river from Underwood. In 1908 he had berries and a truck garden on the lower flat near the railroad. Born in 1849, he died at his home in Hood in 1912. He came from Missouri with his daughter Anna after the death of his wife before 1891. Anna married A.J. Haynes and they moved to Underwood in 1898.

### DeHart, F. W

In 1908 he owned land on the Underwood flat. He built a house and barn. In July 1908 Rev. F.W. DeHart performed the wedding of Millie Barton and Frank Larsen.

### Dieterich, Elder W.

The six-acre Dieterich tract was next to the Cummins farm west of Highland Orchard Road. Mr. Dieterich cleared his land in 1939 using a bulldozer and blasting powder. The land had been densely covered with large stumps and brush. After being cleared, it was planted in alfalfa. Elder died in a car accident near Coos Bay, Oregon in 1952. His wife was injured in the accident. They had a son Wallace and two daughters. The *Mt. Adams Sun* noted that Elder had been an early day steam boat captain on the Columbia and Willamette Rivers.

### Dow, Ann

My mother, Hazel Cranston, and I (Ann Dow), moved to Hood River, OR the winter of 1989. We lived in Hood River for a few months while my son, Jim Dow, built our new home on beautiful Underwood Mountain. We moved into our new home the spring of 1990.

Mom and I were born and raised in Kansas and lived many years in the Midwest. My husband, Richard Dow, was a career military officer so my kids and I lived in many places due to Army moves (Ft. Lewis, WA; Germany; Ft. Benning, GA; Colorado Springs, CO; and El Paso, TX). After my husband resigned from the military in 1964 we moved to Beaverton, OR. We lived in Beaverton for 4 years. We then moved to Seattle and lived there for 21 years.

My husband passed away in 1971 and my dad had died in 1964, so my mother came to live with the kids and me in Seattle.

I have three children. Jim lives in Seattle, Nancy lives in Tacoma, and Susie lives here in Underwood. I have six grandchildren.

Mom and I wanted to get out of the city (Seattle) after I retired from the University of WA. Susie and her family had moved to Hood River in 1983 with the wind surfing people that moved here from Seattle. Susie wanted my mom and me to move down here. So when I retired we very happily moved to this beautiful part of paradise! To keep busy I went to work for a while in the office of Wal-Mart in Hood River.

I am a member of Asbury United Methodist Church in Hood River. I have been doing volunteer work for Providence Hospital in Hood River since around 2002.

I have a dear dachshund named Rudy. My daughter Susie has a dog, Millie. And between us we have four cats.

My mother passed away in 2004, but I still live here on Ashley Drive. It has been a wonderful experience living here and I treasure all my friends and neighbors in this area.

By Ann Dow

**Ann Dow and Rudy**

**Drano, William**

"French Billy" was born April 6, 1834 in France, came to The Dalles in 1864, then to Collins where he worked in the wood yard. Collins was a boat landing on the Columbia River near Home Valley. In 1868 he became a homesteader. He was a contemporary of Amos and Ed Underwood. He died in 1903. Drano Lake is named for William Drano.

**Ericson, Howard and Leona**

When Howard died in 1984 at age 82, he had been an Underwood resident since 1926. He and Leona had two daughters, Jeanne and Bette. Mr. Ericson was an insurance agent, a flutist and a fox breeder.

A May 1928 newspaper advertisement stated, "Wanted: old or crippled horses. Grand View Silver Fox Farm." In 1929 Howard Ericson, owner of the Grandview Silver Fox Farm on Underwood Heights reported four feet of snow at his place. In November of 1933 Moon-Glow Silver Star III, thoroughbred fox of the Grand View Silver Fox Farm of Underwood Heights, won the Grand Show Championship at the International Fox and Mink Show held at Blackfoot, Idaho. Mr. Ericson said that his fox farm is the smallest ranch ever to win the Grand Championship in an open competition. The farm was open to visitors from 1 to 4 p.m. on Sundays.

In February of 1937, Mr. Ericson reported that three of his silver foxes had broken loose, due to crushed fences from a snow storm. The animals were spotted on the road between Bingen and Underwood. Mr. Ericson made a plea that people not shoot them.

From _Mt. Adams Sun_ April 12, 1946 :
_The White Salmon Congregational Church Easter service will feature Harry Card singing "The Holy City" with flute obbligato by Howard Ericson._

In April of 1950, Howard donated a silver fox fur scarf to be raffled for a hospital fund raiser. The hospital committee was deeply grateful for the contribution which raised $129 toward a new hospital in White Salmon.

The Ericson home sat on the bluff at the south end of Ausplund Road. On maps their land is called Ericson View Tracts.

## Estey, Howard and Vera

From *The Enterprise* January 3, 1991:

*The children of Howard and Vera Estey celebrated their parents' 65 years of marriage. A potluck dinner was held at the Underwood Community Center. The Esteys have lived in Underwood for 41 years. Previously they lived in New York State for 20 years. The Esteys have 13 sons and daughters, 46 grandchildren and 35 great-grandchildren. More than 50 family members braved icy road conditions to turn out for Sunday's celebration.*

## Felling, Henry

In 1908 Mr. Felling was foreman for Charles Gibbs, pulling stumps and clearing the ground in preparation for fruit trees.

## Fink, Merlin

(As told to Kathy LaMotte)

Merlin Fink was the son of Glenn and Cleah Fink. The family came to Underwood when Merlin was a young boy. He remembers attending school in Underwood and then finishing with high school in White Salmon.

Merlin married a local girl, Donna Holman. Her parents were Amos and Marge Holman. Her parents owned a home along the bluff in Upper Underwood.

Merlin and Donna raised six children, five boys and one girl. Terry and wife Chris live in Vancouver, Randy and wife Lori live in Vancouver, Russ and wife Sheri live in Vancouver, Mark lives in Underwood on Laycock-Kelchner Road. He has retired due to health reasons. Another son, Joe, passed away a couple of years ago. And daughter Sheri lives in Vancouver. All six children attended school in White Salmon. The oldest son, Terry spent part of his senior year at Stevenson High.

Merlin purchased a farm of 144 acres in Underwood off of Laycock-Kelchner Road which he had for many years. He has since sold that property. However he still has 92 acres of property adjacent to his other property and located on Laycock-Kelchner and Love Road.

Merlin is a veteran of WWII. He has been a member of the American Legion for 36 years.

For 20 years Merlin worked for Broughton Lumber Company. He and family then moved to Vancouver and he worked for the Portland School District for twenty years. He and his wife Donna retired back here in Underwood.

In 1994 Merlin's wife Donna passed away. Sometime later he was re-acquainted with a friend he had known since high school, Francis Anderson. Francis was now a widow, her husband John Anderson having passed away in recent years. Fran and Merlin were married. They have been together now for about 16 years and reside in the Northwestern Lake area.

Merlin & Fran Fink

## Finley, P.T.

In 1905 he owned 80 acres two miles from Underwood, near the station called Hood on the Northbank railroad line. A September 1906 news item said that Knapp Flat (thought to be between Underwood and Hood) had the distinction of having the youngest and smallest workman on the Northbank railroad track. Lit-

**Finley, P.T.** (continued)

tle Bert Finley, eleven years old, tended the switch and drove one of the heavy teams of horses when short for teamsters.

**Forbes**

From the *Glacier* Nov. 12, 1908 :

*We predict that Mr. Forbes will apply for a patent on a watering trough, as he has one that can be used for other purposes than watering horses, as the Greeks have been using it to mix their bread in.*

**Fraine, Walter M**.

Born in 1851 and died in 1916, Walter was in the sawmill business with H.B. Borthwick in Skamania County. The hard times of the 1890's caused the mill to close. He was living in Underwood at the time of his death.

**Frazer, Fred W. and Eva**

Fred W. Frazer was born in Underwood in January 1921. His parents were Fred R. and Myrtle Frazer. Fred R. was born in Montana in January 1884 and Myrtle was born in Fertile, Minnesota in December, 1888. They came to Portland and he worked in the ship yards. Their daughter Frances was born in Portland in July of 1919. They moved to Wellington Orchards in Underwood and had a fruit farm.

Fred W. was a friend of Eva Ziegler's brother LeRoy. They married in 1943 and bought a home and farm from Rev. Henry and Alice Rominger. Fred served 19 months in the army. He worked as a night watchman for Broughton Lumber mill for 22 years before it closed in 1986. Fred and Eva sold part of the orchard in 1963 and lived in the home on Cook Underwood road until 1984. They moved to White Salmon, close to the shopping center.

Fred worked in the Food Bank, delivered Meals on Wheels, drove senior citizens to appointments and gave 18 gallons of blood over the years. When Fred's health began to fail, he went to the Veter-

an's Hospital in Portland and then to the Evergreen Rest Home in The Dalles. He passed away in March of 2005. Eva and Fred had been married for 61 ½ years.

Eva took care of the home and eight children, three of whom were adopted. Their first son Ray was born in April 1946. Then came Carol in November 1947, Evelyn in April 1949 and Joe in March 1951. These children were all born in Hood River. Mary was born in the new Skyline Hospital in White Salmon in November 1953. Also born in White Salmon were Tom in December 1959, Terri in March 1962, and Tim in August 1966.

See I.R. Ziegler for Eva's early family history.

History and photos by Eva Ziegler Frazer

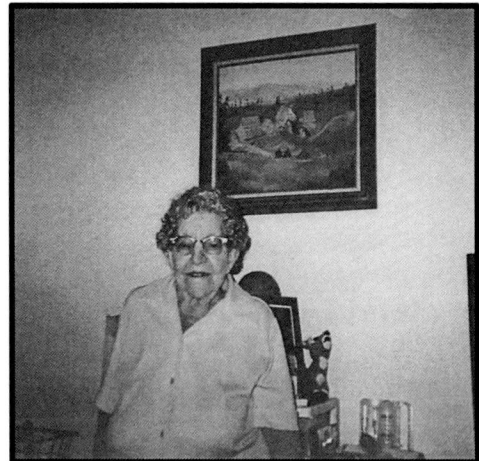

**Eva Ziegler Frazer – 88 years old on November 24, 2012**

**Eva and Fred Frazer 40<sup>th</sup> anniversary**

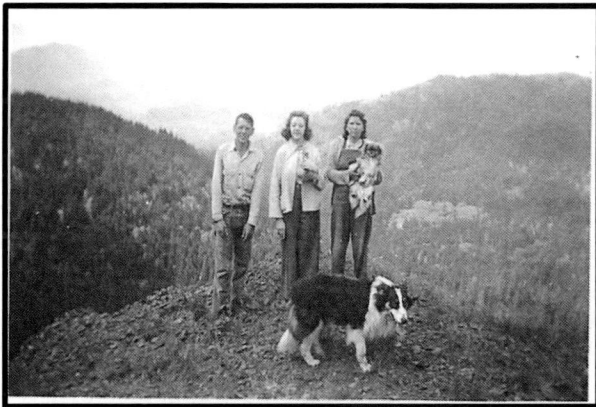

**c. 1941 Fred, Eva and Frances with pets on top of Whistling Ridge**

**Fred W. Fraser home on Cook-Underwood Road**

### Friedrich, Alois and Mary

Mary emigrated from Germany with her Bueche family in 1883. She died in 1919 and Alois died in 1943. They were parents of Frieda who married Ray Meiggs, manager of an Underwood store and service station.

### Germeraad, Donald and Esther (Pete)

By Pete Germeraad

Our daughter Ann and her former husband Bill Swain settled in Underwood in 1978. Bill had graduated from U.C. Davis in oenology and viticulture (wine making) and wanted a place to start a vineyard. They found acreage on Love Road and built a house using contractor Jack Baldwin.

Frequent trips from California to visit our three Swain granddaughters were a drawing card for me, while the great hunting and fishing swayed Don. In 1982 we decided to retire and build here also. I relished the idea of sewing and caring for Mary, Catherine, and Stephanie while Ann taught in the White Salmon and Hood River schools.

Don gave back to the community by involving himself with the Air Rescue group in Hood River. In those days small planes and ground searchers were the means of finding lost hikers and skiers. (Now the Air National Guard with their helicopters does the work.) Don also became involved with the Washington Small Woodland Association while planting trees on our twenty acres.

I spent time taking blood pressures of those who came to get their allotment of government food subsidies at the Underwood Community Center. This Center was the heart of the community then. We had GREAT pot lucks there. Our political aspirants presented their views. Children brought their play toys or roller skates to race around the hall when too many snowy or rainy days followed one another

**Germeraad, Donald and Esther** (cont.)

and moms were eager for a place to vent their children's energy. There were drives to raise money to paint the building, fix the horse arena, install the tennis court, build a larger fire house and develop a park.

Neighbors were true neighbors. Paul Newell Sr. let Don hunt his orchards for deer. Don in turn brought him the livers, which Paul relished. If it weren't for Sadie Fincher and Ira Crawford I don't think Ann would have learned down-to-earth gardening and canning skills and her ability to "live off the land." Both Ira and Sadie were a treasure trove of local doings and history.

After Donald died in 1992, and Ann and the girls had moved away, I stayed in the Underwood house for seven years. When Al Sutton from the Fish and Wildlife identified cougar tracks close to the house, I decided to sell and move to White Salmon.

> **The Underwood Community Center was the heart of the community.**
>
> **Pete Germeraad**

**Gibbs, Charles and Elizabeth**

From a *Skamania County Pioneer* obituary of June 22, 1928:

*Charles Watkins Gibbs was born in 1867 in Portland, Oregon and died in June of 1928. He was educated in the Portland public schools and learned the jewelry business. For many years he owned a jewelry store in Wallace, Idaho and for the last ten years had operated an orchard at Underwood. He is survived by his widow, Elizabeth Ewin and two sisters, Mrs. P.I. Packard and Mrs. Alexander Muir, both of Portland.*

**Charles Watkins Gibbs**

**Goddard E.C**

(From local news articles)

In 1895 Mr. Goddard owned a shoe store on 6th Street in downtown Portland. In 1898 the Goddards bought 320 acres from Mr. Underwood for $6000. Acorn Lodge was on the property. They soon bought another 120 acres. In 1906 they sold 40 acres of the ranch for $75 an acre. Mr. and Mrs. Harry Olsen (Mary Underwood) sold their ranch up on the hill to E.C. Goddard and he was then surveying and dividing it up into small tracts. In 1907 E.C. Goddard had a crew of house raisers, stone masons and carpenters at work on his residence. He also remodeled his reservoir and pipe cistern. Later that year E.C. Goddard's beautiful black dog came to his death by getting some poisoned meat that had been placed out for yellow jackets.

E.C. Goddard left for Portland in October of 1907 after seeing the finishing touch put on the fine residence and installing a nice lot of high grade furniture. The Underwood place was used as a summer home. In June of 1918 a news account states, "In the death of E.C. Goddard, Portland shoe merchant, the Underwood District has lost one of the best known orchardists. Mr. Goddard died June 13 at his Underwood country home at the age of 56 years. He was owner of one of the largest tracts of land in that section, a ranch consisting of 400 acres. It was bought by Mr. Goddard about twenty years ago."

In June of 1928 one of the dwelling houses belonging to Mrs. E.C. Goddard was totally destroyed by fire. The fire was thought to have started from a spark on the roof. The house was occupied by the W.L. McCutchans, who lost most of their household goods, with no insurance. The dwelling was fully insured.

A June 29, 1928 news item said that Mrs. E.C. Goddard and daughter, who were spending the summer in their beautiful residence on the bluff overlooking the Columbia, had placed their entire Underwood property, nearly 400 acres, on sale. Henry W. Goddard of Portland and M.S. Smith of Underwood were handling the property.

### Graves, Charlie

Mr. Graves built the Haselton House in 1910 – still standing, the Lyle Ternahan house in 1915 – burned in 1993, and the Harley Ternahan house – still standing. The three houses are along Cook Underwood Road on the heights.
Source – Barry Ternahan

### Halver, John and Jane

Note: John Halver wrote this before he passed away suddenly in 2012.

John earned a degree in medical biochemistry from the University of Washington and came to the area to design a fish nutrition laboratory in 1950. The lab at Willard was completed in 1953. (See Western Fish Nutrition Laboratory on page 43.)

The Halvers bought the Harry Card house on Cook/Underwood Road. The house was built before 1902 by a German

Columbia riverboat captain. It is one of the oldest houses in Underwood. Harry Card acquired the house and 120 acres of orchards. He moved to Denver in 1958 and the land was divided into parcels.

John and Jane Halver bought the house and the lower 10 acres from the Cards in 1958 and lived there until they moved to Seattle in 1975. They have maintained the house and used it for a summer retreat for many years. The house will remain in the family as it was sold to a daughter, Nancylee Hadley. John and Jane now live in Seattle, where John is still affiliated with the University and travels extensively relating to his research and consulting activities.

The Halvers' children are John 4, Nancylee, Janet, Peter and Deborah. They have all gone on to be industrious citizens. John 4 became an electrical engineer with PUD, Nancylee was a teacher in Texas and later worked for Edward Jones (stock brokers), Janet was an accountant, Peter was a mediator for California electricians' labor disputes, and Debbie was an Army helicopter pilot and military intelligence officer.

Jane came to Underwood with her years of music on the pipe organs of many churches, and was soon involved in music programs in the area. She became the piano and organ teacher of the Hood River School of Music, and then used her home for many children each week to learn the wonders of classical and church music. She donated her time and talents to the White Salmon Methodist Church for over 15 years before moving back to Seattle in 1975. The Halver home was filled with pianos, an organ, flutes, violins, oboes, clarinets, and young and old music voices. Jane also became involved in many local civic activities and joined the "ladies" monthly skiing group to Mt. Hood.

Since their return to Seattle, both have received many honors for their work and dedication to civic activities. John was elected to the National Academy of

**Halver, John and Jane** (continued)

Sciences in 1978, Hungarian Academy of Sciences in 1998, Washington State Academy of Sciences in 2008, and has travelled the world to over 30 countries consulting on nutritional problems for many agencies. He has published over 200 scientific articles in his work with the WFNL and university research projects.

Jane became involved again in music in the Seattle area, and was elected to several offices in civic affairs. She was president of the University of Washington Alumni Auxillary Association, Seattle Women's President's Club, and was on the board of several other clubs or organizations. The first task when moving to her Seattle home was to build a music room addition and install an organ and two pianos. Music and public service has been her life.

The team of John and Jane Halver has been an active addition to Underwood during their long stay in this beautiful community.

**Jane and John Halver on their 64th Wedding anniversary**

**Front: Deborah Halver-Hanson, John and Jane Halver, Nancylee Halver Hadley
Back: Peter Loren Halver, Janet Halver Fix, John Emil Halver IV. Photo taken August 2009**. Photos from Halver family collection.

**Hamlin, H.W.**

Various local newspaper reports mentioned the Hamlins. In October, 1910 H.W. Hamlin had his new house completed and had moved into it. This was the fourth new house that Mr. Hamlin had erected and lived in during the three years that he lived here. In October, 1915 H.W. Hamlin was in Stevenson to attend the Road Bond committee. He had a very busy day and the work lasted well into the evening. Mrs. H. W. Hamlin entertained at dinner on Christmas in 1914. There were several guests from out of town. In 1928 Mr. Hamlin, who was for several years manager of Underwood Fruit Warehouse, lived in Medford, Oregon.

## Hardham, John and Linda

John's love affair with the Gorge started before Linda's. Starting in the early 80s he windsurfed and snowboarded so much with his family that he bought a second home at the other end of the Cook-Underwood Road in Cook. His former wife, Joan, now owns the property. Their family traveled constantly from their primary residence and jobs in Portland to the river and to the mountain for teaching and learning opportunities in the two sports that they loved.

John still is crazy about both, although trips to the mountain have been fewer lately since they've been focusing on the remodel of their Underwood home which was purchased in late 1995, a couple years after he and Linda married. They met at Oregon Health and Sciences University, and the relocation came about because Linda was recruited for a position with Mid-Columbia Medical Center in The Dalles following a prior location in Siletz, Oregon, where they owned a small "gentleman's farm" (and raised a few sheep) and John re-established his video-communications business while Linda had a leadership role in the hospital in Newport.

It seems nearly unbelievable that we've been in this location for 17 years...and we love it more with each passing year. Recently we became Mosier residents for a year during our remodel, and the contrast was wonderful...we enjoyed the community and view of the north side of the river...and we could actually see Underwood from our rental there.

Linda is now enjoying retirement and has developed a small executive coaching leadership business to keep her toe in the water. John continues his video communications work and is really en-joying his new studio in the house. Major landscaping is the theme at the moment.

It is a pleasure to be a member of this community and to know all who make it a great place to live.
By Linda Hardham

## Hanna, Charles

A January 1928 Underwood news note stated that before the roads were broken for automobile travel many in this neighborhood enjoyed riding on Chas. Hanna's sleigh. One day seventeen were counted on it as it left Underwood. Mr. Hanna died in July 1974. Funeral services were held in The Dalles for Charles Hanna, Goldendale, who was a long-time resident of Underwood.

## Harding

In 1909 the Harding place was sold to Rev. H.V. Rominger of Portland.

## Harmsen, Robert and Sharon

By Kathy LaMotte

Sharon Harmsen was best known in the Underwood community for her work as relief postmaster and as The Teddy Bear Lady.

Sharon was born in 1929, in Libby, MT. Her parents were Gwendolen and Sprague Stevens. She had a brother Sprague and a sister Carol. In 1947 Sharon graduated from high school in Boise, Idaho.

She married Walter Dilkes. They had children Ed, Janet, Greg, and Shari. Sharon began writing feature articles for the newspaper. She had a column called, "Shopping With Sharon."

Sharon was divorced in the early 1970's. She later married Robert Harmsen in 1975. They moved to his home in Underwood.

## Harmsen, Robert and Sharon (cont.)

For years Sharon and Robert decorated their mailbox area along Cook/Underwood Rd., changing the scenes according to seasons. After Robert's death in 1998, close friends, the Lampe's next door, also helped Sharon with her mailbox decorating. Unfortunately after several vandalisms, Sharon decided to no longer put out decorations. This was a great disappointment as Sharon felt this was her gift to the community.

In 1986 Sharon was hired as Relief Postmaster at the Underwood Post Office. She would work Saturdays and whenever Wilma McCarthy needed to be away. She loved meeting people and creating friendships with so many Underwood residents. Sharon held this position until 1998, when she retired to help her ailing husband.

Sharon Harmsen was often known as "Grandma Bear." Sharon started collecting "pre-loved" bears in 1990. She cleaned and repaired the bears to their original condition. Her son suggested he take a load back to the ambulance service in Leavenworth, WA. Others began hearing about "Grandma Bear." Elementary schools, hospitals, and emergency agencies all started contacting Sharon requesting bears. Sharon formed the "Critter Repair Crew." They met regularly, washing, drying, and repairing 1,000's of bears.

Over the years Sharon and her helpers recycled approximately 25,000 bears. Sharon was diagnosed with cancer in January of 2010. She delivered her last bag of bears to Skyline Hospital in June. Sharon Harmsen passed on July 18, 2010.

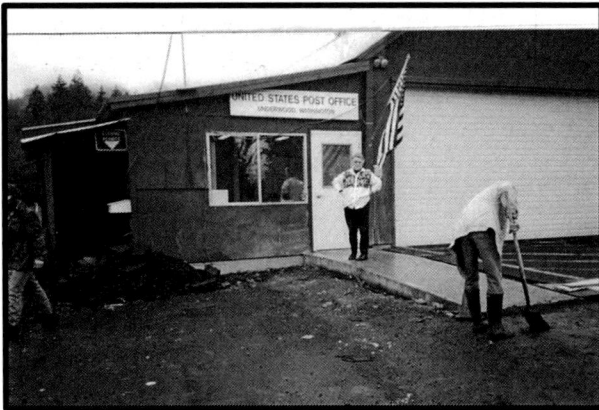

**Sharon Harmsen watches as walkway for new post office is being prepared.**

In 1995 the necessity of continuing a post office in Underwood was being questioned. Two issues were formed: will the post office in Underwood close for good (after 95 years), or can it be relocated? Sharon and her husband Robert were very instrumental in keeping the post office open, writing letters to Senators, Congressmen, and anyone who would listen.

> **Sharon and Robert Harmsen were instrumental in keeping the Underwood Post Office opened.**

## Harmsen, Robert and Sharon (cont.)

**Sharon Harmsen, the "Teddy Bear Lady"**

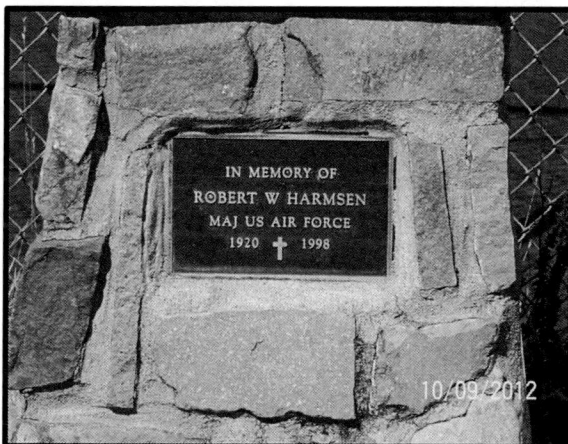

**Drinking fountain memorial to Robert Harmsen near the tennis court in the Underwood Community Park.**

## Haselton, Roger H. and Leta Ruth
### By Hannah Haselton May

Hannah and her twin sister Elizabeth were born in Portland in 1911 to Leta Ruth Smith Haselton and her husband, Roger H. Haselton. Brother Amedee was born in 1913 in Underwood. (*Hannah is 101 at the time of this writing, May, 2012. She lives in Portland. She has submitted these memories of Underwood.*)

As you know, Underwood not only consisted of a few buildings beside the Columbia River...a mercantile store, hotel, the butcher shop, fruit packing house along the SP&S Railway, railway station building and also some houses, but the community covered Underwood Mountain. Apple and pear orchards and farm houses wound over the mountainside. Cattle were raised and alfalfa hay and other farm crops and gardens were grown.

**School:** There were always school buildings in Underwood: one-room, two-room (even three-room when I was in the seventh grade in 1924). Previous to 1917 on Underwood "Flats" there was a simple two-room schoolhouse with two outhouses in back. This was right on the main highway. (Now *Cook Underwood Road*). A new and larger two-room schoolhouse was built in 1917 on a larger piece of property in a meadow, bounded on two sides by the County Road and the Highway.

Community activities centered in the new school, especially after it was raised in 1922, making it a two story building with an auditorium provided on the first floor. Indoor plumbing was added, greatly improving the situation.

The new auditorium space provided an opportunity for boys' and girls' basketball games. One teacher, Miss Josephine Silvers, taught the students to march to the tune of "The Washington Post March" played on a wind-up Victrola; also a dance, "The Virginia Reel." Miss Silvers was fresh out of Washington State "Normal School" and brought new and interesting projects to the 5th, 6th, 7th, and 8th grades room, which my twin sister Eliza-

143

beth and I and our brother Amedee attended. Audubon bird study was promoted. My sister and I especially enjoyed this, for our mother, Leta Ruth Haselton, taught us at home from an Audubon bird guide to recognize and name the many varieties of birds in our neighborhood. Especially we liked to find the bright crimson and yellow Western Tanager and the California Purple Finch.

Teachers are an important part of children's growing-up memories. In my first grade (there were also second, third, and fourth grade students in the same room), we had a fine teacher, Miss Jensen, who was from Chinook, Washington. After Miss Jensen left, another teacher taught whom none of us cared for since she was quick with the punishing ruler on children's hands. It was not until my twin sister's and my 6th grade, that we received a young up-to-date teacher, Miss Josephine Silvers. At this time our father, Roger H. Haselton, was on the school board, along with Olaf Larsen, and Myron Smith. In our seventh grade two new teachers came from the state "normal schools". Miss Emma Christianson taught the 5th, 6th, 7th and 8th grades and her younger sister taught the lower grades. I believe the ninth graders also went to Miss Emma's room for math.

When I was in the sixth grade our school received books from the county or state for a circulating library. We also had music time during the school day. Our mother lent some "Red Seal" records to be played for music period. Especially we loved to hear Madame Schumann-Heink's wonderful contralto voice.

Also at this time, about 1924, a small "teacherage" house was built at a corner of the large meadow that surrounded our schoolhouse. Previous to having their own home, the teachers usually roomed and boarded with Mrs. Hussey who lived on Underwood "Flats."

Recess is always a joy for students. We played tagging games like "Run Sheep Run," "Andy Andy Over," and "Hide and Seek." We even made up one called "Pilgrims and Indians" out in the grassy meadow. A quieter game was called "Statue." My earliest memory was of all the school, from the youngest to oldest, playing with great abandon the various tagging games. As we got older, we played regular baseball during the noon hour. Sometimes there was bullying; for instance my little brother, who was large for his age and had the unusual family name of "Amedee" got teased. However, my twin sister, like a small fierce mother hen, would always scatter his tormentors.

In 1922, when the two-room schoolhouse was raised to provide an auditorium underneath, a third school room was equipped for use. Miss Silvers returned to teach the seventh grade in that room and also a ninth grade, probably the only higher education some children would have. I know Edith Collins from the twelve-member Collins family that farmed at the top of Underwood Mountain, had to live in White Salmon to attend high school. Edith's brother George Collins was my brother's age. Later I heard he became a doctor when he grew up. The Cummins family, whose farm lay far up the highway, solved the high school problem by moving to Hood River so Ellis Cummins could continue his education. When my sister and my eighth grade class were ready for high school, an additional school bus from White Salmon picked us up and drove us back and forth from Underwood to the Columbia Union High School every day.

The Underwood school served as a community gathering place. A monthly meeting, called the "Literary Society" was organized and meetings were held about town business. Various neighbors took turns chairing meetings. The programs also given at the monthly meetings were outstanding and various groups put them on; children recited from the stage or adults put on short plays or a minstrel

144

**Haselton, Roger H. and Leta Ruth** (cont.)

show. Neighbors from Underwood" Flats" put on a funny play. I remember even now the title was "Aaron Slick from Punkin Crik!" After the programs folks gathered at the kitchen window for pie and coffee. Dances were also held and we all whirled around the floor to what I remember was the "one step." At the piano a man chorded out the music assisted by a fiddler!

**Church:** Church services were held in our schoolhouse. Previous to 1921, there had been a rustic log chapel on the "Flats" just up from the schoolhouse, where a visiting preacher from Hood River held forth earnestly. He had to cross the Columbia River by ferry. As a small child I was very interested in watching him pound the pulpit. Also, I watched the other children who were squirming in their seats. I remember Gordon Clark, my age, removed to the vestibule until he could quiet down. (Years later when we were both in our fifties, I met Gordon and his wife at a Mazama campout in the Wallowas at Francis Lake. Instead of climbing peaks and ridges around the lake, he and his wife studied the wild flowers in the area and made a report at the campfire at night.) I noticed little Alice Rine, sitting so good and quietly between Walter and Maude Rine, her parents.

A huge snowstorm in 1921 collapsed the ancient roof of the log chapel. In later years we met in a community church service in our schoolhouse. Occasionally an evangelical minister's family would take up housing in Underwood and assume preaching. Once, the Eastern Oregon bishop, William P. Remington, crossed the Columbia and held services for us. I remember that we seemed always to have good Sunday school classes with two outstanding teachers, Mrs. Lizzie Gibbs Packard and Mrs. Charlie Gibbs. (Governor Gibbs of Oregon was related to Mrs. Lizzie Gibbs Packard.)

Rev. Schuyler Pratt, pastor of Hood River Episcopal Church was active in our

lives and taught us our confirmation class at our home. Also he drove us Haselton twins up to Cove in Eastern Oregon to the Episcopalian summer school each summer of our teen years.

Speaking of the chapel, I remember as a small child, playing outdoors, while inside some of the mothers stitched up and tied comforters for the needy. I heard our mother say that Mrs. Wendland was expecting again and would need a comforter. The Ladies Aid in our community was a strong institution. Quilts also were made and shown at the Skamania County Fair in Stevenson, Washington, and prizes received.

While the mothers stitched, their young children fanned out into the surrounding oak woods to play "hide-and-seek." A very small stream also ran by and we played in that. (Up the road it flowed into a large, moss-covered horse-drinking trough.) Of course, we had to stop and play in that, too, especially since water was scarce on our farm up the hill. A trail ran down through the trees to where an intriguing "style" led up three steps over the barbed wire fence and three steps down the other side.

These open oak woods were also a natural setting for the beautiful Columbia River Gorge wild flowers. On our one mile and half walk to and from school during springtime my sister, brother and I fanned out into the woods to gather "blue bells", (really called blue-eyed grass), buttercups, lupine and lilies. It was like a fairyland!

**Neighbors:** Our neighbors were varied and very interesting, each bringing a rich background and sharing their interests with others. In fact, Underwood was a dynamic community. The Goddards, (Elizabeth) came from Portland to live on Underwood "Flats." Their small home was located close to the bluff overlooking the Columbia River Gorge. To sit on a bench in their front yard gave you a wonderful view down the river to Mt. Defiance, the north side of Mt. Hood and the cliffs out-side Hood River, Oregon. "Acorn Lodge" was a small cabin on the Goddard place. In 1910, my father and mother honey-mooned at the "Acorn Lodge", while the Haselton house was being built that same year, higher up on the mountain.(*The house stands today on the right hand side up Cook Underwood Road above the Little Buck Creek Rd. intersection.*)

**The Haselton house c.1912 before the new "Evergreen Hwy." was placed closer to it.** Photo from the Haselton collection.

Sometimes of a Sunday afternoon we liked to call on another family living close to the Gorge, the Marshes. Their place was located right at the top of the "Hood Grade" Road. Down at the river's edge, along the SP&S railway track, a tiny lum-bering town called Hood was located. Hood was at the foot of the famous flume that snaked down the Gorge cliff side from Broughton Lumber Mill up at Willard, Washington. The lumber floated down the flume and then was piled up by the rail-road to be shipped. The children from Hood attended our Underwood school. They were carried up each day by horse and buckboard along "Hood Grade". The narrow, steep road climbed from the river to the top of the bluff and upon the "Flats" to school.

Also living on the "Flats" was the Wal-ther family. There were Angeline and an older brother and sister. The Hedrick house was located across from the schoolhouse and the highway. A little boy named Dana from there attended school. Another group of children and young people who attended the Under-wood school lived in the Hicks lumber mill town, up on the mountainside. I only re-member the name of one of those young folks, James Miller. He had attended the ninth grade class when our school offered that, and he also attended the freshman class at White Salmon for a while. (Prob-ably he had to go to work in the lumber mill at an early age.)

Beyond the Hicks mill town and the edge of our school district, lived the Cummins and Ausplunds. Before school bus services, Ellis Cummins rode a pony to school. When the Haselton youngsters were young, we had always walked a mile and half to school, back and forth. Once after a snowstorm, we were delighted to have Mr. Cummins come by with horse and sled and drive us down to school over the snowy road.

Other children walked long ways to school: Alice Rine down on the "Flats", Bertha Schweitzer, Helen and Martha Thun down the same road, and the Kapps, who had a large acreage back in that area and raised cattle. Mr. Kapp owned the butcher shop down by the Co-lumbia and White Salmon rivers. Their children that I remember attending the Underwood school were Carl, Max, Julia, Rosa and Maria. (I didn't know Henrietta Kapp, and Heinie worked in the butcher shop). Other school children were Vernon Spears, the SP&S station master's son, and Amel Schwinge. The Thuns lived on the "Flats" next door to Mrs. Lizzie G. Packard. There was a close helping rela-tionship between the two families, I be-lieve. Mr.Thun and his oldest daughter Helen played the violin and piano together. (Helen eventually went on to attend Reed College in Portland. I believe she finally taught Home Economics at Lewis and Clark College, also in Portland.) The Packards were from Portland and he played the cello for community programs. An important man in our community was G.C. Corlie, who delivered mail everywhere.

Up on the mountainside again, Andy Reinland had to walk a long side road before getting to the main highway and the bus. Also up in that area there were the Zieglers. I only remember Reno Ziegler who was about my brother's age. Another two children who lived back on the hillside were Hazel and Eugene. I don't remember their last name. Ray Moore and wife lived in that area too. The Graves lived up the hill from us. Another family was the A.G. Hunters, who lived past the top of the hill above our house and past Peas woods. Up above our farm and the Wess farm, a bachelor named Mr. Freeman lived. He helped on our farm and kept our horse Prince after cars came in. Every spring he prepared our large vegetable garden planting space, harrowing and "floating" the soil.

The Wess family children at that time consisted of John, Katherine (about our ages. We were born in 1911 and 1913.), Rosie and Josephine. I understood that Katherine became a teacher later on. When my twin sister and I were in our teen years, I got a job picking strawberries for Mr. Wess. He knew a lot about farming and horticulture. He liked to graft and grow tree roses. My brother Amedee and John Wess often played or hiked over the mountainside together.

The Romingers lived just up the road from us. They had a large pear orchard and she raised Leghorn chickens and sold eggs. Mrs. Rominger was an accomplished pianist and would play for gatherings at Christmas time while we sang all the favorite Christmas hymns. Mr. Rominger was a retired Congrega-

tional minister from Portland and had traveled a lot. He showed slides from his travels and with a "magic lantern" flashed the pictures up for us to see and lectured with interesting comments.

The Frazers were fine neighbors who lived up past the Romingers and the packing house. Across the road lived the Haynes. Isabel was their daughter who married Herb Ziegler. Their house was large and white on the bluff edge. When my twin sister Elizabeth and I were teenagers we picked apples for Herb Ziegler and also we picked pears for Romingers next door to us.

**Library:** My mother Leta Ruth Smith Haselton provided the "Lending Library" for the community, for she had over one thousand books. These were the only books in the community to be lent. There was no general library, no books in the schools except the few text books that were often shared, no books to be bought without making a trip, and often few funds. Leta's library was the source of entertainment, learning and literature.

My father Roger H. Haselton was a good carpenter and built bookshelves to either side of our fireplace, then down around one side of the living room. One section was devoted to the children's books, which were popular at that time. My mother kept a record of the neighbors' names and the book titles they borrowed and I find it interesting to quote from her record book:

The Bueches who lived down the hill off the "County Road" borrowed some of the following books, popular at that time: Wood Carver of 'Lympus, David Harum, Monsieur Beaucaire, Elizabeth and Her German Garden, The Man From Glengarry, Silas Marner, The Circuit Rider, Wild Animals I Have Known, Told in the Woods, The Inside of the Cup, The Princess Passes, The Virginian, The Hoosier School Master, Tom Sawyer and The Spoilers. To our little two-room schoolhouse the following books: Little Women,

**Haselton, Roger H. and Leta Ruth** (cont.)

<u>A Reader</u>, <u>Tom Sawyer</u>, <u>Lives of the Hunted</u>, <u>The Boy Craftsman</u>, <u>With the Indians in the Rockies</u>, <u>Stories and Poems from Kipling</u>, March "St. Nicolas" magazine, <u>Aesop's Fables</u>, <u>The Three Musketeers</u> and <u>The Book of Joyous Children.</u>

The following list of book borrowers gives a roster of the interesting Underwood neighbors:

Walter McNutt, 14 books; Alice Rine's family borrowed for her 30 books; Thun family, 19 children's books; McKenny (?), 1 book; Forest Slutz, 2 books; Myron Smith, 1 book; Hoge (?), 1 book; Shipley, 3 books; Wendorf (?), 1 book; J. McNutt, 3 books; Gibbs, 2 books; Romingers, 5 books; A.G. Hunter, 26 books; Ross Slutz, 1 book; Reinland, 1 book; Mrs. Roy Moore, 1 book; Thun family, 32 books, mostly children's books; Hazel, 7 books (I don't remember her last name); Rine, 21 books; Miss Looney (?), 9 books; Miss Carr, 1 book (a Columbia Union High School English teacher); CUHS, 2 magazines; Rine, 10 books; Mrs. Putney, 4 books (a CUHS English teacher); Rine, 24 books; Thun, 7 books; Gibbs, 1 book; Wallace, 6 books; and Wess, 8 books.

**Roads:** There were two main roads on Underwood Mountain. Originally there was the "County Road" which ran from Underwood by the river, straight up the mountainside to Underwood "Flats" and finally high along the edge of the Columbia River Gorge bluff. As small children (about 1915 or 1916) my twin sister, brother and I watched from our front porch the "Evergreen Highway" being built past our house. Horses and/or mules were busily moving dirt around. The Evergreen Highway would replace most of the former County Road. (*The road is now Cook Underwood Road.*)

**Apple Harvest:** Early snapshots taken by my mother's fine camera show scenes of how our apple orchard was harvested with horse and wagon partly loaded with filled apple boxes. My early memories were of my twin sister and me riding at the back of the wagon bed, bare feet dangling over the wagon as horses wound up through the fruit trees picking up boxes; then a trip on the main graveled road to the long packing house for the unloading. How exciting that packing shed was to small children! We ran between the tall rows of boxes; we looked at the moving sorting belt where a long row of women sat sorting our apples - only the best were exported to LeHavre, Amsterdam and Liverpool. The Highland Packing House, source of community livelihood and social contact, was located up on the mountain past Romingers' pear orchard and past a road high up to the Wess farm.

October 1913. Roger Haselton on the ladder, the Haselton twins in front of the wagon. The nearest woman is Mr. Haselton's mother, Hannah P. (Gage) Haselton. The other woman is a relative or neighbor.

Photo from the Haselton collection.

148

**Haselton, Roger H. and Leta Ruth** (cont.)

**Roger Haselton in front of a loaded apple tree.**
Photo from the Haselton collection.

**Picnics:** How excited my twin sister and little brother and I would become when we saw our mother get out our well-worn picnic basket with the handles. Then she would put sandwiches into the little tin boxes (no sandwich paper in those days). Always potato salad and fried chicken put in also for a picnic. Then our dad would hitch up "Prince", our faithful hardworking horse, to the buggy, or buckboard if my paternal grandmother was staying with us for the summer on the ranch.

It was a long interesting trip on dusty roads to our favorite campground - Little Cedars on the reaches of the Little White Salmon River among big old-growth red cedar trees.

We passed by the Big Cedars picnic ground, which was especially intended for all the community, also on the Little White Salmon River. The Broughton Lumber Company was also up in that area at the beginning of the famous flume. We crossed over tiny Mossy Creek and farther up into the national forest to a narrow woodsy lane that led to the Little White Salmon. There against a big red cedar tree our father had built a sturdy large picnic table and benches. We would camp overnight, sleeping on fir tree boughs, or just picnic for the day. Always we kids had a wonderful time wading for hours in the icy bubbling stream. Before we got

home at night it would be dark, and our mother would be pointing out the Milky Way, the Big Dipper and the North Star. How bright the stars were in that clear eastern Washington State air!

After my father had a truck and was hauling lumber from Hicks Lumber Mill, he used the truck to take some of our community neighbors for a picnic to the Big Cedars. He put a big flatbed on the truck; chairs and folks rode that way for a picnic on the Little White Salmon.

**Picnicking at Big Cedars near Willard, Washington. Martha Thun, Helen Thun, Elizabeth Haselton, Hannah Haselton, and Amedee Haselton with our two Smith cousins, Mary Louise and Virginia.**
Photo from the Haselton collection.

I can also remember attending a picnic at Husum on the White Salmon River where people from the whole area came by horse and buggy and shared potluck on tables near the river. The Collins family sat at our table, and Mrs. Packard brought a delicious scalloped potato casserole I've never forgotten.

**Haselton,Roger H. and Leta Ruth** (cont.)

Another picnic that happened when we twins were eight years old was on the Columbia River. Our mother's sister (and maybe her daughter, too, my cousin Ruth) came up the Columbia on the *Bailey Gatzert*, one of the paddle wheelers. Our family boarded the boat at Underwood and went on up the river for a picnic excursion all together. We disembarked somewhere up the river. Then I remember the grown-ups laid a picnic cloth on a lawn, put picnic sandwiches on it, etc., and we all just sat around the cloth on the lawn. Of course, we returned to the boat on its return trip and we were dropped off at Underwood.

Another part of our life living on Underwood Mountain was the musical whistle of the trains echoing as they steamed up both sides of the Columbia River Gorge into Hood River and Underwood. What a scenic life!

Elizabeth and Hannah Haselton at Willamette College in Salem, Oregon-1930

**Haynes, Alma James and Anna**

The Haynes were married in 1891 and settled in Underwood in 1898. A.J.'s wife was Anna Debo. The couple had two daughters, Fannie May and Anna Isabelle. Fannie married Claude Davidson in 1911, but died four years later. Isabelle married Herb Ziegler.

In 1903 a high wind storm beached and badly damaged the sail boat of A.J. Haynes, the mail carrier. In 1905 Mr. Haynes had been the faithful mail carrier from Hood River to Chenowith, but his position had been recently discontinued. He was then clearing farm land. In 1906 the Haynes acquired a 160 acre homestead.

In July 1907 it was reported that Mrs. A.J. Haynes killed three rattle snakes, having six, ten and thirteen rattles and buttons. In 1908 A.J. Haynes built an addition to his house. Mr. Haynes was one of the big orchardists of the county, producing 6000-7000 boxes of peaches one year from his orchard.

In 1911 Mr. Haynes had on his ranch a large stable, a covered cistern and an apple house 24 X 70 in which he had canning apparatus. In 1915 A.J. Haynes harvested a fine crop of Winter Banana and Delicious apples from seven and eight-year old trees. Both Anna and A.J. Haynes died in the 1930s. In 1951, Harry Card bought the Haynes ranch.

**Hogue, Frank**

In September 1917 his name was drawn in the draft and he left for Camp Lewis at American Lake. *The Pioneer* of January 1917 reported,

*A wedding of much interest to Underwood residents took place in Portland Christmas Eve when Miss Rachel Anne Brooks was married to Sgt. Frank Hogue, formerly a young business man of Underwood but at present stationed at Camp Lewis. Sgt. Hogue is a member of the firm Adams and Hogue of this place (Stevenson presumably). The new Mrs. Hogue has completed her course at Radcliffe College.*

**Holtmann, Jerome and Lorraine**
As told to Kathy LaMotte

In about 1947-1948 Fred and Nellie Holtmann moved here from Nebraska. Two of their ten children stayed in Nebraska. One son was already out here and working in the fruit industry for Underwood Fruit Warehouse. Mr. Fred Holtmann had come out to visit. He liked what he saw and decided to move his family out here to stay.

The Holtmanns pointed out the double 'n' at the end of their name. This is the German pronunciation. A couple members of the family have since dropped the second ' n'.

The Fred Holtmanns first lived in Upper Underwood in an old home for a few years. It had been the Kellendonk homestead. Fred Holtmann was working for Broughton Lumber Company. After a few years the family moved down by the mill at Hood. There were several houses behind the mill. They were in that home for a while, before moving over to a new home just built on property owned by a Mr. Johnson. They had a large area there, which was good, having a large family. They raised cattle and always had a large garden.

Several of the sons of Fred and Nellie also eventually worked for Broughton Lumber. They were Fritz, Ramey, Kenny, Rick, and Jerome.

Lorraine is the daughter of Jay and Delia Robbins of Husum. Both parents have since passed away. Jerome and Lorraine met at a dance in White Salmon. Jerome was already out of school and Lorraine was a junior in high school. Jerome married Lorraine Robbins in 1960. They moved into a home on property Jerome had off of Laycock-Kelchner Road in Underwood. They lived there for two or three years. They were not really satisfied with this location because there were not any neighbors at the time. So they moved into a brother's place in White Salmon. Both of their children, Jay and then Becky were born while living in White Salmon.

Jerome worked for a time with the automatic stackers at the Broughton mill at Hood. At some point they wanted him to run the dry kiln for the mill. To do that he had to live at the mill, being called on for emergencies at any time. So Lorraine and Jerome moved their young family to a home at the mill. Lorraine recalls that living by the train tracks was always worrisome. Once when Becky was about four, Lorraine noticed she was missing. She immediately started looking toward the tracks. She spotted their Dalmatian and rushed that way. Sure enough, Becky was with their dog, and actually on the tracks. She had been picking berries.

After their family got older and in school Lorraine went to work in fish marking. They were contracted by the US Fish and Wildlife to tag and clip fins of fish, so as to track age and location of fish being released from hatcheries. Lorraine worked at this from the 1970's until 2006.

Jerome recalls that in the last place they lived by the mill there was a flume bell. It was important to check the water flow. There were a couple of men working on this at the time. As Jerome explained, the flume was designed in the form of a V.

## Holtmann, Jerome and Lorraine (cont.)

Up above Drano Lake a gate was constructed on one side of the flume. If the electricity went off it tripped this gate. One side of the flume opened up at the gate and anything coming down, water, or also cants (if it was during working hours), would drop down into Drano Lake, thus perhaps preventing a disaster at the mill. The flume bell was in another residence as well, and they never knew, of course, when it might go off. This last home they lived in near the mill later burned in the fire of Sept. 2007.

Jerome worked for Broughton Lumber from 1955 until it closed in 1985. He then went to work for SDS for a few years before retiring.

Upon leaving Broughton's, Jerome and Lorraine had planned to build on their property off Laycock-Kelchner Road in Underwood. However, they ran into difficulty because of the Gorge Commission. They were unable to build at that time. So they bought a home and property in the Pucker Huddle area of White Salmon.

Since then regulations have eased somewhat. Both their son Jay and his wife Wendy, as well as their daughter Becky and her husband Tim Woosley have built homes on their property in Underwood.

The Holtmanns have two grandsons, two granddaughters, and a great grandson, Kaleb.

Both of Jerome's parents, Fred and Nellie Holtmann have passed away.

Since the time Jerome, and later Lorraine, moved to Underwood the main difference they have noticed is all the houses. They recall when there seemed to be only a handful of houses up the hill. They remember events often taking place at the old gym, now the Community Center. Skating was big. Skaters could rent clamp-on skates. Families would take turns running things. For a while there were many musicians up in Underwood who enjoyed getting together. One weekend they might play in Willard, and the next in Underwood.

As many know, the winter ice storm of 2012 did much damage to property owners in Underwood. The Holtmann's property was hit hard as well. Many loads of downed trees were taken from their property.

From their home in White Salmon Jerome and Lorraine can look over and somewhat spot their property on Underwood Hill.

**Lorraine and Jerome Holtmann**

# Horn, Joe

From The *Enterprise*, September 16, 1976, page 11:

*The year is 1913 and the sternwheeler JN Teal is churning its way up the Columbia River between Portland and The Dalles. A full day's journey. When the boat stops near Underwood, Washington, 21 year-old Joe Horn is there to meet it. As an employee of Herman Friedrich, who owns the Underwood Livery Stables, it's Horn's job to pick up freight, put it on a four-horsepowered wagon, and drive to Trout Lake and Glenwood to make deliveries. Today, 63 years later, 84 year-old Joe Horn still holds memories of those good old days of stages and sternwheelers fresh in his mind.*

*He was paid $45 a month, plus board and a place to sleep in the hay loft of his employer's livery stable, to haul supplies ranging from carpentry tools and groceries to feed for cattle. He also carried mail from Underwood to Chenowith, a now-obsolete town west of Underwood near Broughton's mill.*

*Horn started work at 7 a.m. when he went down to the boat landing near Underwood to get enough rope and halters for his four horses. When the boat arrived, he picked up "general freight for country stores"—groceries, dry goods, and feed for cattle and sheep, he says. Sometimes he transported passengers. Requirements for the job, according to Horn, were being able to "read and write, understand the English language and converse with people. I didn't have to take an exam."*

*On the days when he journeyed to Trout Lake, he got as far as Husum at noon and spent his lunch hour there. After eating, he went on to Trout Lake, unloaded his freight, and then came back to Underwood. "It was a long day," he sighs. It also could be a lonely day. Between Husum and Trout Lake he sometimes just met the stage coach and nothing else.*

*On his way to Glenwood from Underwood, Horn traveled the first 15 miles to Gilmer, where he stayed in a half-way house owned by George Gilmer. Russell Kreps lives in the old house today, he says. The next day he arrived in Glenwood, where he unloaded his freight at the town's two stores, one operated by August Kuhnhausen and the other by a man named Fitzgerald (he can't remember the first name.) "I stayed overnight at August's, then started out at 6 a.m. and got to Underwood late at night," he remembers. On the way back to Underwood he stopped at noon at Gilmer. Two stage coaches, one from Underwood and one from White Salmon, met there to exchange mail and passengers, then went back to their respective places.*

*Winter snows caused Horn to vary his routine. "Once or twice at Gilmer when there was a lot of snow," he says," I had to transfer the load from the wagon to bobsled to get over the mountain. Then when I got over down to Laurel or wherever I could find a wagon, I'd go on down to Glenwood. Then I had to come back and repeat that again."*

*Horn, a small spry man with a sharp recall of the past, also tells of leisure activities which supplemented his work. "We had a baseball team over there and we played a pretty good game," he smiles, "We played Stevenson, White Salmon. . . Hood River beat us 4-3. I remember the score. We played Sundays and holidays.". . .*

*The dance hall in Husum, which Horn says he thinks might still be standing, was popular place on Saturday nights. "Boy, when I hauled freight out of Glenwood, I'd load up and get out to Gilmer. . . I had a girlfriend there." He took her to dances in Husum on Saturday nights, and after taking her back home to Gilmer, he'd go home to Underwood. "The sun would be shinning when I got there!" he laughs.*

## Horn, Joe (continued)

*One year Horn picked up small pox and went to a doctor in Hood River to be examined. "They examined me and decided, "Joe, you got the small pox." I said, "I wouldn't doubt it. I feel kind of funny." When he asked how he would get back to Underwood, the doctor said simply to get on the ferry and "don't say anything to anybody." Horn took the doctor's advice and when he got on the ferry, "crawled to the back end as far as I could get." The ferry operator, though, was a friend of Horn's, and told him to come up front and talk to him. Horn declined repeatedly and the ferry operator asked, "What's the matter with you, Joe, you got something the matter with you?"*

*"I said," Yes, I have small pox, so he turned the boat around and dumped me off on the sandbar!" Somehow Joe made it to his family's home in Oak Grove, where he was quarantined.*

## Howell, Bud

In April 1939 it was reported that Mr. and Mrs. Bud Howell have moved from the hotel to the Love Ranch on the Underwood Heights.

## Hunsaker, Jake

In 1905 Jake Hunsaker, later postmaster of White Salmon and general store merchant, owned property near Cook, known as Hunsaker Flats. Each year several local men had work bailing hay for Hunsaker. J.W. Overbaugh and Captain H.C. Cook worked the hand bailer every year for Jake. He later sold the property to Mr. Knapp.

## Hunsicker, Frank

No relation to Jake Hunsaker, however, Frank bought 80 acres from Jake's son in 1904 and the land clerk thought he was a family member and the name Hunsicker was misspelled, so the land title came back as Frank Hunsaker. It was decided to permanently change the name.

## Hussey, Henry A. and Grace

A *Glacier* news article of June 1, 1911 reported that Mr. Hussey, whose 30 acre ranch one mile back from Underwood station, was a successful orchardist and has a business of raising squabs (pigeons) for the market in Spokane, Portland and Seattle. He had about 1500 cooing birds in his pens. Mr. Hussey formerly manufactured shoes and boots in New England.

In October 1917 H. A. Hussey, of the Avalon orchards, started harvesting his splendid orchard crop. Mr. Hussey and the other ranchers who had water for irrigation for the first time that year were more than pleased with results.

## Jackson, Chief Johnny

By Kathy LaMotte

Johnny Jackson was born February 2, 1931, in Wahkiakus, WA, about 3 and 1/2 miles above Klickitat. He attended school in Klickitat, WA. Jackson is one of four chiefs of the Columbia River tribes along the river. Chief Jackson has been a fisherman all his life. He has also worked in logging, on the railroad, and in cold storage packing.

Sla-kish was Jackson's great, great grandfather. He was Chief of the Klickitat tribe. His father was Andrew Jackson. He was an enrolled Yakima Indian, and was from the Cascade Villages Klickitat Tribes. Inez Sla-kish Jackson was his mother. His grandmother on his mother's side was Mattie Sla-kish. Jackson's Indian name is Tawatosh, after the Chief. He is Chief of the Cascade Tribe of the Yakima Nation. Chief Wilbur Slockish of the Klickitat Tribe is his cousin. Chief Jackson has one son, Peter Dean Jackson.

Jackson's ancestors are on both sides of the river. His people are buried on both sides of the river, including sites at Lyle and Bonneville.

Johnny Jackson was designated Chief in 1988. He is part of the Council of Columbia River Chiefs, formed in the 1980's, to work together to advance the common interests of the tribes located along the Columbia River.

**Jackson, Chief Johnny** (continued)

As a small boy, Chief Johnny Jackson lived at the mouth of the White Salmon River during fishing season.

**Indian Village on White Salmon River 1936**
Photo from Gorge Heritage Museum archives

Jackson is quoted as saying, during his boyhood,

*This used to be a village here. There were lots of people living here, buildings from where the road is (Washington Highway 14). The road entering the fishing village used to be further up the hill on Underwood Road. Drying sheds were down here. My two grandmothers had drying sheds and my mother would be here in summer until way late in the fall. Then we'd move home... I was 7, 8, 9 years old. The river used to run the other side of the bank. When I was a kid I used to stand over there and throw rocks at the fish."*
From *Empty Nets* by Robert Ulrich.

After the Bonneville Dam pool filled in and flooded the low land at the mouth of the White Salmon River, many of the Indians left. Jackson also moved away at first. But the Bureau of Indian Affairs (BIA) used to burn the drying sheds that were left, and they had to rebuild. Jackson moved back to protect the sheds. He is the only resident living there year round.

He watches over the boats, drying sheds, and nets. Chief Jackson lives at the in-lieu sight at Underwood to ensure that non-Indians and visiting fishers respect the property.

Since becoming Chief, Johnny Jackson has worked on many issues affecting the Cascade tribes. His duties include sitting in on Columbia Gorge Commission meetings, although he is not a member. He also works on representing his history correctly. His cousin Wilbur Slockish and his wife, work to revive the teachings of language, songs, dances, stories and cultures of the Columbia River Tribes for next generations.

**Chief Johnny Jackson stands in front of cleaning station at his home in Underwood.**

Sources: *Empty Nets* by Robert Ulrich
*Oregon Voices*: Oregon Historical Society
Energy Facility Site Council – Testimony

**Johnston, Ray and Darla**
By Darla Johnston

What an adventure our family has experienced on our acreage in Underwood! While Ray and I both grew up in Phoenix, Arizona, Ray became driven for an adventure. The next thing I knew was that he was dreaming of moving to Alaska, a frontier. Unfortunately for him, but lucky for me, there were no teaching positions available there at that time. The dark, dreary winter would have been diffi-

**Johnston, Ray and Darla** (continued)

cult for me, but the part of the year with mostly sunshine would have been perfect.

However, Washington had an opening for a business teacher in Forks. This is where Ray made his home for three years and I shared it Fridays through early Monday mornings. I had an apartment in Aberdeen where I worked for the hospitals as a medical technologist. Ray came up on Wednesday nights and left Thursday mornings. Thank Goodness this schedule was only for one year. After our son Jay was born, I took two years off of work and lived seven days per week in our home in Forks. It was surrounded by miles of trees, running creeks, mountains, and many animal trails on which we hiked during our non-working hours. We were about two miles west of Fairholm Resort which was located on Lake Crescent, a very scenic area. The people were wonderful and we have many fond memories of our time there.

When Ray accepted a job at Stevenson High School, we moved to Underwood where we have lived since 1972. Ray retired from the Stevenson position in 2004 and I retired from Skyline Hospital in 2000. Underwood was a great area for a family. Ray's dream of a having a mini farm and a self-sufficient life of living off the land was realized in Underwood. I remember going into the post office at the bottom of Cook-Underwood Road just west of the White Salmon River by Bud Cumming's Auction and asking Ruby Sooter if she knew who owned all the property south of Ellson's Trailer Park. She informed me that Mick and she were the owners and invited our family to come over. They agreed to sell us the land and a lasting friendship was formed.

Our children, Jay and Shawna, along with us were kept busy with the gardening, canning, raising chickens for meat and for eggs. We purchased an Alpine goat from Robert Morby in Underwood because our kids needed goat milk. From there, we purchased day-old steers and a

cow, had Mabel, a goose, and Gus, the gander, along with mallard ducks. When Jay was very young, Ray, Shawna and my parents went to the Trout Lake fair (I had to work that day) and Jay caught and hung onto a greased pig. This was our final addition to the farm until the kids were in 4-H and decided to raise rabbits. Underwood has allowed us to go back to a life of self-subsistence and reap the pride that comes from doing so.

Our next adventure was building our octagon home. While the animal phase, the gardening, and fruit harvesting have gone by the way side, the house still has remodeling that gets addressed from time to time along with trim that still needs to be done. This is the house that VISA built. We charged only the supplies that we would need for the next month and paid VISA off totally each month for years.

In 2002 I went back to college and picked up a teaching certificate from Pacific Lutheran University in Tacoma. I enjoyed both the After School Program and the Alternative School in which I had the opportunity to be involved with the teaching and with students' and parents' lives. I have subbed mostly and find that I really enjoy working with students and staff. It has been very rewarding with the positive impact I feel that I have been able to share with some of the students. I know Ray felt loved his many years of teaching and working with students. We were also fortunate to share our love with our two children and their spouses (Jay and Laurie and Shawna and Mike) and five grandchildren (Wesley, Sophie, Derek, Griffin and Taryn). All live locally which is a real blessing.

Ray and I have enjoyed raising dahlias and other flowers, fishing, playing baseball, horse shoes, tennis, swimming, camping and hiking while we were raising our family. We have made so many friends through the years and I continue to do so. I cannot imagine having raised our family anywhere else.

**Johnston, Ray and Darla** (cont.)

**Shawna and Jay with harvest**

**Jay, Darla, Ray, Shawna Johnston**
Photos from Johnston collection

### Judd

The 1934 Plat Map of Underwood shows the Judd place next to I.R. Ziegler on Little Buck Creek Road in the Climax area. A July 1944 news item:

*White Salmon Marshall John Splawn, accompanied by several local men, left at 4 o'clock yesterday morning to join the hunt for the Judd girl reported lost on Underwood Heights.*

### Kapp, Carl and Neretta

Carl was born in Underwood in 1905. He attended the school built in 1905 that sat in the vicinity of where the new Underwood fire station is now. He married Neretta Estes in 1928. They had a daughter Carlie and sons Ron and Don. The family lived for many years in the farm house on the Kapp ranch on Laycock-Kelchner Road.

Carl Kapp at school c. 1912

In the 1930's Carl worked for Skamania County Road Department, then worked at Broughton Lumber Co. until his retirement in 1974. He was a fire warden for a time and raised and butchered cattle and pigs. Carl worked into his 90's cutting fire wood. After his wife Neretta died in 1973, Carl married her sister Nerissa.

Carlie Kapp Holmes told about these memories of Underwood to Mary Kapp in 2008: Carlie remembered the one-room Climax School and the Climax Mill with a skid road made of cord wood. She knew Bessie Quiemps and the Sohappy family. Her grandmother Christiana Kapp told her, "Behave or I'll turn you over to the Greeks." Carlie's parents talked about the boys throwing rocks at the Greeks building the dam on the White Salmon River. Carlie heard that most of the Greek dam builders were political prisoners shipped over here to work. They came with a Greek interpreter and were sent back to Greece when the dam was finished.

Carlie also had heard that the captain of an Underwood ferry boat was a rum runner. He would haul liquor to the Koberg Beach dance hall and hand it up through a trap door.

## Kapp, Heinrich Sr. and Christiana
### By Jack Kapp

My grandfather Heinrich Kapp was born in Geislingen, Germany in 1862. He came from a long line of master and journeyman butchers. When he came to the United States, he worked in Chicago, probably in the stock yards, and then he moved west before 1900. In that year he married Christiana Bauerle. She was born in Oberstenfield, Germany in 1873 and came to the United States as an infant. Her family settled in Portland.

In 1901, they moved to Underwood where they produced three sons and five daughters. The oldest daughter, Henrietta (Betty) was born in 1901, followed by Heinrich Jr. (Henry/Heine), Karl (Carl), Julia, Max, Margaret, who died before age one, Rosa and Maria.

Heinrich operated a meat market in lower Underwood near the hotel and mercantile building. He raised and butchered cattle on the family's 15 acres off Orchard Lane.

Deed records indicate he purchased 52 acres at $2.50 per acre in 1905. The total paid was $130. The land was situated at the first tunnel going west on Highway 14. At that time there was neither the tunnel, the highway, nor the Bonneville Dam, so there was land along the river's edge. The story is that while the family lived there, Heinrich would row a boat up the river to tend the meat market. The store had a house built on the back, so it is assumed that the family lived there for a time. The building burned in the Underwood fire of 1946 and was rebuilt with a flat roof by the eldest son Henry. The building is still there and can be seen on the left as you travel up the Cook Underwood Road.

Buried in the Underwood Chris-Zada Cemetery, along with baby Margaret, are Max, who died on July 5, 1929, as a result of a fire cracker accident; Christiana, who died in December of that year; and Heinrich Sr., who died a month later. It was left to Henry, the oldest son, to run the meat market/butchering business and care for his younger sisters Rosa and Maria, who were still in school. Carl, Rosa (Reinland) and Julia (Thomas) are also buried in Underwood, having lived long lives.

Henry Kapp, Jr. remained in Underwood and acquired acreage up the mountain, fencing his large Hereford cattle ranch and building a barn. He married Erma McHan, whose grandparents were Iver and Anna Wang, Norwegian pioneers in Trout Lake. The couple lived above the butcher shop in "Old Town" Underwood and had a daughter Shirley and a son David. After moving to White Salmon, their son Jack was born in 1939. Henry kept the butcher shop in Underwood until 1950 when government regulations would have made it too costly to keep it open.

**The Kapp cattle brand - quarter circle K**

## Kapp, Heinrich and Christiana (cont.)

**Heinrich Kapp, Sr. and daughters c. 1917**

**Kapp meat market, store and gas station in Underwood. Burned in 1946 fire. Rebuilt with a flat roof.** Photos from the Gorge Heritage Museum archives.

From the *Pioneer* Editor – August 1911:

*Heinie Kapp, the accommodating Underwood butcher, touched the heart as well as the stomach when he sent us down a nice roast of beef cut from the anatomy of a tender young heifer. Mr. Kapp also understands the needs of the average country editor,* too, *for the proportions of the roast were very generous. He has our thanks for the same and we will always extend our kindest thanks for any other donations along that line.*

A July 1931 news item related that *Mr. Anderson, who owns the trucks that are hauling logs for the Pacific Logging Company moved from the Gleneree Orchard to the Reed place at Underwood. The place now belongs to Henry Kapp, Jr.*

### Kapp, Jack and Mary
By Mary Olsen Kapp

Although Jack, born in 1939, grew up mainly in White Salmon, he did live in Underwood on occasion and rode the bus to school in White Salmon with teacher and bus driver Mr. Richardson. Jack also spent many hours and days helping his father Henry Kapp, Jr. with the meat market in Old Town Underwood and on the family cattle ranch up Laycock-Kelchner road. After graduating from Columbia High School in White Salmon, Jack played college football and graduated in math education at Central Washington College in Ellensburg. He received a master's degree in math education from Western Michigan College and taught in Airway Heights, Washington and Turner, Eugene and Redmond, Oregon. He coached football for most of his 33 years of teaching.

Jack and Mary were married in the Bethel Congregational church in White Salmon by Rev. Clevenger and Rev. Olsen, Mary's father. He was pastor at the White Salmon Methodist Church for three years. Her mother was a nurse at Skyline Hospital in 1957-1960. Mary got a BA degree from Eastern Washington College in Cheney and a master's of library science at the University of Oregon. She was a teacher and school librarian in central Oregon for 26 years.

**Kapp, Jack and Mary** (continued)

Their daughter Kelley Taylor is living in Gresham with her husband Sean. Their two sons, Jake and Jared are away in college. Kelley is a respiratory therapist at Legacy Emanuel Hospital in Portland.

Jack and Mary's son Beau lives in Medford, Oregon with his wife Karen and high school daughters Megan and McKenzie. Dr. Beau received a dental degree from Oregon Health Sciences University and has a practice in Medford.

After retiring, Jack and Mary moved from Redmond to the Kapp ranch in Underwood in 2005. We cleared five acres of the large Douglas fir trees that had taken over the hay field and built a metal storage shed with the help and supervision of 80 year old Cliff Duffy from The Dalles. Then we purchased a modular home from TLC in Goldendale and had it set on a foundation built by Darrin Kenoyer. We moved into the house in August of 2005.

Jack keeps busy gardening and doing chores with his tractor. He has built a green house, a barn, a water tank shed, another storage shed, and a three-room peacock condo. Friends and relatives have helped on these projects, as well as the pole fence around the hay field.

Mary gardens and is involved in the White Salmon United Methodist Church, P.E.O., Friends of the White Salmon Library board, Daughters of the American Revolution, weekly violin practice with the Gorge Strings, the Gorge Heritage Museum Board and three book clubs. The book club she and her friend Cathy Crummett started in Underwood in 2006 now has 14 members.

Front: Sean, Kelley, Jack, Mary, Beau, Karen
Back: Jared, Jake, McKenzie, Megan
At the ranch in Underwood, 2011

**Kelchner, Harvey and Blanche**

Harvey was born in 1892 in Pennsylvania. He and Harmony "Blanche" Root were married in 1920 and moved to Underwood where they were fruit farmers. They both had served our country during WWI. Their two children were Richard and Alice. Alice married Clyde Redmann and lived in White Salmon.

Blanche died in 1953 and Harvey remained in Underwood until he died in 1974. They are both buried at Willamette National Cemetery in Portland, Oregon. Their son Richard served our country during WWII and is also buried at Willamette National Cemetery. He was married to Mary Phelps.

Harvey spoke with a Pennsylvania Dutch accent, constantly smoked cigars, and was extremely proud of "Non-Irrigated Underwood Fruit."

## Kelchner, Harvey and Blanch (cont.)

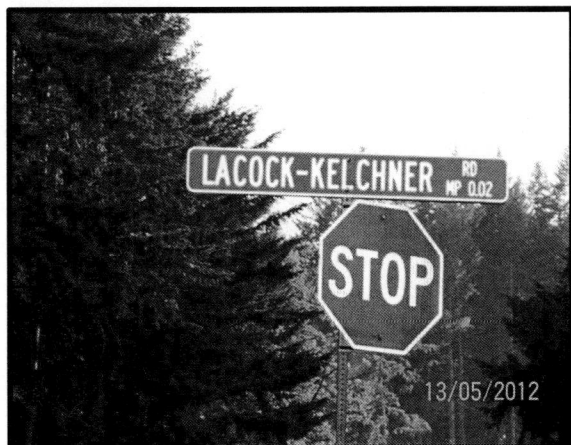

**Note: The spelling Lacock is not correct if the road is named after Edmond Laycock who lived nearby c. 1910-1920. The Kelchner part is named for Harvey.**

Harvey Kelchner

## Kellendonk, William and Franziska

Born 1842 in Germany, William came to America in 1881 with his wife Franziska and two children. They settled in Underwood in 1888 and in 1896 he bought 160 acres. Mrs. Kellendonk died in 1900 at Underwood's Landing. Their son Henry had drowned a year earlier by falling off a log in the White Salmon River. Their other children were William, Mary Ann, Magdalena, Elizabeth and Katherine.

In October 1903 Miss Kate Kellendonk and Miss Phoebe Lyons were both laid up at their homes as a result of a horse and wagon accident. Eleven young people were on their way to a dance at White Salmon Falls when the wagon slipped over the bank beyond Mr. Cameron's. Several of the party were badly hurt but no bones broken. In September 1905 Mr. Kellendonk lost 3 or 4 cows from eating skid grease. His son-in-law Charles Walther also lost his best "milch" cow (an old term for giving milk). William, Sr. moved to Estacada, Oregon in 1910 and died in 1919. He was residing with his daughter Lena Underwood at the time of his death.

## King

In 1905 Mr. King and his wife moved onto their homestead on the mountain.

## Knapp, George

In 1903 Mr. Knapp returned home after a visit to some friends in Alberta, Canada. In 1905 he owned a good farm along the river with 40 almond trees. In 1906 a local news item reported that Mr. Knapp left for Hillsboro after a few days' visit with his daughter Mrs. Sorenson. His granddaughter Selma accompanied him and intended to spend a few weeks in the hop fields and then a trip to the coast.

## Knutson, Knute and Julia

Knute was born in Norway in 1848. He immigrated in 1853 and acquired a homestead of 160 acres on Underwood Mountain in 1902. Their son Gilbert Knutson acquired a 160 acre homestead in 1904. He was married to Lucile Chapman of the Glenwood/Troutlake area. Charles and Mattie Knutson also had homesteads near family on the northeast side of Underwood Mountain called "Norway."

## Kollock, G. C. and Maude

From the *Glacier* October 19, 1906: "Mr. Kollock has a band of 17 (Japanese) clearing his land for apple and peach trees in the spring." In 1907 Mr. Kollock and Mr. McInnis established a line between their properties by survey. An October 1915 news item reported that Dr. G.C. Kollock, a dentist, formerly of Madison, Wis., is now on his ranch in the Underwood district. In December 1952, the *Mt. Adams Sun* reported that Maude Kollock was recovering from pneumonia at Skyline hospital.

Mr. Kollock owned property at the west end of the road that bears his name. The property was sold to Bill and Russ McVeigh and later sold to Donald Campbell.

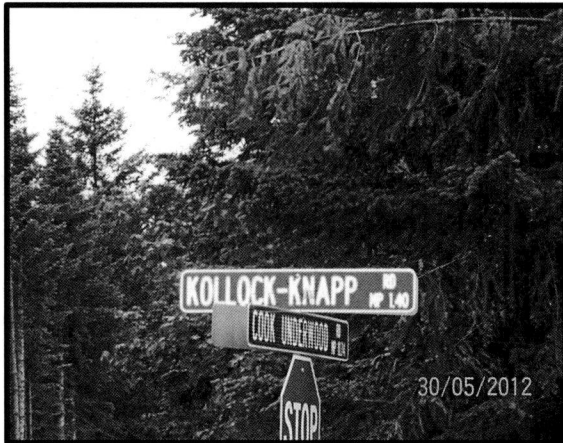

**Road named for G.C. Kollock and George Knapp**

## Kramer, C.E.

In 1928 Mr. and Mrs. C.E. Kramer and Mr. and Mrs. Herman Preggs returned from a very pleasant trip to the sea shore. Mr. Kramer was building an addition and making improvements on the dwelling on his ranch recently purchased from M.S. Smith.

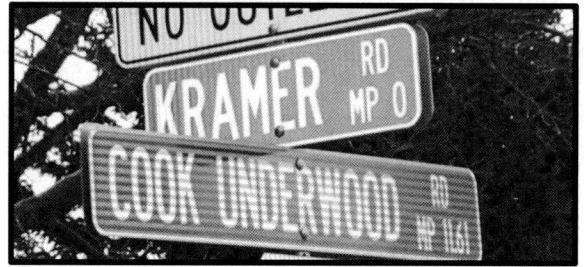

**Road named for C.E. Kramer**

## LaMotte, Ed and Kathy
By Kathy LaMotte

Ed and Kathy LaMotte came to this area in 1985. They resided first in a home on the property of Spring Creek National Fish Hatchery. In 1992 they bought a home and moved into the neighborhood on Ashley Drive in Underwood.

The LaMottes came to this area because of Ed's employment. He took over as manager of the Spring Creek Fish Hatchery. Along with them came their daughters Darcie and Leslie. Darcie started 6th grade at Henkle Middle School and Leslie started 4th grade at Whitson Elementary.

The first winter they lived in Underwood there was 'tons' of snow. The relatives had a great time while visiting over Thanksgiving. The snow remained, even at their home near the river, until March.

*Snow in lower Underwood - 1985*

**LaMotte, Ed and Kathy** (continued)

Ed and Kathy both were raised in California, Ed in Southern California and Kathy in Northern California. They met while both attended Humboldt State University in Arcata, California. After Ed finished military duty by serving time in Vietnam, he returned to the states and his employment with the US Fish and Wildlife. Edward LaMotte and Kathy Johnson were married in Arcata, California in 1970. Kathy finished her undergraduate studies at Montana State University with a degree in teaching.

The LaMottes began moving around the U.S. with Ed's employment. At times Kathy was employed as an elementary school teacher. They resided in Montana, Washington, Colorado, New Hampshire, Massachusetts, Arkansas, and back to Washington. Both their daughters were born while they were living in Colorado.

In 1989 Kathy began working as a 5th grade teacher at Henkle Middle School in White Salmon. There she would remain teaching for 17 years.

After graduating from Columbia High daughter Darcie went on to graduate from Linfield College. She later married Casey Waage of Beaverton. They live in Portland with one daughter Bennett Marie.

The younger daughter Leslie graduated from Columbia High in 1994. She went on to graduate from Washington State University. She now lives in Bend, Oregon with husband Ken Archer and children Edward, Sydney and Elsie.

After 37 years with the US Fish and Wildlife, Ed retired in 2002. He now spends part of his time volunteering with the local American Legion. Kathy then decided to retire from teaching in 2006.

Their Underwood neighborhood has become quite closed in since they moved to Ashley Drive in 1992. But they can still enjoy the view of beautiful Mt. Hood.

**Kathy and Ed LaMotte**

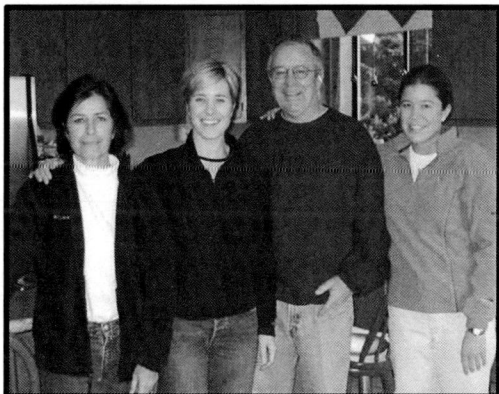

*2003 – Kathy, Leslie, Ed and Darcie*

**Larsen, Christian and Mary**

In 1889 Christian acquired a 120 acre homestead above the White Salmon River. Christian was born in Norway in 1853. He had charge of the fish hatchery for many years. In October 1903 a local newspaper reported that little Amos Larsen broke his arm by falling from a bicycle. Medical aid was summoned from Hood River. On May 27, 1922, Christian and Mary Larsen celebrated their 40th wedding anniversary. Nearly all of their children and grandchildren were present. Their children were Nora, Zada, Frank, Olaf, Aaron, Lewis, Amos and James.

## Larsen, Christian and Mary (cont.)

In February 1931 Mr. Aaron Larsen was building a house down by Hood and expected his family to move into it in a few weeks. In April 1939 Mr. Lewis Larsen injured his knee when the west-bound train ran into the work train on which he was working.

In August 1971 Olaf C. Larson, who lived at Underwood all his life, passed away and was buried at the Chris-Zada Cemetery in Underwood. His wife, Rose Hanna Larsen survived her husband. She came to the White Salmon area as a teenager to work in a cook house at a logging camp. She met Olaf in Underwood and they married in 1917. She later married Ross Shepeard and lived to be 100.

**Road named after the Larsen family**

## Laycock, Edmond E. and Mary

From census records: Edmond and Mary were married in 1880. A daughter Mable died in 1890. A son William was born in 1891. Edmond was a house carpenter in 1900 in Portland and Alaska. In 1910 he was a fruit farmer in the Husum precinct of the Columbia Forest Reserve, Klickitat, Washington. Their home was quite a bit north on Little Buck Creek Road. Ken Ziegler related that the remains of the home years later had a beautiful spiral staircase. In 1917 Miss Blanch Kuchenthal was a luncheon guest at the home of Mrs. E.E. Laycock. In the 1920

census the Laycocks were in Underwood, Edmond a carpenter. By 1930 they had retired to Portland. Lacock-Kelchner Road (see photo under Kelchner, Harvey) is apparently partly named for the Laycocks; however, someone misspelled the name.

## Leach, Clyde and Connie

By Clyde and Connie Leach
April, 2013
"How We Found Underwood"

While staying at a rental house in Hood River on a windsurfing vacation in August of 1990 Clyde looked out from the porch of the rental to the other side of the Columbia River and picked out his spot, his idea of a perfect place to have a home. We found a realtor, came to the Washington side, found Wess Road and Clyde's perfect lot. A real estate lady was just placing a for sale sign on the property. We told her to remove the sign, please, we were ready to purchase the lot at full price.

That is how we began our eventual move to Underwood from Studio City, California. We returned to California and spent two years negotiating with the Columbia Gorge Commission to approve a simple basic plan for our new home. When the C.G.C. finally relented and allowed us a livable foot print for our lot, we found a home designer in Portland, OR, Michael Barclay, to flesh out our plans and get them approved by the C.G.C. It took two more years to build our home, mostly because building was halted during the winters. We were able to move into our home in August of 1994.

The January 1994 earthquake in Los Angeles devastated our San Fernando Valley area, especially in Sherman Oaks, where large apartment buildings and many very nice homes were destroyed. The four story office building where Clyde had his dental practice was closed due to damage. We had a view of the valley from the deck of our home and early that morn-

## Leach, Clyde and Connie (continued)

ing we watched the loss-of-power darkness wave come toward us across the valley floor. The water sloshed out of our pool and our poor dogs were as completely traumatized as we were. We were ready to leave the land of earthquakes, congestion and riots for Washington. As it worked out the quake gave us the opportunity to lease out our undamaged home in April 1994 and move.

Clyde retired from his tenured assistant professorship and his position as assistant dean at the University of Southern California School of Dentistry. He is a retired dentist, class of 1959 with a DDS degree and a master's degree in education MSed from USC class of 1985. Connie attended USC, was president of her sophomore class of 1958. Clyde and Connie married in 1958. Connie went on to pursue her art endeavors by studying at USC, UCLA, LAVCC, and Otis Art Institute in Los Angeles. As a professional artist her art was exhibited and sold in galleries in Los Angeles, Beverly Hills and San Francisco. Her work is in major collections. She is past president of the Los Angeles Printmaking Society (1984), a national organization of artists. Connie was also the founding president of the alumni support group, USC Trojan Affiliates in 1966.

We enjoyed the experience of building our home while we lived in a small trailer with two large dogs. We did not know a soul here in Underwood except our immediate neighbors and our contractor and crew. We met people at the Underwood Community Center by attending meetings and making friends, especially with Don and Tommy Campbell. The Community organized a very active campaign to keep our Post Office and we helped. It was a very successful endeavor, with everyone in Underwood participating. That was the beginning of our community service here in our new location.

At Tommy's suggestion Clyde interviewed for the position of P.U.D. Commissioner in early 1996. He was appointed by the two serving Commissioners in April and was formally elected the following fall as P.U.D. Commissioner, District 3. He has served for seventeen years and hopes to continue as long as his health allows. The Underwood water system has been greatly improved during his tenure. When we moved here we had days when we were completely without water and the pressure was only twenty pounds when we did have water.

Since then we have two new large reservoirs for water, the Huber tank and the Connie tank. Connie was responsible for a grant from the state through our legislators, Jim Honeyford and Bruce Chandler. That gave the P.U.D. $365,000 toward the cost of the Connie tank. The P.U.D. was able to fund the rest. SDS donated the land for the tank site. These two tanks increased our supply substantially. Leaks in the system were another problem needing to be solved. Through leak detection we have lowered our leaks to a manageable number with increased new pipes, hydrants and upgrades to the system design.

Representing Underwood and Skamania County as a P.U.D. Commissioner has been a great privilege. It has also been hard work but overall it has been good to make a positive contribution to our community. We have met and enjoyed some wonderful people here and throughout the State of Washington.

## Leek, Steve and Darlene

By Darlene Leek

We moved to Cook, WA in 1968 from Spearfish, SD, and moved to Underwood in 1980. We have two children and three grandchildren. Steve worked as a fish health biologist in the Lower Columbia River Fish Health Center at Little White Salmon National Fish Hatchery (NFH) and in 1988 moved the lab to the Spring Creek NFH. Steve retired 1/2/1992. Darlene worked in the Auditor's Office at the Skamania County Court House in Stevenson. Darlene retired in 10/15/1994.

In August of 1979 we purchased 10 acres in Underwood from Mick and Ruby Sooter. We fenced the property and cleared stumps and trees. During the fall of 1979 we hired Jack Baldwin, a Hood River contractor, to build our home. He had it completed in April 1980 and we moved in on May 17, l980 the day before Mt. St. Helens erupted.

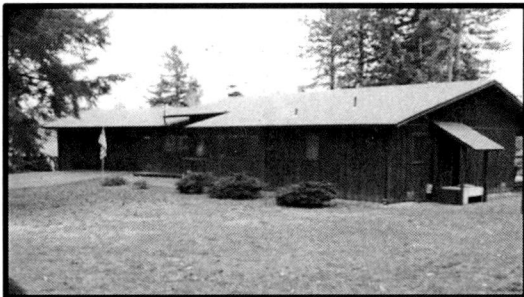

Jeff and Shellie Leek, Steve, daughter Michele, grandchildren Jade, Darlene, Kelsey and Casey

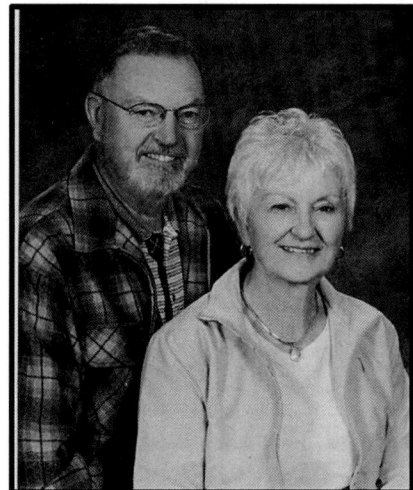

Leek Family Home in Underwood

Steve and Darlene Leek

## Lehmann, Theodore and Martha

Martha was a daughter of Louis and Emily Thun. Born in 1915, she went to school in Underwood and lived here most of her life. Martha was a cemetery commissioner for Underwood, doing much volunteer work at Chris-Zada. Ted was born in 1907 in Minnesota and came to the area in 1913.

166

**Lehmann, Theodore and Martha** (cont.)

Martha and her husband took over the Thun Underwood orchard management after Louis and Emily retired. They also had a logging operation and owned the White Salmon Auto Supply for years. Their children are Ted, Robert, and Richard.

The February 7, 1957 issue of the *Mt. Adams Sun* ran a story about the Lehmanns' honeymoon, which almost ended tragically due to the weather. Ted and Martha were married January 31, 1937 in the White Salmon Congregational Church. The snow was 30 inches deep and still falling during the wedding at 2:30. They started out at 4:30 for their honeymoon in Portland.

Ted's convertible Ford car had neither a heater nor defrosters. They bought gas in Stevenson and were told that since they had made it through the snow over Cook grade in Underwood, they could probably make it over Cape Horn.

After North Bonneville, the blizzard increased and finally stopped them. They began to fear being frozen to death on their honeymoon. After being pushed out of a snow drift by a CCC truck, they came to a standstill on top of Cape Horn hill, the carburetor frozen.

Ted started walking to look for shelter and came upon a car stuck at the foot of Cape Horn hill. Ted struggled back to get Martha and they joined the three men in the car, Martha having to sit on Ted's lap. It was now 8:00 p.m. This car did have a heater, but they couldn't run it all night.

At 11:00 the next morning, help came with blankets from a near-by farm house. They walked through the snow, where the hosts warmed and fed 21 guests, mostly highway men, until the road opened two days later. The newly-weds found their car packed solid with snow, dug it out, got the engine started, and were on their way. They were married for 26 years, until Ted died in 1963. Martha lived until 1988. They are buried at the Underwood Chris-Zada Cemetery.

News note of September 1972 – "Mr. and Mrs. Ted Lehmann had the Grand Champion Mare at the Skamania county Fair. She is 'Five Oaks Seasoned Pepper,' a leopard appaloosa."

**Lowden, Harry C. and Adelaide**

In 1909 he purchased land from William Morrow, originally owned by Amos Underwood. (*The site is behind the new Underwood firehouse.*) It was reported that Harry Lowden had the best barn in Underwood and was in the market for a team and a Jersey cow. In April 1909 Rev. H.C. Lowden accepted the pastorates of the Stevenson and Underwood churches. A 1910 news article commented, "Judging by the number of new vehicles that Mr. Lowden has purchased, they must be contemplating going on the road."

In October 1914 Rev. and Mrs. Lowden held a reception to exhibit the collection of watercolors and ceramics which would be on sale in Portland. Mrs. Lowden's work was much appreciated in the east and the local exhibition and sales were a treat to all lovers of art. In October 1917 H.C. Lowden left for Carson to become principal of the school there. In October 1928 James Meneilly purchased the Lowden fruit ranch.

**Love, Henry K.**

In 1909 Mr. Love owned half interest in the "Bear Springs Ranch". He returned from Portland with a shipment of furniture. He and his partner Gerald Beebe had everything in good shape to take some new members into the firm of Beebe and Love. Both Henry Love and Gerald Beebe were graduates of Yale. Henry Love's mother Patsy came to live in Underwood. She planned to stay with the boys at Bear Springs Ranch for some time. George Darting sold his team to Beebe and Love to keep their orchard in "apple pie order" all the time.

**Love, Henry K.** (continued)

In December 1909 Henry Love left for Chicago and did not expect to return until spring. In October 1914 a news report stated, "Mr. H. K. Love is the envied owner of the only bearing walnut tree in town. He is gathering a crop of extra fancy nuts and his friends are delighted to get them at retail prices." In 1918, "It is a source of regret to their many friends in this community that Mrs. Patsy Love and Henry Love are leaving Underwood this week to make their home elsewhere. Their immediate destination is Portland. They leave their picturesque orchard property in charge of J.J. McNutt."

*(The following is from the Sexennial-1910?- record of the Class of 1904 Yale college):*

*Henry King Love*
*Home Address, Underwood, Wash.*
*Business Address, 848 First National Bank Building, Chicago. Born April 23, 1883, in Des Moines, Iowa, the son of Henry King Love, who was president of the Iowa National Bank of Des Moines, Iowa (died in 1891), and Pattie B. Thomas Love. He prepared at St. Paul's School, Concord, N.H. He is un-married. He writes "After leaving college I entered the employ of N.W. Halsey & Company, bankers, 49 Wall Street, New York City. The confinement of office work proving bad for my health, I left the above firm May 1, 1908, going west and knocking about the lumber woods of the coast for the next six months, three months of which were spent in the Redwoods of California with a camp of timber cruisers. In November, 1908, I went into partnership with Gerald E. Beebe, '04, in Bear Springs Ranch, Underwood, Wash., where we spent the next year raising fruit. In December, 1909, I came to Chicago to look after some property interests here and am temporarily engaged in selling fruit land for the Bitter Root Valley Irrigation Company. It is my intention to*

*return west and raise fruit as soon as circumstances will permit, so you can put me down as a fruit grower by profession. When in New York I was a member of the Essex Troop and the Yale Club."*

Henry Love, his wife, Marjorie Pond, and his mother Patsy Love are buried at Idlewilde Cemetery in Hood River, Oregon.

The Love house and barn burned completely in 1952 while Mr. and Mrs. Andy Abrams were renting it from owner Henry Kapp.

Love Hill (also known as Green Mountain) is the round bare hill with the power lines. It is believed to be a volcanic cinder cone. The Love place was on the southeast side of the hill.

168

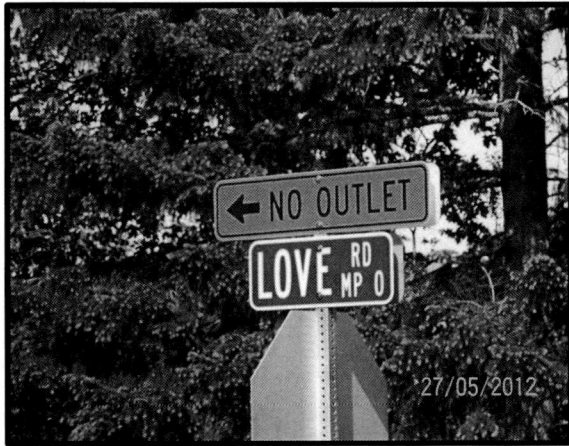
**Love Road named for Henry Love**

## Lusk, Hugh

In October 1903 a white pine squirrel was shot by Hugh Lusk. The report stated, "White squirrels are seldom seen and this one would no doubt be greatly appreciated by some taxidermist." In January 1904 a cougar was seen by Mrs. Lusk making away with one of her chickens.

## Luther, Norm and Roz
By Roz Luther

**Roz and Norm Luther**

Norm and Roz became residents of Underwood when they retired here in 1998 after 17 years in Hawaii. They bought the corner house on Cooper and Sooter Roads, and have lived there happily through 2013.

Norm was born in Palo Alto, CA, and grew up in Salem, OR, with his parents at Willamette University. Roz was born in Tacoma, WA, and grew up in Claremont, CA. They met at Stanford and married before he started graduate school at the University of Iowa. Norm received a Master's and Ph.D. in math; Roz graduated and trained for a year as a medical technologist for lab work. Their first son was born in Iowa City Christmas Day 1961. Following those education years, they had one year in Berkeley for a post-doctoral position, where their second son was born.

Then Norm was hired at Washington State University in Pullman, where they spent a total of 19 years teaching in the Math Department. In that time, they adopted two girls to complete their family and also spent a fascinating year (1971-72) in Albany, Georgia, teaching at a black college, Albany State.

A desire to broaden his work to mathematical demography (population study), led Norm to get a sabbatical at the East-West Center in Honolulu. The years there were exciting, broadening in many ways, and lots of hard work! It's not all playtime for the residents. The challenging adventure included trips to China, Japan, Sri Lanka, Thailand, Indonesia, Australia and nine trips to India for Norm. Roz went on some of them. The oldest son married an Indonesian girl and that let them be part of a fascinating wedding in the middle of Java, in Solo. That couple is now living and raising their sons at the World Vegetable Center in Taiwan. The other son is an ER doctor in Coeur d'Alene, ID; the oldest daughter is the Senate journalist in Hawaii, and the last daughter lives in Georgia, ill with MS.

Retired in Underwood, Norm has been active in the middle-school after-school program in White Salmon, and has worked to get grants on behalf of that. He also is interested in promoting micro-loan businesses here in the Gorge. Both Norm

169

## Luther, Norm and Roz (continued)

and Roz attend the United Methodist Church in White Salmon. Norm has served on the board of the Gorge Community Foundation. Roz was an active outrigger canoe paddler in Hawaii, but here stays busy with lots of gardening, making quilts for the seven grandchildren, and Underwood Book Club. In the summers, they host several of the grandchildren from Taiwan and Hawaii for most of their time out of school. They also enjoy traveling and are active in the state Democratic Party. This is a wonderful place to be and they love the change of seasons and friends here.

## Luthy, Fred and Martha

Fred was born 1856 in Switzerland; Martha Bueche was born 1863 in Germany. Fred immigrated in 1884 and Martha in 1883. In 1901 they acquired a homestead of 160 acres. Their children were Elma, Fred, Rose and Erwin. In August 1903 a large bear was seen above Mr. Luthy's place. In 1905 the news reported that Mr. Luthy grew excellent tomatoes and cherries. September 1906 found Fred Luthy, Jr. slowly recovering from an attack of typhoid fever requiring the assistance of a trained nurse from Portland.

## Lyons, Ed

An August 1903 news article said, "Ed Lyons attempted to shoot a rattle snake with a revolver when something flew up and struck him over the eye. The snake escaped uninjured, but Lyons carries a very sore eye."

## Manners, Dr. W.S.

In July 1909 Dr. W.S. Manners of New York City made arrangements to purchase the Jansen place. In April of the next year Dr. W.S. Manners lost a lot of cord wood by fire and a day or so later lost a horse that was killed by falling off the bluff. The 1933 Plat Map shows the Manners place on the Underwood heights between the Marsh and the Shipley place. He grew alfalfa and wheat and planted young trees. In 1917 Dr. Manners built a barn.

## McCall, Lawrence R.

*The Enterprise*, February 1967:
*Lawrence R. McCall, 23, of Underwood, a "fast draw" victim of his own shooting ability, made a stab for a fast draw, shot his own right leg at the top of the calf. The bullet, a 22 short, came out the lower part of the calf above the ankle.*

## McCutchan, W.L

From *The Pioneer* July 1928 :
*Mr. and Mrs. McCutchan, who recently lost their home by fire, have moved on to the Laycock place.*

## McNab, Pete and Jamie

Jamie Kreps met Pete McNab in 1973 during college, Jamie graduating from Oregon State University, and Pete from Portland State University. They married in 1977. They bought a lot from Ruby Sooter and lived on Circle Drive in Underwood. Their two children are Ryan and Molly. Jamie grew up in White Salmon, close to Whitson School where she attended kindergarten through grade five. Later, she taught school at Whitson for 34 years. Her father Bill Kreps had the Sportsman Barber Shop in Bingen and White Salmon. Pete took over the Partridge Inn restaurant in Underwood after his mother Nora retired in 1982. He stopped the restaurant business in 1988 to work for United Grocers. Jamie and Pete converted the Partridge Inn building into a home and moved in.

Pete McNab passed away suddenly in 2010 at the age of 56.

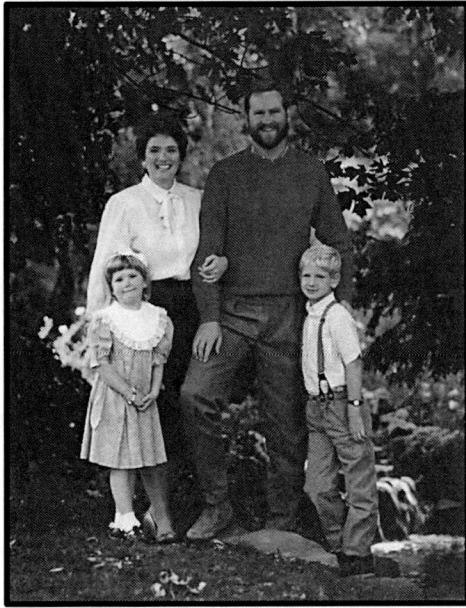

**Jamie, Pete, Molly and Ryan McNab**

### McNutt, John Joseph (J.J.)

In 1918 he was in charge of the Bear Springs Ranch property of Henry Love. In the same year it was reported that his brother Walter McNutt, formerly of Underwood, now of Camp Lewis, while visiting his mother in Camas, was taken seriously ill with pneumonia.

### Meiggs, Raymond and Frieda

He was born in 1886 in Rhode Island. He married Frieda Friedrich in 1914. In 1922 Ray Meiggs attended the automobile show in Portland. A 1923 news report said that Ray Meiggs was under bond of $1000 and was to appear in superior court, along with Forest Slutz, for injuring deputy sheriff Underwood's back in a "rough and tumble mix-up." (*The sheriff must have been one of Ed and Isabelle Underwood's sons.*) In September 1928 Ray Meiggs sold his garage business to John Von Carnop, a first class mechanic from White Salmon. Mr. Meiggs continued to run his filling station and Auto Supply store in Un-

derwood. Their children were Elizabeth, Raymond and Vernon.

### Moore, C.D.

In 1907, along with a Mr. French, he bought William Wendorf's farm of 80 acres, to put in peaches.

### Moore, Ray G. and Nita

The *Mt. Adams Sun* of September 22, 1955 ran a story about Ray Moore of Underwood. This is the opening to the article:

*Back in 1899 the mother of Ray G. Moore packed him off a boat at Underwood landing, nothing but a clump of trees on the beach. They came to visit his uncle, William Wendorf, who homesteaded the Paul Newell place where the old log house still stands.*

The article gives a short history of Underwood, saying that by 1905 the area had been logged off by the Oregon Lumber Company and the land was cleared for orchards.

Ray's father, Capt. John T. Moore of the Portland Police department, bought the Valley View Orchards in 1911. Ray lived there since March 1919, when he was discharged from the Army after WWI. He had enlisted in 1918 as a radio operator.

Ray married the former Nita Hilstrom of Portland. At the time of the *Sun* article she was still working during the week in the SP&S railroad accounting department in Portland and coming home on the weekends. The article notes:

*Last weekend Nita was baking a cake to celebrate Clark Ziegler's killing of a 259 pound black bear in the pear orchard.*

In 1928 Ray completed building a swimming pool on his ranch. In May of 1946 Ray Moore's old house burned, perhaps in relation to the fire that devastated the old town of Underwood a couple days before. The new home of the Moores was not burned.

Twenty-five of Ray's 40 acres were planted to apple and pear orchards. His biggest yield was in 1947 when he marketed 7,800 boxes of D'Anjous, 45,000 boxes of Boscs, 15 tons of Bartletts and 15,000 boxes of apples.

Ray helped organize and was a director of the Underwood Soil Conservation District. He belonged to the original Fruit Growers Association of the White Salmon Valley and the Underwood Growers Association, Inc. from 1920-1941. He was director of Star Fruit for six years. He had nothing but good to say about the farm laborers from Mexico he hired for years.

## Morby, Robert and Betty Jean

**Robert Morby**
By Kathy LaMotte

Mr. Morby was born in 1929 to parents James and Ida Morby. He was born in Chenowith, WA. There were nine children in his family: Mildred, Ronald, Bud, Frank, and Jack, born to Ella Palm, and Bonita, Donald, Shirley, Robert and Larry, born to Ida Harris. All of his siblings have passed on.

Robert's parents came to this area from Utah in the late 1800's. At the time there were several mills springing up in the area, and many Mormon families came out to this area for work. There were mills at Chenowith and Willard; with Mill A and Mill B, and one behind what is now the county garage. Also there was Climax Mill, up Buck Creek Rd.

Mr. Morby has lived all of his 82 years in the Chenowith/Underwood area. He attended first grade in a school in Chenowith. He attended second grade in Underwood. The school has long been removed but the gym is still there today. He then went on to spend third through eighth grade in a school in Mill A. It has since burned down, but the modern day Mill A School we know today sits on the same property. Mr. Morby recalls there was also a school about ¼ mile above Big Cedars, that was known for being one of the best in Washington.

Mr. Morby married a local gal, Betty Jean Abrams, in 1949. She was the daughter of Andrew and Stella Abrams. She attended school in Underwood. She then finished high school in White Salmon. Betty passed away in November of 2000.

The Morbys raised four children, Beverly, Donald, Nancy, and Robert. His wife Betty and daughter Nancy have passed on. The family received their schooling in the White Salmon School District, with the exception of eldest daughter Beverly who attended Stevenson High for a short while. The Morby family bought their home on Cook/ Underwood Road, just south of the Buck Creek Road turnoff. Mr. Morby added many additions to his place. It is the property with all the beautiful sunflowers each year.

Mr. Morby worked for the Skamania County Road Department for 35 years. Mr. Morby is proud of the fact that three generations of his family have worked for the state and county road departments:

his father, he and his brother, and his two sons.

Mr. Morby then went to work for Broughton Mill in Willard until it closed in 1985. Following that he went to work for SDS Lumber Co. in Bingen, where he is still employed. While working for SDS, he helped build the new road above Willard that will access the area being planned for installing wind turbines.

Robert recalls there were only six or seven families living in the area of Underwood when they first arrived. Some of the names he shared were the Graves, Shipleys, the Cummings orchard, and the Dieterich orchard. He recalls there were packing sheds built in several places along the main road to accommodate the orchards. One in particular, the foundation still existing, is just south of Kramer Road on the property of the late Sharon Harmsen.

When asked about the postal service, Mr. Morby recalls the Underwood Post Office being down by the railroad. He said the train went through twice a day. If there were passengers, or cargo to be dropped off, it would stop. Otherwise there was a large hook attached to the side of the building. If the train was not going to stop, a crew member would reach out and attach the mail bag as they rode through.

Robert also recalls that originally a township was planned and platted in Underwood Flats, in the area off Cooper Road today. But the plan did not prosper. Those moving into the area bought land for orchards and built their homes on the property instead of the planned town site.

All of the neighborhoods and almost all homes standing today in Underwood have been built within Mr. Morby's lifetime of living in the area.

* * * * * * * * *

Here is additional background of the Morby family: (*Courtesy of the Find a Grave web site and Ralph Brown*)

Robert Morby's grandfather Moroni Morby was born on May 6, 1853 in West Bromwich, Staffordshire, England. He died on October 3, 1902 in Skamania County, WA. He is buried in Chenowith Cemetery.

**Moroni Morby**

Moroni Morby's parents were David Morby (1825-1885), born in England, died in Utah, and Emma Williams Morby (1823-1904). She died in Utah also.

Moroni Morby married Harriet Clark on June 10, 1883. She was born on November 15, 1865 in Henefer, UT. *Harriet was married a second time to Willard B. Young (buried in Underwood Chris-Zada Cemetery). Harriet Clark Morby Young's life extended from 1865 to 1950. She died in Gresham, OR.*

The Moroni Morbys first lived in Upton, Summit County, UT. They moved to Washington in about 1894/95. They had two sons, Henry and James, and three daughters, Harriet Pearl Morby Peck, Cora Morby Yandell, and Goldie Morby Willis. It is believed that Goldie was the only child born in Washington.

Robert Morby is the son of James Morby. James was born in Utah in 1884. He died in 1960.          After moving to

## Morby, Maroni (continued)

Skamania County he was employed for many years by the Skamania County Road Dept. James was first married to Ella Palm Morby. They had four children, Mildred Morby Young, Ronald, Frank, and Jack. This first wife died in St. Helens, OR in 1922.

James later married Ida Harris in 1923. She is the mother of Robert and other younger siblings, Bonita, Donald, Shirley Morby Parson and Larry. Two children from this union, Donald and Bonita, died as infants.

After James Morby died in 1960, Ida Harris Morby married Herbert Miller, who outlived her by 15 years. He was 105 when he died.

From the James and Henry Morby families there are still many Morbys living in Washington and the extended Northwest.

## Moteki, Makoto and Hatsu

The Moteki family joined the Underwood community in approximately 1953. Makoto and his wife Hatsu lived on the grounds of a peach orchard, at the very east end of lower Orchard Lane. The property originally was part of the Edward Underwood homestead.

Mr. Makoto Moteki was born March 18, 1880, in Fukushimo, Japan. Mrs. Hatsu Moteki was born May 18, 1893, also in Fukushimo, Japan. She was the daughter of Mr. and Mrs. Yashiki Takahashi.

Mr. and Mrs. Moteki (pronounced mo-ta-kee, long a) came to the United States in approximately 1906. They first lived in Colorado. They then moved to the Tri-Cities, WA, area. Mr. Moteki worked in farming; trees, fruit, and vegetables. Mrs. Moteki was a homemaker. The Moteki's began raising a family of four children. Mary, born in 1921, George, born in 1923, and Ruth, born in 1928, were all born in Kennewick, WA. The fourth child Robert was born in Pasco, WA, in 1933.

When WWII broke out the family was sent to the Gila River Internment Camp, 30 miles from Phoenix, AZ. George was the only member of the family not be interred, as he was already serving in the Air Force, 442nd regiment, 2nd battalion.

The Motekis moved to this area, first to White Salmon, and then settling in Underwood, to be near their daughter Ruth, now a registered nurse. She lived in Hood River with her husband Robert Sumoge. The Sumoges would soon have two children Gerald and Theresa.

The Motekis were already retired when they moved to Underwood. They were active in the community, making many friendships. Mrs. Moteki became an active member in the Japanese Methodist Church.

After the war, at some point, Robert enrolled at Portland State University. He also spent time in the Army. When he returned from Korea, he spent 3-4 months with his parents in Underwood. After college he moved east.

Mary, the oldest child, moved to Colorado. She never married. Due to an illness she passed away in Denver, CO, in the 1970's or 80's.

After his time in the military, George Moteki took a job that required much traveling. He lived in NJ, and was married. While traveling, George would often stop to spend time with his parents in Underwood. At some point George was divorced. He later moved to Japan and remarried. He lived in Japan 5-6 years before his death in 1993.

In 1960, Makoto Moteki passed away, at the age of 80. He was buried in Chris-Zada Cemetery here in Underwood.

In 1961, daughter Ruth Moteki Sumoge tragically passed away from a brain tumor. She was only 33 years old. She left behind her husband Robert, her two children Gerald, five, and Theresa, three, her mother Hatsu, and three siblings. She was buried in Hood River.

**Moteki, Makoto and Hatsu** (cont.)

Mrs. Hatsu Moteki continued to live in Underwood near the pear orchard. She had many friends in the area. One young neighbor at the time, Kathy Brown Layman, recalls going to her house at Halloween. Mrs. Moteki loved seeing the children and prepared bags for each child containing beautiful little cookies.

During the last days of her life Mrs. Moteki lived in a care facility in Goldendale, WA. She passed away in 1980, at the age of 86. She was buried alongside her husband Makoto in the Chris-Zada Cemetery in Underwood.

There is one surviving child, Dr. Robert Moteki, a clinical psychologist. He lives in Brooklyn, NY, with his wife Violette, and daughter.

There are three grandchildren. Gerald (Jerry), son of Ruth and Robert Sumoge, lives in Beaverton, OR, Theresa Jan Sumoge, daughter of Ruth and Robert Sumoge, lives in Portland, OR, and Winona Moteki, daughter of Robert and Violette Moteki, lives in Brooklyn, NY.

*Told to Kathy LaMotte by Dr. Robert Moteki* and *Gerald Sumoge*
*The Enterprise*, White Salmon
*The Hood River News*, Hood River

The Moteki home was located on what is now the Sam and Sue Davis property. It has unfortunately been torn down and a primary home built on the property. It was hoped that the cabin would be saved as a historic site.

The home sat on property originally belonging to local Native Americans. Later I.L.Iverson acquired the land in 1875, then Ed Underwood purchased it in 1892. Next the land was owned by P.I. and Lizzy Gibbs Packard and later Louis Thun. The Thun descendents (Lehmann) held the property from 1958 – 2003. The Davis Family purchased the land in 2004.

The Moteki Home, on Packard Farm, in later years before it was torn down.

175

**Moteki, Makoto and Hatsu** (continued)

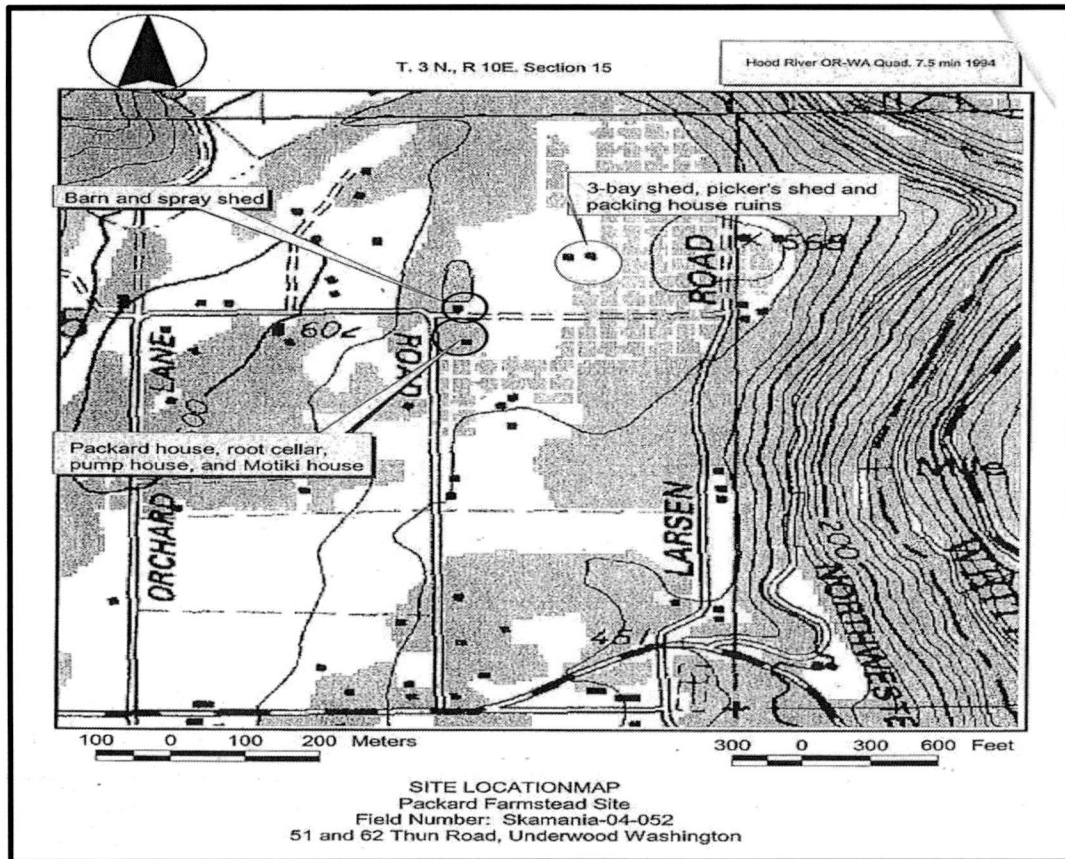

SITE LOCATIONMAP
Packard Farmstead Site
Field Number: Skamania-04-052
51 and 62 Thun Road, Underwood Washington

This small 600 square foot residence had a low gable roof covered with asphalt shingles and wood shingles siding. It faced toward the primary residence, the Packard house. According to written record by Ted Lehmann, Louis Thun's grandson, he believes that the house was built sometime after WWII for Makoto and Hatsu Moteki. The couple were friends of his grandparents and during WWII they had been interned in a relocation camp.

*Home photo, property ownership, and Site Map location information courtesy of Sally Stillman.*

### Munch, Nels M.

In 1905 Mr. Munch, born in Denmark in 1878, acquired a homestead of 160 acres on Underwood Mountain. In 1908 he bought 80 additional acres. In August, 1908 N.M. Munch had his residence nearly completed and planned to move in soon. In 1905 a John Benjamin Munch moved to Underwood. This is from his 1934 obituary. (Perhaps a cousin of Nels.) John Benjamin married Nama Newman and they had four children: Clara, William, Ruth and John.

### Nelson, H.

IN 1908 he was reported to have a nice new place of about 40 acres on the flat, neighboring Mr. DeHart. He had cleared out much of his land and had it about ready to put out berries, potatoes and fruit trees.

176

## Nielson, Dean (Leona) and Walter

In August of 1953 they wrote a book titled Thelma, about one of their 350 foster children, who came to them at their foster home in Pasco when she was thirteen. The Nielsens now lived in Underwood and wanted to write the story of the White Salmon girl who ran away from home and wound up in the clutches of an Idaho madam and her pimp son before finding security with her foster parents. (*2013 – 2 used copies of the book found on Amazon.com, one for $75.00 and one for $200.*)

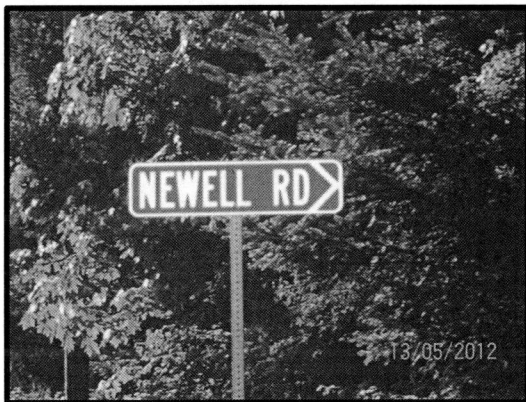

## Newell Family

*The following information shared by Sally Adkisson Newell and Jayne Newell Allen. Photos are from the Newell family collection.*

**Alma Asbury Newell and Paul E. Newell – about 1959.**

Paul E. Newell was born in 1903 in Nebraska. He married Alma E. Asbury (born in 1905), daughter of an itinerant sheep shearer, in 1924, in Kennewick, Washington. The couple first lived in Couer d' Alene, Idaho, where they had met and courted, and where their families lived. They then moved to Edgerton, Canada, where their first child Verne was born in 1925. The family came to Stevenson, Washington so that Paul could work on the Bridge of the Gods. The rain there caused his bones to ache, he said, so the little family moved to BZ Corner, Washington, and in 1927, their daughter Cecile was born. Later that year, the family moved to Underwood where Paul went to work as foreman for C.W. Gibbs, who owned the orchard the Newells would eventually buy. A brief history of the place and its surroundings was written by Cecile in 1984:

### Hunky Dory Orchards

In 1882 a man named Kellendonk (German immigrant, born 1842, lived for a time in South Dakota before arriving in Underwood with four children) had a homestead on the other side of Amos Underwood's homestead. They built and lived in the house where Mrs. Griffin lived on Orchard Lane, now (2012) the home of the Craig and Leslie Haskell family, just above Pete and Ava Grove's new home. (Ava Grove and Alma Newell were sisters, and that house now belongs to Gerald and Deborah Grove.)

Kellendonk sold a large part of it to Mr. Keely and Mr. DuBoise. They are the ones who built the log house that used to be in the Gravensteins (in the Newell orchard). There was also a barn where they kept livestock. Their property now (in 1984) belongs to Paul Newell. The other part, Kellendonk sold to Berrong, Cannahan and possibly others.

After DuBoise's death from a heart attack, Keely sold the property to C.W. Gibbs and his wife. Gibbs was a retired jeweler from Wallace, Idaho. He was the son of Addison C. Gibbs, who served as

**Newell Family** (continued)

governor of Oregon from 1862-1866. The rocking chair he gave the Newells was one the first governor of Idaho (George L. Shoop, served from 1889-1890, when the territory became a state) used to sit in when he came to visit. They were good friends.

The Gravensteins were full-grown trees at that time. They were planted by the Indians, and their age is estimated to be over 120 years. The rest of the orchard was planted by Gibbs, who named it Hunky Dory Orchards.

Gibbs built a house where Paul Newell's barn now stands (barely! It is north and a little east of the house the Newells built in the 1950's). It was considered one of the finest in the country.

Paul Newell Sr. came to work for Gibbs in 1927. Mr. Gibbs suffered a fatal heart attack in 1929. Mrs. Gibbs stayed on until 1933, but she was not well, so she sold the place to a widow named Gibson. Her son, Miles, ran the ranch. He hired a new foreman, so the Newells moved to a house near the grade school (now the Underwood Community Center). That house is gone now, but the property belongs to the Rodgers family. Paul worked for the county and did some orchard work for Thun and Packard.

Gibson knew nothing about running an orchard; he could not make a living from it. When the fine house Gibbs had built burned to the ground, he sold the place to Mr. Glover, who owned the General Mercantile Store in Underwood. He asked Paul if he would take it over and try to build it up again. He would work the place and buy it from Mr. Glover from the crops. Paul made the final payment in 1941, and his dream of owning the ranch came true at last.

**Paul E. Newell (Grandpa) in orchard- 1970's-doing what he loved**

**Left: Alma Newell, Cecile Newell Farrar, Verne Newell, Paul E. Newell**

Verne's daughter Jayne Newell Allen (who gathered most of this information) and her brother Paul M. Newell add this:

After the birth of Cecile, our grandparents moved their family to Underwood, where they resided most of the rest of their lives. Another daughter Elizabeth was stillborn in 1939, and that was very hard for them.

Still, they greatly enjoyed Verne and Cecile, calling them, "a team and a half," taking them on fishing and camping trips, and berry picking on Mt. Adams. They found enormous satisfaction in tending and harvesting their apples and pears, and there was a large patch of asparagus which Grandpa always said saved the place from the Great Depression. Verne and Cecile both attended the old Underwood School. Verne remembers a story from his childhood about his dad and Cecile:

*When we were very young, Dad took us down to the bottom of Underwood to the Columbia River, where he kept his rowboat. Crossing the Hood River Bridge cost ten cents, and back then you could buy a lot of groceries with that. So he would row his boat across the river which back then was very swift, because it was before The Dalles Dam was put in. We kids would wait by the river while Dad rowed over to Hood River. One time he bought a phonograph player made of oak that stood about 4 feet high. You could store your 75 rpm records in the bottom part. It must have been very heavy and awkward, but Dad put it in that row boat and rowed it back to the Washington side. We could hear him whistling a tune long before we could see him returning.*

Maybe that record player was what inspired Alma to urge her children to take up music. Cecile learned to play piano, and Verne took up the violin. As a young man, he was quite a fiddle player and played for many dances in the local area.

Grandpa Newell was glad when his grandchildren got old enough to help out in the orchard, and he also employed neighborhood kids from the Rodgers and Deo families. There was always a large garden to put by, and Grandpa also carried the mail for the Underwood route.

Paul M. remembers Grandpa Paul E. taking him along on the mail route sometimes. In those days, the post office was along the tracks at the bottom of the hill, in a little wooden building just west of the bridge. The train would slow down as a railroad worker would grab the outgoing mailbag off of a hook outside the post office and throw the rope on the incoming mailbag over another hook and leave it there for Grandpa and Postmaster Ruby Sooter. Grandpa always had hard candy to give to the kids who would wait for him by their mailboxes, Paul said. He would also deliver groceries for folks who phoned the Mercantile with their orders. He was the Underwood mailman for decades, finally handing the job off to Verne's wife Betty, who handed it down to their daughter Sharon, leading a family legacy that lasted for 36 years.

For some time, Grandpa's dad, Charles Newell, lived with him and Alma. When Charles finally had to be moved to a rest home, it was in the old Columbia Gorge Hotel, and Paul M. remembers visiting him there, where Charles' roommate was Chief Tommy Thompson of Celilo.

**About 1957 at Bench Lake – Front – Tim and Paul Newell. Back – Verne, Paul E. and Great Grandpa Charles Newell.**

Grandpa Newell also served his community as a weatherman of sorts, keeping records of Underwood rainfall,

**Newell Family** (continued)

snowfall and temperatures for local newspapers from Jan. 1, 1939 through Dec. 31, 2000.

After 37 years of marriage, Alma died in 1961, after a long illness. She'd suffered a stroke and Paul tenderly cared for her at home.

Following her death, Paul was pretty lost, and often ate supper with his children and grandchildren. In 1965 he married Maybell Clara Montgomery White of White Salmon. Mother of two grown daughters, she shared his love of gardening and harvesting fruit from their ample orchard. She took good care of Grandpa and was his full partner.

One of his great sources of pride was the Gravenstein tree that he claimed covered a half-acre of ground. There was also a holly tree and some roses near the tumbledown old homestead those early folks had left. Also cherished was his 1930 Ten-Caterpiller tractor, which was restored by Caterpillar and donated to the Columbia Gorge Interpretive Center in Stevenson. In 1992 the orchard was all pushed over and burned to make way for a vineyard. Grandpa Newell was 90, blind and unable to work in his orchard any more. They sold it, but retained a life estate on the home they loved, living there while new owners Peter and Faye Brehm established White Salmon Vineyards on the former orchard property.

The Newells also owned about 80 acres of timber north and west of their house, and sold that about the same time. Grandpa had been practicing sustainable forestry on it for years, selecting a few big trees for harvest every so often, but it was logged off pretty well when they sold it. The buyer divided it into three parcels and sold them for folks to build new homes on. When Grandpa's health began to fail, he and Maybelle moved to White Salmon, where he passed away in 2001 at the age of 97.

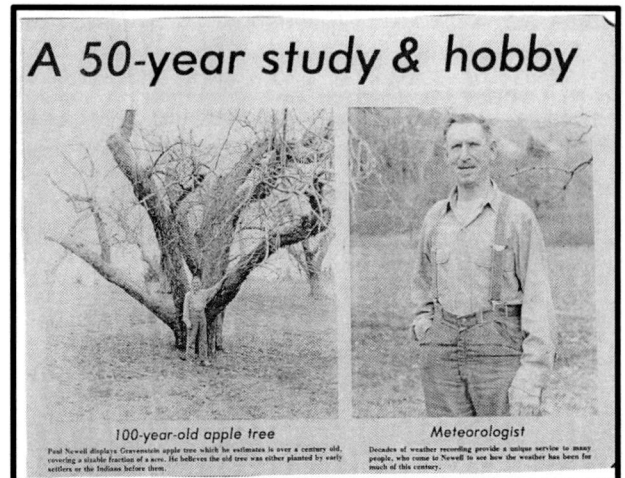

**A 50-year study & hobby**

100-year-old apple tree · Meteorologist

**Grandpa Paul E. Newell in newspaper clipping, showing fruit tree that spanned much of an acre.**

**1950's or 60's–Grandfather Paul E. Newell in home he built all by himself.**

Grandpa Newell was an able, intelligent farmer, who continued to climb ladders and tend his orchard well into his 80's, until his doctor advised him to stop. A kindly, gentle jokester, grandpa loved to tell stories, (some true, some real whoppers) and he would sing old songs and recite poetry, too. He loved his family dearly and we all miss him.

\*\*\*\*\*\*\*\*\*\*\*\*\*\*\*\*\*\*

**Newell Family** (continued)

Verne Newell's 82<sup>nd</sup> birthday

Verne Newell was born at home in 1925 in Edgerton, Canada to Paul E. and Alma Asbury Newell. Paul E. wrote down some of his recollections of his son Verne:

*Verne was a healthy, mischievous child. He made friends with everyone and he teased and tormented every one of them; they loved him. They called him "the Brain" at school. Verne was just average himself, but he seemed to know the answers. Verne was given a farm deferment during World War II, so he did not serve in the armed services.*

*Verne worked on our place and a neighbor's place (Louis Thun) for about 10 years. He bought 30 acres on Orchard Lane (Mary Walther's Homestead) close to our place in 1947. Verne and his wife Betty built a new home on this property in 1964. He went to work for Broughton Lumber Company (lower mill, Hood) in 1951, where he has worked ever since, doing everything from saw filer, millwright and foreman of the resaw. Toward the end of his working days he worked at the Willard mill. When the mills shut down, Verne retired at age 65.*

In August of 1946, Verne married pretty Elizabeth Ann (known mainly as Betty) Wess, whose family farmed strawberries and other fruit on their farm high on what is now known as Wess Road. That place has largely become a subdivision of fancy homes with beautiful views.

The young couple set up housekeeping in a little house on Verne's folks' place and started their family with the arrival of Cecilia, born in 1947. Next was Sharon, born in 1949. Paul M. was born in 1950. Timothy came along in 1952. Jayne was born in 1955, and the family was complete when Lester was born in 1959.

Verne was a good cook, and usually did the cooking on the weekends to give Betty a break. He was a good-humored, happy man, good at repairing most anything that broke, and that was a good thing, because there were lots of kids, and money was always tight. The family was open-handed with friends and family though, and often invited neighbors or the priest to share special occasions.

In 1966, Verne and Betty took over the mail route. In 1970, as their children were reaching marriageable age, the Newells divided their 30 acres, and gave each of their six children 2 acres. Five eventually built homes on their land, and as their children arrived, four generations of Newells were living in Underwood. They dubbed Verne's original 30 acres, "the Newell Compound," and it's still a delightful place to grow kids. There's another generation of Paul and Alma's descendants growing up there (and nearby) now.

Rosa Zellner Wess, Betty Wess, and John Joseph Wess

181

**Betty Wess and collie on Wess Rd. at homestead**

**Grandma Rosa Wess with Paul, Tim, Cecilia, and Sharon Newell.**

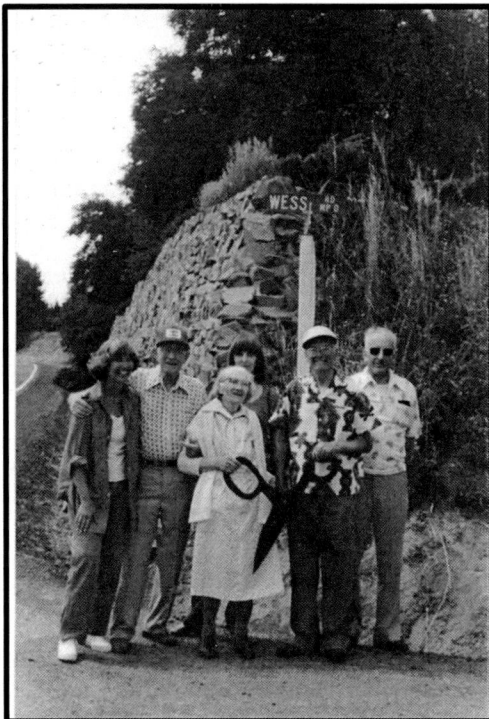

**Ribbon cutting ceremony when the Wess Rd. was named. Left: Betty Wess Newell, Cecil Combs, Rosa Wess, Anna Rose Matteson Haralampas, John Adam Wess, Paul Matteson.**

Verne and Betty divorced in 1981. She left, and Verne continued to live in the family home. In 1985, he married Charlene Junker. She had a son William Junker, born in 1975. They lived in the home on Orchard Lane during his retirement until 2007, when Verne's health failed and they moved to The Dalles, OR, where Verne resided at Columbia Basin Nursing Home until his passing at age 87 on May 29, 2013.

*******

**Betty and her kids**

**Newell Family** (continued)

**Cecile Newell Farrar**

**Cecile Newell**

Cecile Newell was born in 1927 to Paul E. and Alma A. Newell. Her father remembered some things:

*Cecile was born on one of the stormiest days I have ever seen. It snowed so hard we could not see the hillside only fifty feet from our house. Again we were lucky; we had a nurse living nearby. She came over and the baby was five hours old by the time the doctor arrived. We lived at BZ Corners.*

*Cecile was a gentle, loving sort of child, and just the opposite of Verne. They never quarreled nor fought, but were always together. Verne never picked on her for the simple reason that when she had been driven too far, she would simply explode. Once, when she was two years old, an uncle of hers, a year or so older than she, was playing in the dust with her in the orchard. He picked up a handful of the hot dust and poured it over her head. Without a word, she picked two handfuls of dust up, and in one movement, threw it all into her uncle's eyes.*

Cecile went to beauty school in Portland after high school and worked as a beautician for two years. It was during this time that Cecile met Clinton (Dick) Farrar on a blind date. Dick was a sailor from upstate New York, who had enlisted in the Navy at age 19 during World War II. His adventures included Normandy. Cecile was swept off her feet and the couple married in 1948. Dick stayed in the Navy for 20 years, taking his family to his different posts, including a stretch in Hawaii. Grandpa Newell visited them there and brought home tales of paradise.

There were children, too. Norma was born in 1949, married Alan Hawley and now lives in Mosier, OR. Carol was born in 1952, married Tony Henderson and lives in Willard, WA. Tammy was born in 1958, married John Hoffman and lives in Hood River, OR. Donald (Donnie) was born in 1965 and died in 1992. Cecile and Dick had five grandchildren and three great-grandchildren at the time of Cecile's passing. They loved every one.

Cecile and Dick returned to Underwood to raise their family on his retirement from the Navy. Grandpa sold them a little piece of land along Orchard Lane where they built a home (Peter and Lori Nelson's place now) and lived happily for many years. He went on to work at the Spring Creek Fish Hatchery for 17 years. Their kids got to know their Newell cousins, and holiday dinners with the whole clan became larger, louder affairs.

**Grandpa Paul E. Newell with Norma, Tammy and Carol Farrar.**

183

**Newell Family** (continued)

Cecile and Dick loved the outdoors – he hunted, fished and gardened, especially enjoying his roses. Cecile loved gardening also, and she was quite the mushroom hunter, too. They loved Underwood, loved being in the woods. They celebrated their golden (50$^{th}$) wedding anniversary the year Uncle Dick died in 1998. Cecile moved to Hood River to live with Tammy and John. Verne and Cecile were loving siblings to the end. She passed in 2001, our adorable little auntie who gathered a lot of the history we remember here.

*******

**Children of Betty and Verne – Left: Cecilia, Sharon, Paul, Tim, Jayne, and Lester Newell**

Verne and Betty had six children, four of whom still live in Underwood.

Sharon Newell married Jim Bryan in 1967. The couple lived in San Diego while Jim was stationed there in the Navy. Later, they moved back to Underwood and built a lovely home on their two acres in the Newell Compound. Their son, Troy was born in 1969. He lives in White Salmon. Traci, their daughter was born in

1975. She married Johnny Deo (the boy from almost next door) in 1999. They live in Klickitat. Jim worked for the Washington Department of Transportation until retirement a few years ago. He drives log truck now. Sharon took over the Underwood mail route in 1981, and continued until 1988. She has worked for Northshore Medical Clinic for many years and will retire from there soon. Sharon is the early bird runner in the family, but you have to get up really early to catch her running around the neighborhood in her safety vest. Following a milestone birthday a few years ago, Sharon climbed Mt. Adams! Jim and Sharon love riding Jim's Harley-Davidson motorcycle and panning for gold on their claim in eastern Oregon.

**Wess Four Generations – back: Sharon Newell Bryan, Betty Wess Newell, front: Rosa Wess, Troy Bryan.**

**Newell Family** (continued)

Paul Newell married Debbie Hodge in 1971. She had a son Jason Hodge who was born in 1969. He now lives in Redway, CA with his wife, Dorothy. Paul and Debbie had a daughter, Melanie, who lives in Underwood. She married Rich Julian in 2005. She has two children, Kamryn Ruthardt and Grace Julian. Paul and Debbie divorced. He married Sally Adkisson in 1987. She had two children, Claire Smith, born 1976 and Colin Smith, born 1982. They live in Portland and The Dalles, respectively. In 2007, Melanie, Claire and Colin all had babies within a period of two months. Colin's daughter, Ilaina, Claire's son and Gracie, Melanie's daughter were all born in 2007. Colin's son Zane followed a year later. Colin is married to Lurel Pinheiro and Claire is married to Robert Graper. Paul and Sally lived in the Newell Compound in the house that Paul built for several years while the kids were growing up. In 1989, they bought 40 acres on Green Mountain, overlooking Orchard Lane. The land had belonged to Earl and Jane Strode, who retained a life estate on their home on Orchard Lane, and the Newells built a home on the upper part of the property. They sold their house in the compound to Jack and Doreen Hotchkiss.

Paul worked for Broughton Lumber Company at the Willard Mill until 1981, when he lost his leg on the headrig. He retrained and is hoping to retire soon from his IT job with the phone company. Sally works part-time as librarian for Mill A School. They raise hay and sheep on their property and ride horses for fun. They love to pack in with their horses to high country haunts on Mt. Adams.

*******

Timothy Newell married Karen Morley in 1973. They made their home in the little white farmhouse on the northeast corner of Orchard Lane until Tim got their house built in the compound. Their son Matt was born in 1975. He lives in Carson, is married to Lisa Meese, and they have two daughters, Addison and McKenna. Tim and Karen's daughter Jilyn was born in 1977 and is married to Jeremy Wood. They have three children, Karter, Karlie and Abigail, and they live in the home they built on two acres originally given to Tim's sister Cecilia Stone. She passed away in 1988, and Jeremy and Jilyn bought the property. They are the only ones of their generation to build in the compound.

Tim went to work for Broughton Lumber Company right out of high school. When Broughton folded, he went to work for SDS Lumber Company. He sells retail lumber at the mill and hopes to retire soon. Tim bought some additional acreage from his dad and planted Christmas trees on part of it. His passion is cutting firewood and playing with his grandchildren. Karen worked at the high school in White Salmon for many years, but now she's at McCoy-Holliston Insurance. She keeps a gorgeous yard and likes those grandkids, too.

**Five Generations – left: Matt Newell, Addison Newell, Tim Newell, Verne Newell, and Paul E. Newell.**

**Newell Family** (continued)

Jayne Newell married Scott Allen in 1975. They moved onto their two acres in 1975. Scott worked for the Skamania County Road Department out of the Underwood shop starting in 1977. Jayne helped Sharon with the mail route as needed. Danny Allen was born in 1979. He married Lindy Tolbert (the girl from almost next door). They had a daughter Taylor in 2007 (the Year of the Baby in the Newell family) and Fletcher in 2009. Danny bought his grandparents' home on Orchard Lane, and he and his family live there. His sister, Jolene was born in 1981. She married Tim Tolbert (Lindy's brother, also from Underwood) and they bought a lot on Orchard Lane from Ben and Melody Van Horn and built a beautiful home there. They have two children, Hailey (born early 2008) and Calvin (2010).

Scott retired from the county in 2007 after 30 years, and currently hires out with his Kubota tractor and backhoe. Jayne works for the White Salmon School District as a sub for classified employees – she likes the library at the high school best. They love helping to raise their grandkids and keeping a beautiful yard for them to play in.

Lester Newell married Wendy Campbell (the girl from almost next door) in 1977. They had one daughter, Rikki, who lives in Trout Lake with her husband Matt McNeely and their sons Tanner and Wyatt. He married Karen Spooner and had a son Timothy, who lives in White Salmon, works at SDS and is lately returned from his tour in Iraq with the Army. He married Misty Wilkerson and had a daughter Mackenzie, who lives with her mother and sisters in Carson. Lester married Shelly Kerber and they live in White Salmon.

Lester built a home on his two acres, but moved away following his first divorce and the property was bought by Clyde Knowles, whose stepson, Vince LaGrander lives there now. Les has been a millworker, an underwater welder, a fisherman, a mechanic and a musician. He is a talented mechanic and works at Smokehouse Products. Shelly is an aircraft technician at Insitu in Stevenson. Les and Shelly love to run and kayak together.

Great Grandma Rosa holding Dan Allen

**John Joseph Wess, father of Betty Wess Newell Boileau**

**Newell Family** (continued)

**Grandma Rosa Zellner Wess making strudel - 1958**

**Carl Anderson, Virginia Wess Anderson, and Virginia's father John Joseph Wess**

\*\*\*\*\*\*\*\*\*\*\*\*\*\*\*\*\*

**Nicolai, George**

In 1900 Edith Nicolai bought 160 acres and George bought 120 acres. By 1904 Mr. Nicolai had been in the saw mill business for several years with R.D. Cameron.

**Olsen, Harry (also spelled Olson or Oleson) and Mary (Underwood)**

In 1904 the local news reported that Captain Harry Olsen was back on his ranch, "Oak Cliff." Mrs. Olsen spent the summer visiting relatives in Iowa and Kansas and put in fourteen days at the St. Louis Fair. In 1905 Captain Harry Olsen was erecting a fine hotel along the river.

**Ohnemus, Doug**

As told to Mary Kapp

Our family moved from South Dakota in 1938. We settled in Hood and lived in a large house owned by the Johnson family. Later the Holtmann family lived in that home. I was the third oldest of ten children. All of our names started with the letter D.

My father Omer worked at Broughton's mill as a sawer until 1946. The log blocks came down the flume from Willard and the mill workers below fashioned them into useable shapes. Larry Campbell was one of the bosses and a man named Fraley was the office manager. The company owned about 15 to 20 houses for the workers and their families and there was a cook house for the unmarried men. Before we moved to Hood there was a school house near the railroad tracks and also a train depot.

There was a road to Underwood flats from Hood, used for mill vehicles. The children also walked up the road to attend school. I went to the Underwood school from 1941 until it closed in 1945 or 1946. We had 32 students in eight grades, divided into two rooms. The rooms were upstairs. Barry Ternahan's mother taught grades one through four and a man taught the upper grades.

**Ohnemus, Doug** (continued)

A fire destroyed most of the buildings in the town of Underwood in 1946. From Hood we could hear explosions coming from Balsiger's store, Harm's restaurant, and the service station. The store moved to the train depot building after that before it was rebuilt.

In 1949 our family moved to White Salmon on Strawberry Mountain. Our father worked for SDS at the time. I graduated from Columbia high school in 1952 and worked at Boeing in Seattle for some years before moving back and living in Carson.

**Orser, William**

In 1901 Miss Sadie Orser of Chenowith was attending the Portland Business College. In 1905 the Orsers had a fine farm, and their daughter had a fine homestead nearby. Sadie married C.H. Cromwell. The Orsers owned 160 acres. In February of 1908 road supervisor Orser with a few neighbors blasted and removed the large stones from the road caused by a slide. In March 1912 W.A. Orser had cleared and was ready to plant an orchard of standard apples and offered odds that he would live to market premium pippins from these young trees.

**Ostroski, Chet**

A *Mt. Adams Sun* article of July 1952 told about Chet's cougar hunting hobby. Chet shot a 150 pound cougar in the Trout Lake area, using his three cougar hounds.

**Packard, P.I. (Ivan) and Lizzie**

A February 1908 news item said,

*Mr. Packard has promised to conduct a singing class here in the near future. Mr. Packard sings in the Taylor Street Methodist church in Portland. It is hoped all our young people will avail themselves of this opportunity.*

In 1909 Mr. and Mrs. Packard left to visit friends in Victoria, B.C. where they formerly lived.

According to a National Parks Service description of the historic home and land of Ed and Isabella Underwood, P.I. and Lizzie Packard purchased the place in October 1909. They established an orchard on part of the property. The Packards sold the property to Louis Thun in November 1912. The place remains "Five Oaks Farm", named by the Thuns. The new owners live in the home built by Ed Underwood and added on to by Louis Thun in 1935.

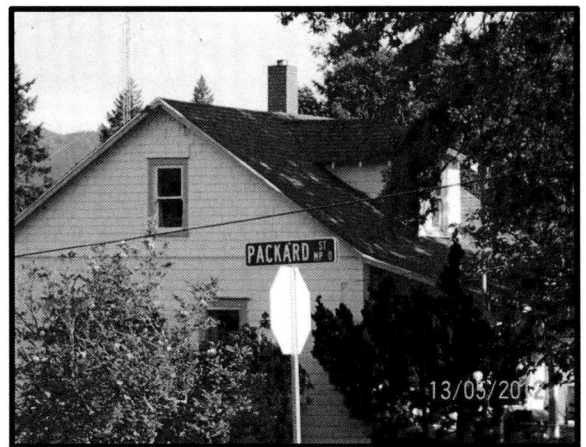

Packard Road, believed to be named after P.I. Packard

**Perry, Martin and Elizabeth**

They were considered pioneers of Underwood according to their obituaries of 1927 and 1930, respectively. Their sons Sol and David lived on the farm on Cooper Rd. for years. In February 1931 Mr. David Perry was reported to be sick with quinsy (a throat infection).

**Reed, E.L.**

In 1917 the Reeds, who left the past year to make their home in Portland, were complimented by a cheering-up party September 29th when about 35 of their neighbors dropped in unexpectedly to extend their best wishes to these popular old-time friends and express the regrets of the community at losing them.

## Reed, Eddie and Louise
Gathered by Kathy LaMotte

(Not related to E.L. Reed on previous page?)

**Eddie and Louise Reed**

(*As shared by Wilma Brown and son Ralph Brown*)

*Wilma* - Louise and Ed Reed lived just down the road from us in the big farmhouse, the second house east of Orchard Lane. (*More recently owned by the Steve Hurn family*). I don't know when they came to Underwood, but our kids were very small. They were like grand-parents to the kids. They had one son, Edward P. Reed, who became a lawyer and later went to Olympia and was a District Judge. Louise and Eddy Reed later moved to Vancouver. They were rather quiet people and never made waves. They were very helpful, and were friends with everyone.

I remember one night when our daughter Kathy was probably less than two years old. She was very sick and ran a very high temperature. We had to stay up all night to bathe her every hour. The Reeds came over and stayed with us all night. We played poker in between taking care of Kathy.

**Louise and Eddie Reed**

**Reed's home in Underwood**

After the Reeds moved to Vancouver, we kept in touch for many years.

*Ralph* – Eddie and Louise Reed's son went on to become an Appeals Court Judge in Olympia. (Edward P. Reed, Jr, District Judge).

Edward Jr. was maybe ten years older than I. I looked up to him. I think he was in Scouts or maybe had an electronics project in school. He gave me a crystal radio he had built, which piqued my interest in electronic stuff. When Ed went off to Law School and gave me his crystal radio it was a catalyst in my career. When I joined the Navy I used the electronic knowledge to get into Guided

189

**Reed, Eddie and Louise** (continued)

Missile Control, and later the knowledge helped me in my career with the telephone company.

The Reeds, Eddie and Louise, were very well known and active in the Underwood community in the 1940's and 1950's.

*Additional* – Eddie Reed, Sr. was born in *1905. He died in Vancouver, WA* in 1986. Marie Louise Reed was born in 1907. She died in Tacoma, WA in 1998.

While living in Underwood Ed Sr. worked for SDS Lumber. Louise Reed helped at the post office.

Edward P. Reed's first job as an attorney was in White Salmon. He practiced law there from 1950-1965. While going to law school he would come home for the summers and work in sawmills and logging camps. He met his wife Margaret while attending Willamette University. They had 3 daughters and 1 son. Their daughter Paula died in a fire while attending college. Margaret Reed passed away in Tacoma in 1996. Judge Edward Reed Jr. died in 1999 of heart problems, in Tacoma at the age of 73.

*The Columbian, Vancouver, WA*

*The following told by Kathy Reed, daughter of Ed and Margaret Reed, granddaughter of Eddie and Louise Reed.*

Those early years in Underwood/White Salmon are deeply imprinted on me. I have vivid memories. A couple of years ago my brother and I drove there and revisited all the familiar places.

My grandparents lived in Underwood during the war and my father joined the Navy in 1945. He met and married my mother in 1946 at Corvallis Ore. and then went to law school in Salem on the G. I. Bill at Willamette University. He moved to White Salmon, WA in 1950 to set up his practice. My brother and sisters and I all spent a lot of time at our grandparents' place in Underwood, just across from the Eyrie where we first lived.

However it is my brother and I who remember it the most.

**Eddie Sr. and Ed Reed - 1954**

**Ed Sr. - 1956**

190

**Reed, Eddie and Louise** (continued)

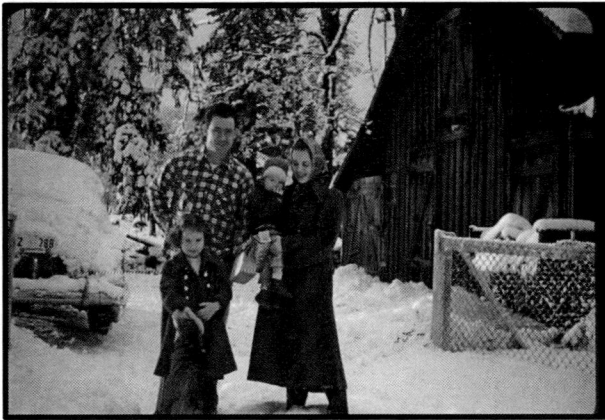

**Ed and Margaret Reed with children Kathy and Alan, at Ed's parents' place. -1951**

**The swing on my grandparents'porch**.

The Browns lived two doors to the west and I played with the Brown girls, Beverly and Kathy, for many hours, making mud pies, swinging, playing all kinds of ball games, hopscotch, playing house, you name it. Of course when we were school age we all went to the same schools in White Salmon. When I stayed with my grandparents I would ride the Underwood bus to school with them. Red Richardson was the bus driver...he had all redhead daughters. I remember roller skating in the community hall and watching my grandparents square-dance with their friends. They were friends with the Brown's, the Baker's, the Ziegler's, Halver's, Ternahan's, others I can't think of at the moment. I used to listen to their radio and now whenever I hear the Tennessee Waltz, the McGuire Sisters, Hoagy Carmichael or Rosemary Clooney I get teary eyed. All friends and neighbors looked out for one another.

I have vivid memories of the details of the house as it was...from the staircase banister, the kitchen where I used to help with canning and making cookies, to the bathroom upstairs where I watched the full moon in the trees from the bathtub many a night; to the bedrooms and hiding places and back porch where Granny used to read to me on the porch swing. I played all over the maybe two acre property with the dogs, chickens and helped Grandpa milk the cow. We made butter, cream and ice cream with the old butter churn on the porch off the kitchen. I remember the dining room so clearly. Many holidays were spent in the old farm house.

**Left: Alan, Kathy, Granny (Louise), Margaret (wife of Ed), and Ed – in the dining room**

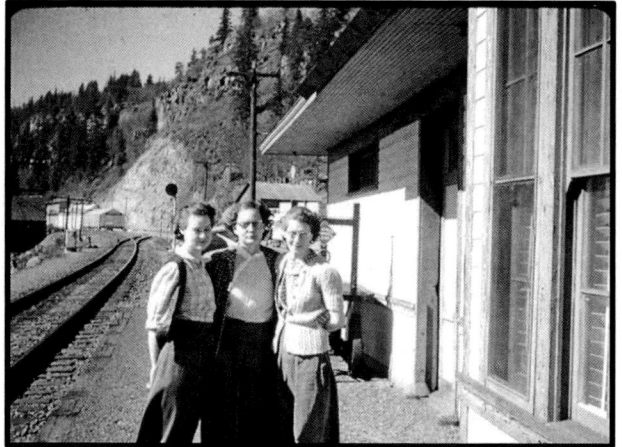

**Right to left: Louise Reed, Ruby Sooter, and unidentified lady at the Underwood train station. Underwood Fruit Warehouses in the distance.**

Grandpa chopped wood and worked in the SDS lumber mill where he had one finger cut off accidentally with a saw.

Grandma worked at the Post Office during the war...it was located exactly beside the railroad tracks midway between the White Salmon River and the Columbia and sat between the little grocery store and the Eyrie bluff.....with Ruby Sooter; mail bags would be dropped off and loaded while the train was moving at a slow pace.

I remember band-aided-scratched knees, the sound of the train whistle and picking all kinds of berries. I also remember how deep the snow was those early winters.

Each time a sibling was born meant we would spend a lot more time at Underwood. Besides myself and Alan there were two more sisters: Paula, born in 1952, and Shelley, born in 1954.

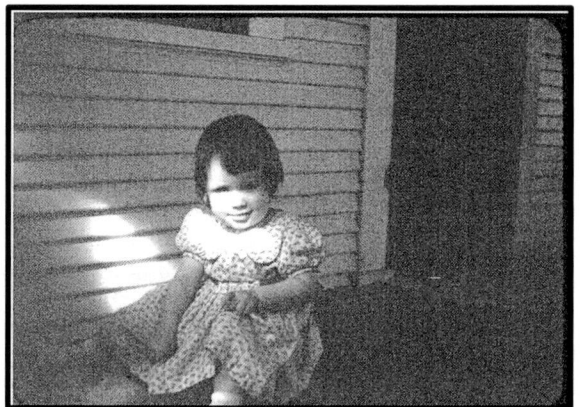

**Paula Reed in 1953**

**Reed, Eddie and Louise** (continued)

During that time many young families thrived after the war raising their families there....now, most are gone, but a few still live to tell stories.....and we of the baby boomer generation have a lot of priceless memories growing up during that time. I believe some never left that ideal place; some left and went back.

**Alan Reed – 2007 – Visit to Grandparent's former home in Underwood.**

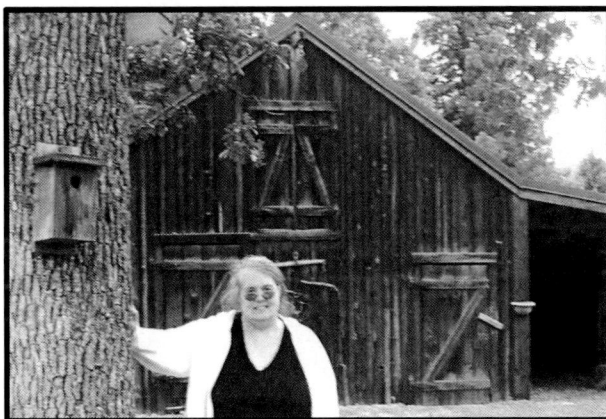

**Kathy Reed – 2007- In front of the barn at Grandparent's former home in Underwood.**

**Reinland, George and Katherine**

The Reinlands emigrated from Hungary in 1909 and moved from Portland to Underwood heights in 1923. Katherine Reinland was the sister of Rosa Wess. They purchased an apple orchard and packing shed and converted the top floor to living quarters. The building is still being used as a residence on the AniChe winery property off Little Buck Creek Road.

The Reinland children were Andrew (Andy), Joe, Kate and Teresa. Teresa married Reno Ziegler of Underwood and lived in Underwood most of her life. Andy married Rosa Kapp of Underwood and lived in Underwood for some time before moving on to manage sawmills in other parts of the Northwest. The children of Rosa and Andy were (Ronald) George, Andy Jr. (Little Andy), Rosalie and Max.

Andy Reinland Senior 1930

**From the Columbia High School year book in the Gorge Heritage Museum archive**

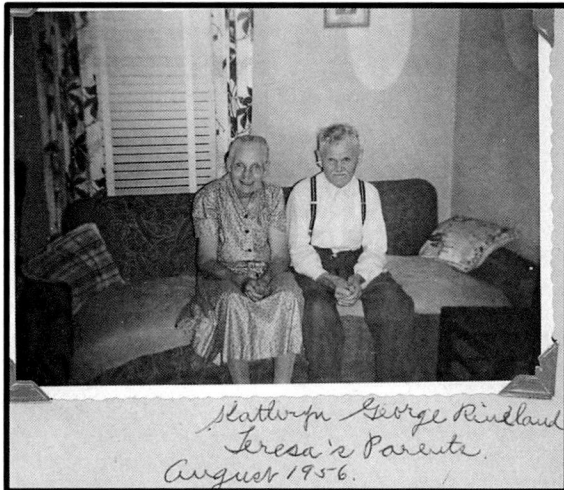

Slattorn George Rindland
Teresa's Parents.
August 1956.

**Katherine and George Reinland in 1956**

## Rice, Isadore E. and Mary

He was on the 1900 census for Underwood but probably didn't live here for long. He was on the 1850 census as a 3 year old in Missouri. Mary Snowden Rice died in 1901 in Isadore, Oregon. She had traveled to Oregon in 1852 with her parents. They settled near Drain, Oregon. She married Isadore in 1868.

## Richards, Pete and Judith

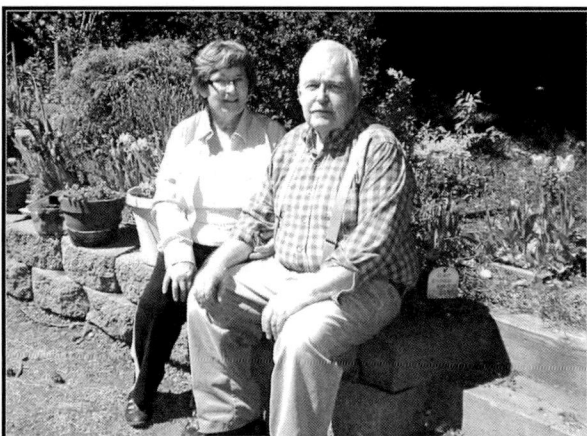

**Judith and Pete at home in Underwood**

Pete and Judith Richards moved into their place on Weather Rock Rd. in Underwood in 1992. Pete (legal name, Harold) was born in Newport, WA just north of Spokane. He is a retired industrial arts teacher. Judith was born in St. Paul, MN. She is a licensed clinical social worker and also a Presbyterian minister. The Richards moved to the area in the '80's when Judith pastored two churches, at Trout Lake and Mill A. Pete was still teaching at Richland, WA, and with the challenges of travel they decided to make their permanent dwelling here in Underwood. Pete had an opportunity to teach at Stevenson, WA after teaching 27 years in Richland, WA and the surrounding area.

After retiring from teaching Pete used his skills and built homes in the area. Soon he realized that building was hard on his body and gave up building to have hip and knee replacements. He discovered his joy is in carving, and he would enjoy sharing his art with you. He commonly likes to carve Northwest Coast Native Carving. (While in Ketchikan, he loved having the opportunity to carve with the native carvers).

From Trout Lake/Mill A Judith went to Moscow, Idaho in 1988, to Central Point, Oregon, to Ketchikan, AK and finally to Gresham, OR. She was an Interim Pastor in all but one of these points of ministry. Because of family concerns with a grandchild, it was decided to stay closer to home, and she began a Clinical Pastoral Practice in The Dalles, OR (1991) where she was licensed by the State of Oregon and Washington. She also holds advanced certification as a Fellow in the American Association of Pastoral Counselors. In 2007 Judith retired from active ministry but continues to receive invitations, and responds, to officiate at weddings, renewals of vows, memorials and so forth.

## Richards, Pete and Judith (continued)

Pete and Judith raised four daughters, one of whom (Gwen) lives here in Underwood. The other three with spouses and children live in Bellevue, Moses Lake, and Boulder, CO. Our children were raised in Richland where Pete taught school. They all have active lives, and would you believe that they are wonderful people?

If you are curious about how Pete named himself, just inquire and he will tell you a cute childhood story.
*By Judith and Pete Richards*
*(Pete suddenly passed away in August 2013)*

## Rine, Walter B. and Maude

The Rines were from Humboldt, Iowa. In March 1909 they purchased the Sunderland tract of thirty acres on Underwood flat. In January 1915 Mr. and Mrs. Rine were dinner guests of Mr. and Mrs. Reed for the holiday.

## Rodgers, Pauline

From the March 16, 1967 issue of the *Enterprise*

*Miss Pauline Rodgers, daughter of Mr. and Mrs. Carl Rodgers of Underwood, received her cap from the Emanuel Hospital School of Nursing.*

## Rominger, Henry V. and Alice

In 1909 the Harding place was sold to Rev. H.V. Rominger of Portland. In 1910 they decided to make Underwood their home. Mr. Rominger, who was formerly pastor of the Congregational Church in Portland and Rainier, OR, arrived with household goods and chickens. In November 1918 Mrs. Rominger reported that her pen of Rhode Island Reds had been at the All-Northwest Egg Laying Contest for the past year. Two of her hens laid 230 and 243 eggs each in eleven months of the contest, more than twice as many eggs as the average hen in the United States. In 1938 Mrs. Rominger was reported driving a new 1938 Ford coupe.

## Rosenkranz, Charles and Katharine

Mr. Rosenkranz was born in Germany and came to this country when he was twelve. He was a cabinet maker by trade. He married Katharine Eichorn in 1908. She had come to the United States from Germany in 1903. They had one son, Carl.

In 1906 Charles had acquired an 80 acre homestead in the Underwood area. In October of that year Chas. Rosenkranz was reported slowly recovering from a severe attack of lumbago at the home of Mr. and Mrs. Luthy. In April 1908 C. Rosenkrantz was preparing to get his lumber on the ground to build a new house. A May 1908 news item states,

*What do you suppose Charlie Rosenkrantz will do next? Since returning from an extended visit east he has cut his mustache off.*

In 1911 Charles sold his property on the east side of the White Salmon River and purchased 40 acres of his original homestead on the west side on Underwood Mountain.

## Rosenkranz, Carl and Edna

Carl was born in 1909 and raised on Underwood Mountain. He married Edna Davis and moved to the Willard area in 1937. Carl was a faller for Broughton Lumber Company for 38 years. They had a daughter Katherine. A 1929 news note: "Norton Judd and Carl Rosenkranz are working on the Willard Bridge."

## Rowland, Ira

In 1904 he bought 20 acres from Jake and Ed Thornton, intending to plant 400 peach trees.

## Rutherford, Tom and Carol

By Carol Rutherford

Tom and Carol moved to Underwood in 1978, along with their two daughters, Teresa and Christine. Tom and Carol still reside on Hale Drive.

Tom was born in 1943 in Havre, Montana, to Thomas A. and Geraldine Rutherford. Tom and his father moved to West Stayton, Oregon, when he was in the 7th grade. Tom has two sisters. Janet currently lives in San Antonio, Texas, and Beverly lives in Portland, Oregon.

Carol was born in 1944 in Beatrice, Nebraska, to Edward and Verna Bauman. Carol moved with her parents and siblings to Salem, Oregon, when she was a senior in high school. Carol has a sister, Janice, who lives in Dallas, Oregon, and a brother, Steve, and a sister Jane, who still live in Salem.

Tom and Carol married in 1963 in Salem. Tom worked in the logging field until he suffered a logging accident in 1967. His doctor refused to release him to return to work in logging, so he went back to school and got a two-year degree in Forestry. Once he received his degree the family started moving to better his job opportunities. The family lived in Redmond and Albany, Oregon, before moving to Longview, Washington. They then moved to Underwood, WA.

Even though they were purchasing their home in Underwood, Tom went to Alaska several times. The first time the family lived on the Prince of Wales Island, Craig, Alaska. The next move in Alaska was to Yakutat, but the family remained in Underwood. Finally, Carol and Tom moved to Cube Cove, Alaska (located on Admiralty Island not far from Juneau) and lived there for approximately seven years.

With both girls married and grandchildren arriving, it was time to return home to Underwood. Teresa married Tod Dechand of Glenwood, WA, and they have two sons. Teresa currently works in White Salmon for a dentist. Christine married Dale Kloster and they have one daughter. Christine works in White Salmon for Harvest Market.

Once their traveling days to Alaska were over Carol returned to banking. She retired from First Independent Bank in Bingen, WA. Tom is still working part-time driving truck, which became his second occupation.

**Tom and Carol Rutherford**

## Rylander, C.J.

In August 1928 C. J. Rylander, the railroad station agent and Heinie Kapp attended the Shriner's picnic at the Oaks in Portland.

## Schweitzer, Kendal

In 1928 the former postmaster was here visiting his parents Mr. and Mrs. Wm. Schweitzer.

## Schwinge, John and Hilda

John was born in Germany in 1891. He married Hilda Wendland. The couple had two sons, Robert and Norman. A former resident of Underwood, John had been operating an Auto Camp and filling station at Mitchell's Point on the Columbia River Highway when he passed away in 1928.

## Shepeard, Rose

In March 1995 Rose Shepeard of Underwood celebrated her 97th birthday. Her nephews Melvin Fowlers of Kelso, and Ray Nunacker of The Dalles, Oregon were present at the celebration. Others attending the family get-together were Agnes Nunacker, Doris and Lily Murray, Bob and Nelva Denton and Leonard and Charlotte Lutje, all of The Dalles, and Sharon Carrie, Portland.

In March 1998 centenarian Rose Larsen Shepeard, formerly of Underwood, marked her 100th birthday at the Hood River Care Center. Born in 1898, she married Olaf C. Larsen in 1917. The couple lived in Underwood for over 50 years. The couple had two children: Ivan C. Larsen of Battle Ground and the late June Cleo Smith. After Olaf died shortly after their 50th wedding anniversary, Rose married Ross Shepeard. Mrs. Shepeard had five grandchildren and 10 great-grandchildren. The birthday open house was hosted by granddaughter Sharon Corrie. Rose died in 1998 at age 100. She is buried in Chris-Zada Cemetery in Underwood, which was partly named for Olaf Larsen's sister Zada.

## Smith, Myron Soules and Cora

Born in 1851 in Parishville, NY, Myron Smith attended the United States Military Academy at West Point. His cousin was president Grover Cleveland. Mr. Smith was engaged in the mercantile business in Underwood and was an agent for the Phoenix Insurance Co. of Hartford, Conn.

In 1905 Mr. Smith became the owner of the mercantile store in Underwood. He sold it in 1911 and acquired it again in 1918, along with a group of local men. In 1909 he had land adjoining A.J. Haynes on the north. He and George Sandel had 15 acres ready to plant.

On January 25, 1915 Mr. and Mrs. Smith gave a family dinner. It was a merry occasion. The evening was taken up with cards. Everyone voted it a great improvement over bachelor days.

In July 1915 it was reported that Miss Dorothy Hall was taken suddenly ill with ptomaine poisoning but was recovering. She was the daughter of Mrs. M.S. Smith. In 1929 Mrs. Lucia Hall, a Bellingham High School teacher, visited her mother, Mrs. M.S. Smith.

In May 1938 the news reported that M.S. Smith backed his Chevy Coupe over the boulder-strewn banks of the Underwood Heights road in front of the Heine Kapp store. In April 1939 Mr. and Mrs. M.S. Smith had returned to their cabin on Northwestern Lake to enjoy the summer. Myron died in 1940 and is buried at Idlewilde Cemetery in Hood River. He and his twin sister Myra had planned to celebrate their 89th birthday together later that year.

## Sohappy, David and Mryna

*From his obituary in The Enterprise, May 9, 1991; the Oregon History Project website; the Seattle Times, May 7, 1991*

David Sohappy was a Yakama Indian who gained national attention for challenging state and federal fishing regulations. In the mid-1980s he was imprisoned for a year under allegations of salmon fishing violations. He was incarcerated at the Sandstone Federal Prison in Minnesota, 2000 miles away from his family. David Sohappy was sent to prison for involvement in selling illegally caught fish to an undercover agent. He and four other Columbia River fishers claimed they were entrapped by federal law enforcement officers. The case was referred to as "Salmonscam." He was not released from prison until his wife Myrna and others were able to enlist the support of Senators Daniel Inouye from Hawaii and Dan Evans of Washington. After his release, he continued to fight for the fishing rights of his people, the Mid-Columbia River Indians. In addition to his contributions to Indian fishing rights, Sohappy served in the U.S. Army during World War II.

197

## Sohappy, David and Myrna (continued)

Mr. Sohappy, or otherwise known as David Tucknashut, an Indian name meaning Provider, was born in 1925 in Harrah, Washington. His parents were Eliza (Wahpenoyah) and Jim Sohappy. He married Myra Agnes Charlie in 1946. They resided on Cook's Landing where he was a fisherman.

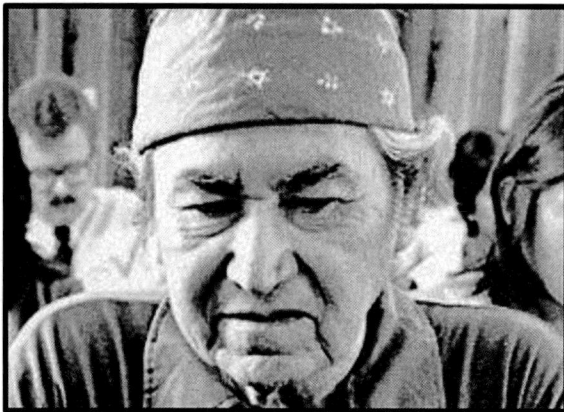

**David Sohappy photo from The Oregon History Project web site**

Mr. Sohappy's resistance to fishing regulations and his insistence upon living permanently on the northern bank of the Columbia River at Cook's Landing created enemies for him, but also many admirers. Tom Keefe, a lawyer and friend said, " He was one of the unique leaders in the Pacific Northwest, known internationally as a fighter for Indian fishing rights."

Mr. Sohappy died at age 66 in May of 1991 from the effects of a stroke. He was survived by his wife Myrna and seven children. He is buried in White Swan, Washington, on the Yakama Indian reservation.

## Sooter Families

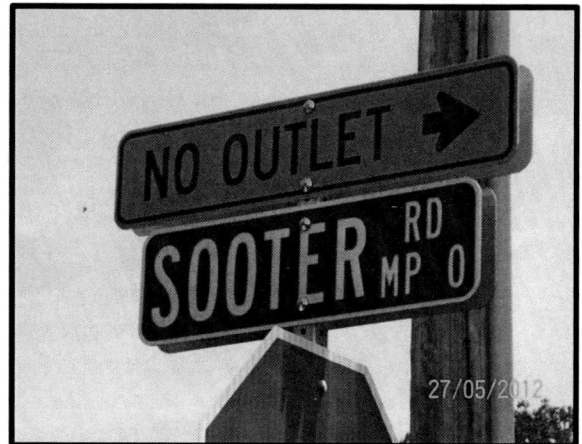

**Road named after the Sooters**

By Kathy LaMotte

Elbert and Elmer (Mick) Sooter were brothers. Their parents were John F. Sooter, originally from Tennessee, and Julia Belle Poindexter Sooter from Texas. The brothers and their siblings were born in the Cherokee Nation Territory of what is now Oklahoma. The family moved west in 1900. After several moves they settled in Idaho.

Elbert married Elva Skeene and Elmer (Mick) married her sister Ruby Skeene. Elva and Ruby were from Walla Walla. There were seven girls in Ruby's and Elva's family.

In about 1939 Elbert and Elva lease-purchased 100 acres in Underwood. The property ran from Cook/Underwood Road, to the bluff, and to School House Road. At the time of Elbert Sooter's purchase they were not yet living in Underwood. They were living in Washougal where Mr. Sooter was farming. They needed to complete the season of farming before moving to their property in Underwood. After moving to Underwood, Elbert continued farming. He would haul milk down the hill to be transported by train. Elva worked at Skyline Hospital in the 1970s.

198

**Sooter Families** (continued)

The Elbert Sooters had two children, Howard and Virginia. Both were born near Walla Walla, Virginia in 1922 and Howard in 1929. Virginia married Paul Tate. (See Tate Family.) Elbert died in 1948 at age 60 and Elva died in 1983. They are buried in Walla Walla.

In 1942 Elmer and Ruby Sooter joined their brother and sister Sooters, moving to Underwood. After moving to Underwood, Elmer (Mick) and Ruby Sooter built a home on what is now Circle Drive. He went on to build other houses as well. Mick was a Veteran of WWI. He served with a horse-drawn artillery outfit with the American Expeditionary Forces in France. Mick's wife Ruby took over as post master, when Clifford Cordier died. She was then the post master from 1942 until 1976.

Mr. Elmer Sooter died in 1980. Ruby Sooter passed away in 1996, at the age of 88.

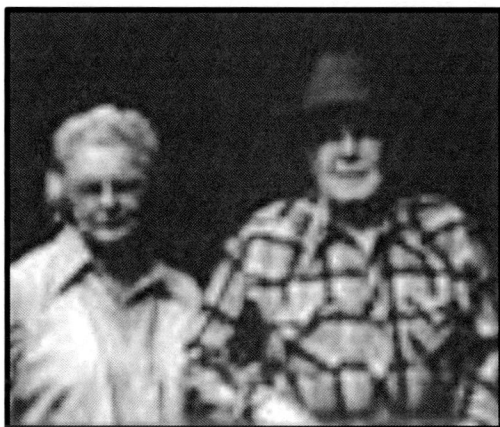

**Ruby and Mick Sooter**

In the late 1940's Elbert Sooter became ill with cancer. He decided to sell off most of his property. Part was bought by his brother and sister-in-law Mick and Ruby. Part by his son-in-law and daughter, Paul and Virginia Tate, and part by a

man named Zilka. Don Thomas later bought the property from Mr. Zilka.

## Sooter, Elmer E. "Mick" and Ruby Dolly (Skeen)

By: Darla Johnston

Ruby first laid eyes on Mick as a young girl when he came to work as a ranch hand at her father's place in Landing, Idaho. Ruby told me that she had fallen head over heels in love with Mick and had made up her mind to marry him. As Mick was 14 years older than Ruby, he told me he originally viewed her as a child. However as Providence would have it, many years later they were destined to meet again in Walla Walla, WA. You will read more of this story later.

From the *Skamania County Pioneer*:

*Mr. Sooter was born November 25, 1894 in the Cherokee Nation territory of what is now Oklahoma. His father, John F. Sooter, was originally from Tennessee and his mother, nee Julia Belle Poindexter, was from Texas.*

*In 1900, when he was six years old, Mr. Sooter moved west with his parents and they lived first near Lyndon, Washington and later in British Columbia before homesteading near Landing, Idaho. When he was 18 he went to work for a horse breeder near Grangerville, Idaho, who sold horses to the French and British armies.*

*He enlisted in the army early in World War I and after training at Camp Lewis (now Fort Lewis), Washington, was sent to France with the 346th Field Artillery, where he continued working with horses and riding with the teams pulling the guns and caissons.*

*After the 1918 Armistice, Mr. Sooter returned to civil life and worked for a Montana cattle rancher. When his employer was*

## Sooter, Elmer and Ruby (continued)

*elected sheriff of his county, Mr. Sooter was appointed deputy and served in that capacity for a time. As a young man he was given the sobriquet "Mick" by a saddle-pal in Montana who thought he looked Irish. He carried the nickname for the rest of his life, although the name Sooter is believed to be of Swiss origin.*

*He was a past president of the Skamania County Saddle Club and a member of the White Salmon Posse. He will be remembered for the many years he carried the flag with saddle club riders in the annual Stevenson parade."(1)*

Ruby's family had moved to Walla Walla where she graduated Cum Laude from Whitman College with a degree in Romance Languages and a Teaching Certificate. I can certainly see that her degree in Romance Languages probably was useful in lassoing her future husband. Mick had an exciting life before his arrival in Walla Walla. He moved there because his brother Bert Sooter was ranching there and Bert's wife Elva Sooter was one of six of Ruby's sisters. On August 24, 1936, Ruby's life-long dream came true as Mick and Ruby were wed. As Mick told me Ruby had set her mind on marrying him so "what could a fellow do?" This time the circumstances were right.

Ruby worked in Walla Walla at various jobs as Mick ranched, ran a gas station and an automotive shop where he repaired cars. In 1941 Mick again followed his brother Elbert, this time to Underwood where he was able to purchase property from a man who lived in Portland. The land adjoined his brother's property to the south of it on the Underwood Flats. According to Robert Morby: "Mick raised about 15-20 cattle and when ready for butchering loaded 7 to 8 at a time and drove them in his 1 ½ ton truck to Swift in Portland across the interstate bridge."

The big oak tree at the corner of Sooter and Corner Roads was a favorite place for Mick. He told me of raising his own alfalfa on his property for his horses and cattle and of his fond memories for the shade of this tree where he always stored his lunch for the day. As his thoughts of noon time approached, he was looking forward to the beer that was awaiting him there for his lunch break. He asked Ray and me to make sure that tree was never cut down.

The gas station along with an automotive repair was also owned and operated by Mick. It was located at the bottom of Underwood Hill. Years later, Home Valley boys, among them the Collins boys, have memories of coming to the house that Mick had built his wife Ruby on the north side of the turn-around at the end of the pavement on Sooter Road. Just west of the home is a gigantic barn-automotive repair area with many drawers for keeping his tools organized. There Mick entertained the boys for hours as they worked with him on a 1956 or 1957 classic Chevy that he would buy one at a time. Gail Collins said he always had one available. When one of the boys wanted to buy the current one being worked on, Mick would go and buy another one.

Another thing that he will be remembered for is his never ending passion for coffee. I never saw Mick drink anything except coffee...never any water--- amazing he lived 85 years! Darlene and Steve Leek tell the story of going out to dinner with Ruby and Mick. Mick set out a penny on the table and when the waitress came by he told her: "This is your tip if you do not keep my coffee cup filled." When he came to my house which was two or three times per day on days that I did not work at Skyline Hospital, I kept his coffee cup full and enjoyed his reminiscing about "bye-gone days."

I never tired of the cowboy songs he sang to me and our children Jay and Shawna. Upon entering our home, Jay or

Shawna was most of the time riding the spring rocking horse and Mick would walk over and put his hat and leather gloves on whichever one of them that was on the horse. Mick gave me a new lassoing rope to give to Jay when he was older along with a picture of him. Mick always remained a cowboy at heart. It was obvious that some of Mick's favorite memories were riding the range on his horse, heading cattle to market while sleeping out under the stars and singing around the camp fire.

Both the Leeks and I laugh when remembering Mick driving his old 1947 yellow Chevy to our houses. As Mick had macular degeneration, he did not have vision in the center of his eye---only peripheral vision. Both of our families had warned our children to stay far away from "Old Yellow" and run in the opposite direction until it had come to a complete stop... It was a good thing that his Chevy was made like a tank as Mick had hit many rocks that Steve had put in strategic areas to keep Mick on the roadway when driving to his home. Mick felt like he had the right to drive on the roads in Underwood flats because after all this had been his property or his brother's!

Working at various jobs in Underwood until she was appointed Postmaster for Underwood, Ruby's dream was to have a beautiful view home on the bluff which she and Mick were planning on eventually having built. Unfortunately, Mick did not live to see the home finished as he passed away in 1980 living to be 85. But Ruby paid her nephew from central Oregon to come up and build her fabulous home for her on the bluff.

Ruby worked 34 years for the postal service. She started when the post office was inside the railroad station just west of the White Salmon River. Bill Manly, longtime White Salmon Postmaster, remembers when there were six trains a day that delivered the mail. Our Underwood mail came from the Bingen Post Office along with the mail for Cooks and Mill A. (White Salmon Post Office had contracts to deliver mail into Glenwood, Trout Lake and Dock's Grade.) The mail came in everyday, but only went out every other day. It was quite an interesting operation. A metal arm extended towards the tracks and a Catcher Pouch was filled half-way full of mail then was hung on this metal arm. Then someone in a baggage car had the job of hooking the straps on the Catcher Pouch and swinging it into the car. What an amazing skill for the person retrieving this pouch because the train did not slow down! Of course a person was hired to walk about ½ mile in the direction that the train was traveling to pick up any of the mail that may have fallen out of the pouch. Zippers were not used in clothes until after World War II but one wonders why other forms of closure had not been incorporated onto the Catcher Pouch. The mail delivery via moving trains to platform was eliminated in 1970.

Riding her Appaloosa horse was one of Ruby's favorite pastimes. As a masterful leather worker and knitter, she enjoyed making many crafts. She was an avid reader and a great conversationalist. She was knowledgeable in so many subjects. She was a member of the Book Club, and was involved in the creation of the Gorge Heritage Museum in Bingen. (2)

The post office where I first met Ruby was attached to the Bud Cumming's auction building on the north side of Highway 14. Bud had purchased this building from George Balsiger when The Underwood Grocery Store was closed. Bud built his house on top of the building and opened up his auction. He drove back to the Appalachian Mountains and various places in the north and south buying eloquent furniture with marble tops and fancy wood workings from home owners to be auctioned off by his auctioneer that came from Portland for every Saturday evenings' auction. This was a very well-attended weekly event. He had wanted

## Sooter, Elmer and Ruby (continued)

my husband Ray to be his accountant because Ray was a frequent Saturday night patron. Many people's yards were landscaped with the unique trees and bushes that Bud had brought from wholesale nurseries. Local homes were furnished with unique and beautiful furniture from the auction. In fact Ruby had purchased from Bud her Erard grand piano that she had in her game room in her new home on the Bluff. (Erard pianos were favored by Haydn, Beethoven and Liszt, all composers with whom Ruby was familiar.)

Ruby always gave us citrus-sugared candy strips that she had made and her special recipe of seasoning salt for Christmas every year. She would not share her recipe, but told me anytime I needed more to let her know and she would make me some. This was a wonderful deal for me at the time. Shawna remembers looking at Ruby's collection of glass globe paper weights. Ruby had a doll that she said looked just like Shawna and that she was setting it aside from her fabulous doll collection for her.

Mick checked his fence lines everyday even though he no longer had any cattle. Our upper acreage west of our house was part of his original barbed-wire fences that he had built many years ago with the squares where he had built a support for firming up the T-post and barb wire. The boxes were filled with rock and the wire at various areas were attached to these heavy boxes. Seeing the few head of cattle that we raised enclosed by the barbed-wire fences he had made, pleased him immensely.

Mick also gave us a window from the old Underwood Church that we installed in our home. He passed away in November 17, 1980 living to be 85. Ruby enjoyed her new home on the bluff for many years before passing away in August 24, 1996 at 88 years of age. Mick and Ruby were from an era of gentle speaking people who valued their family and friends.

Information for this article was obtained from my personal stories with Mick & Ruby, Steve & Darlene Leek, Bill Manly (White Salmon Postmaster), Clark Ziegler, (1) *The Skamania County Pioneer*, Stevenson, WA, November 28, 1980, page 5 (Mick) and (2)) August 28, 1996, page 2 (Ruby) recorded by Jeffrey L. Elmer on the Chris-Zada Cemetery Rootsweb page.

## Stultz, John

In 1937 Mr, and Mrs. Stultz moved from Bingen to the Haselton place on Underwood Heights.

## Sutherland, L.F.

In 1909 they moved up from Portland to their ranch in the "Norway" country.

## Tate, Paul and Virginia
By Kathy LaMotte and Darla Johnston

Paul Tate was born in Goldendale in 1922, to Minnie Maude and Edwin Anderson Tate. The family later moved to Washougal where Paul Tate graduated from high school in 1940. He then worked in Umatilla, building igloo concrete bunkers used to store toxic waste and bombs. Paul later enlisted in the Navy, and spent two years as a ship fitter and two years in the Naval Reserve. He was a welder the rest of his life, working for Broughton Lumber from 1950 to 1972 and Skamania County until he retired in 1984.

Paul Tate and Virginia Sooter met while in school in Washougal. They were high school sweethearts. Virginia Sooter was valedictorian of her class. Virginia later went on to business school in Portland. In 1942 Paul Tate and Virginia Sooter were married. Paul and Virginia lived in an old home east of the Fire Station in Underwood. While Paul was away in the service, Virginia did the books for her father's business and worked for the Fruit Company.

The winter took its toll on the house and the roof caved in. Virginia moved in with her parents Mr. and Mrs. Elbert Sooter while Paul was still away. During

**Tate, Paul and Virginia** (continued)

WWII Paul and Virginia bought property by her parents – the Elbert Sooters.

The Tates had seven children. One daughter Nicholette passed away at age three months. Another daughter Paula passed away at age 17 due to a car accident. The other five children are Dan, Karol, Judi, Bill and Vicki.

The Tate children were raised on the property their parents had bought. The road being Tate Road. Their home was in the timber. Dan Tate told Darla Johnston that as kids he and his siblings rounded up cattle and raised a few chickens, pigs and horses. They had open space to play with the Ellson kids. Their favorite sledding hill was just north of the Ellson home, still used by Underwood Flat kids. Since Vernon and Ella Ellson had the first black and white television in the area, all the neighborhood kids would congregate at their house.

Darla Johnston remembers taking her children to "Trick or Treat" at Virginia's and Paul's house. They gave out massive amounts of candy: big candy bars, Sugar Daddies, Smarties.

Bill Tate, son of Paul and Virginia, lived in Underwood for some time. He eventually sold his property of one acre and moved with his wife Judy to Mill A. They have three children. One daughter still lives in Underwood.

Bill Tate recalls being told that his Uncle Howard Sooter was in the last graduating class in Underwood. Howard lived in Underwood. He worked as a surveyor for the Corps of Engineers. He retired in 1974. He had a son, Elbert. At the time of his death he was survived by his wife Con'E. He passed away in 2001, at the age of 72.

Bill Tate told about the train and how it used to stop in Underwood. He and his mother were on the last passenger train to stop in Underwood. They were coming home after visiting family in Walla Walla. After that passengers had to use the stop in Bingen.

Bill also recalls his dad Paul, telling him about the fire that burned the hotel in lower Underwood. He said that Edgar Boyers came down the hill and saw the fire. He drove up to the hotel, jumped out of his truck and rushed to help. When he came out he found the heat had melted much of his truck.

Virginia Tate passed away in 1989. In 2001 Paul Tate sold his property and moved back to his birthplace, Goldendale, where he bought a city block. He passed away in 2010. He was survived by his second wife of 17 years, Jean Tate.

In 1965, Dan became the proud owner of the old Underwood school house bell that his dad had salvaged from the building when it was torn down.

**Ternahan, Barry and Carolyn**

Barry, the son of Lyle and Rosalyn Ternahan, attended the University of Washington, joined the army and served in Japan as an analyst for the Counter Intelligence Corps. After returning, he spent 20 years in production management for newspapers in Kent, Portland, Bellingham and Olympia. Upon the death of his father, Barry returned home and became general manager of *The Enterprise* newspaper in White Salmon. He was PR director for the phone company for 13 years and then the media writer liaison for Luhr Jensen in Hood River until the company was sold.

The Enterprise of January 21, 1993 reported that forty firefighters were helpless to combat the blaze as fire destroyed the Barry Ternahan house, one of the oldest houses on the Cook-Underwood Road. Fortunately, no one was inside the house. The Ternahans left around 6 p.m. and returned at 7:30 to find the total destruction of their home. There was 18" of snow on the ground at the time.

## Ternahan, Barry and Carolyn (cont.)

On February 19, 1994 *The Enterprise* ran a story on Carolyn Ternahan's singing career, which began in White Salmon's Columbia High School choir. Music teacher Bernie Bursette recognized her talent and enrolled her in an Oregon music competition where she won first place. After marrying and raising three children, she entered Sacramento State University with her oldest daughter and graduated with their top music award. Further instruction from masters in voice, diction, drama and languages propelled her to sing opera in such venues as Vienna, New York, San Francisco, Munich and Hamburg. She then returned home, married Barry, and moved to Underwood. In the Gorge she started the Showcase Singers, performing for fairs, festivals and organizations. She started the Junior Showcase Singers for youngsters and gave voice lessons from her home.

## Ternahan, Harley and Bonnie

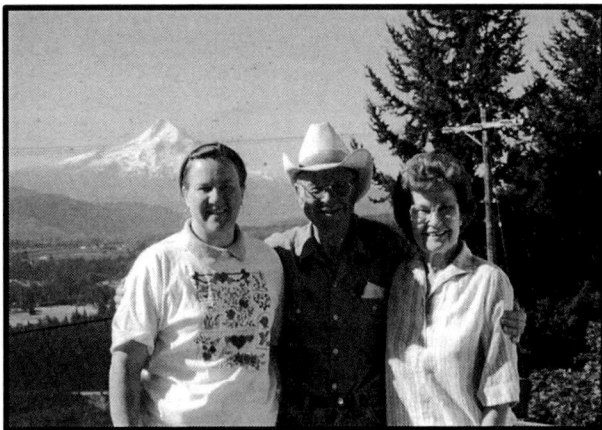

**Harley and Bonnie Ternahan with daughter Sally**

Harley Ternahan returned from overseas and was stationed at Camp Maxey in Paris, Texas, when he met Bonnie, a student attending Southeastern State College, in Durant, OK. They were married in May of 1946 in Boswell, OK.

Harley was born in Nez Perce, ID. He grew up around Pullman, WA. His father was a wheat rancher and his mother lived in Pullman, eight miles away. She managed the care of the family and took in boarders, i.e. college students from WSU, thereby giving the older brothers and sister the opportunity to pursue a college education.

The family, now just the three youngest children, relocated in Eugene, OR. Harley graduated from high school in Eugene.

Later the family moved back up to Spokane, WA. Harley and his father owned property there. In 1942 Harley was inducted into the army. Most of his time was spent in the South Pacific; New Guinea, New Britain, and Guadalcanal. He was on the last rotation home before his Company went into the Philippines.

Harley was discharged in 1945, and was visiting his brother, Lyle Ternahan and family in Underwood. His brother said, "You don't need to go back to Spokane. There is a widow-lady down the road that wants to sell her place." So the deal was made. They purchased 60 acres from May E. Graves, widow of Charlie Graves. In later years they had the opportunity to buy the Kramer Road property from Harry and Margaret Card.

Harry Card was a good man for the community. He was very active in promoting the Underwood Water System and the Public Utility District. Prior to this, almost all of the water was captured on roof tops into cisterns. There are very few successful wells in Underwood.

Harley always loved the farm life and was partial to Black Angus cattle. Mean-

## Ternahan, Harley and Bonnie(continued)

while, both he and Bonnie found employment in the area. Harley retired from the Skamania County Road Dept. Bonnie worked at the Western Fish Nutrition Lab in Willard, WA for 14 and ½ years, and McCoy-Holliston Insurance for 17 years.

Bonnie said they always stressed good citizenship and education to their kids. Philip, the oldest, graduated from CWSC in Ellensburg, was in the Peace Corps for three years, and retired from the US Navy after 24 years. He obtained his master's degree from Cal State University. He is currently working for the government, and is a minister in the Episcopal Church in Ventura, CA. He was ordained as a priest in 2009.

Jeanne retired from teaching in the Reedsport, OR, schools. Kathie and Sally received college educations and found work, and husbands, and families.

Bonnie says, "We feel so fortunate to live in Underwood, among good neighbors and friends. We are very proud of our county roads and the PUD. We had lots of snow in the 1960's and 1970's. I never missed a day of work due to snow while working at the Willard Lab."

Many changes have occurred in the past 65 years. Harley has had his 99th birthday. He recently remarked, "If I were a young man I would like to be a farmer."

*(Harley Ternahan passed away on May 15, 2012 after this article was written.)*

## Ternahan, Lyle and Rosalyn

The Ternahan clan (Lyle, Rosalyn and son Barry) moved from Goldendale to Underwood in 1939. Lyle was County Extension Agent for Klickitat County but wanted to get away from the paper work of a government career and start a farm of his own. They found a beautiful place on the bluff in Underwood Heights built by Charles Graves for a doctor in Portland. After commuting for a couple of years, he quit the County and went to full-time farming.

Rosalyn resumed her teaching Career in the early 40's teaching in Underwood, Husum and Bingen, retiring in the 1950's Lyle experimented with many different forms of livestock including cattle, flocks of several thousand turkeys and even 2,000 laying hens lodged in an old white house on the property. In 1956 he became District 3 County Commissioner for Skamania County, a position he held for more than 15 years.

**Lyle Ternahan's turkeys**
Photo from Gordon Baker family collection

## Thomas, Diane Henry

Diane Henry Thomas was born to Alvin and Pauline (Nystrom) Henry in 1935. They lived near the highway in Lower Underwood. There were four Henry children born to Alvin and Pauline; Dean, Diane, Donald, and Darlene. Pauline (Nystrom) Henry came from Minnesota with her family. She was born on January 8, 1915. She had ten brothers and two sisters. Alvin Henry went to work for the CCC Camp in 1938. In 1939 Alvin and Pauline were divorced; he joined the military, and later settled back east after WWII.

Diane began school in Underwood, along with brother Dean. She recalls it was a two-room building, one room for primary grades, and the other being grades up to eighth. She only attended school there for the first grade. Her teacher was a Mrs. Clark. That was the last year the school was open. The following year she began second grade in Bingen.

The Henrys and the Larsens had been neighbors for years. In 1942, Aaron Larsen (who had lost his wife Anna tragically in 1928, and who was the father of two grown children, Elmer and Esther), married Pauline Nystrom Henry. Aaron now had four very young stepchildren. A short time later three new Larsen children were born: Linda in 1943, James in 1946, and Sandy in 1952.

After living in Bingen for a time, the family of Aaron and Pauline Larsen moved into the two-story, white house that had been built by Aaron's father, Christian E. Larsen. This house sits near highway 14, just west of the fish hatchery.

The road originally ran down below the Larsen home. Later when the permanent road was built, many curves were straightened. This put the highway north of their home where it is today. The new highway also cut straight through the middle of the Larsen property.

Diane has fond memories of her stepfather Aaron Larsen. Aaron came from a large family. He was the son of Christian and Mary (Cline) Larsen. She recalls her stepfather saying he came west with his parents when he was three years old. They first lived in Sweet Home, OR, before homesteading in Underwood. (This story differs slightly from the recollection of daughter – See Esther Larsen Yarnell). Aaron's siblings included Olaf, Amos, Frank, James, Lewis, and sisters Nora and Zada. Zada died as a very young girl when she became ill. Her death followed only weeks behind her classmate's death (Christina Dark). Being the first to be buried in the newly established cemetery in Underwood, it was decided to name the cemetery after the two small girls, hence - *Chris-Zada Cemetery.*

Diane recalls her mother often packing a picnic lunch and she and her siblings would walk the short distance to the fish hatchery where Aaron worked. Many a day they would sit on the lawn and enjoy their picnic during Aaron's lunch break. She recalls her stepfather being employed for 30 years at the fish hatchery. His father, Christian Larsen, was one of the original employees at Spring Creek National Fish Hatchery which opened in 1901.

Diane says that Aaron also had his marine license and was an accomplished ferry boat pilot on the river.

Diane recalls a little about Aaron's siblings. Amos was a meat cutter by profession. Olaf, who died in 1971, was married to Rose (Hanna). They lived up in Underwood on their namesake Larsen Road. Lewis was married to Clover. Both Lewis and Clover worked for the railroad.

In 1943 the Aaron Larsen family moved to Bingen. Pauline (Diane's mother) bought a tavern. She would then own a tavern off and on for the next 50 years.

In 1948 Aaron decided he wanted to move his family back out of town. So he and Lewis traded houses, Aaron and his family moving back into the white house by the river, in Underwood. Diane was in 8th grade at the time and was not keen on the idea of moving. The two-story, white house has been owned now for years by Diane's half-brother James and his wife Helen. Diane shared that James took care of his dad, Aaron, and their mother, Pauline, until they died.

In later years, after husband Aaron's death, Diane's mother Pauline married Howard Lea. They lived in the Bingen/White Salmon area. On August 02, 1998, Diane's mother Pauline Nystrom Henry Larsen Lea passed away. She is buried in the White Salmon Cemetery under the name Pauline Marie Lea.

In 1953 Diane married Lloyd (Buddy) Thomas. They have one son, Steven, who

206

**Thomas, Diane Henry** (continued)

lives in Hood River. Lloyd passed away in 1996.

Diane has worked in fruit packing off and on since age 19. Still today she works for Underwood Fruit, where she has been employed for many years.

"I have no reason to quit," she said "I have friends there, I enjoy what I do, and you have to stay active."

**Diane Henry Thomas**

Other Underwood Families remembered by Diane Henry Thomas:

Bob and Francis (Hunsaker) Hill ran a café and service station in Lower Underwood. They have two daughters Marty and Mary.

Mr. and Mrs. Harvey Kelchner lived in Underwood. They were parents of Alice Redmond. Alice and Nick Redmond lived and worked for AAA Orchards. They lived in a cabin on the property. They had four children.

Mr. and Mrs. Hatch lived up across the road from them when they lived by the river. They were an elderly couple. Mrs. Hatch was very friendly.

Diane recalls that Jim Hore and family lived at Broughton's Lumber Co. in Hood. Also living there was the large family of

Omer and Margaret Ohnemus. She also recalls the Sturtevants lived up just behind the Underwood School. They owned a large pasture.

**Thomas, Donald C. and Jean**

Donald Thomas will be remembered for heading Broughton Lumber Company from 1970 to 1986 as well as his civic duties. In 1962 the Donald Thomas family hosted the first American Field Service student at Columbia High in White Salmon. His name was Kristoffer Lien from Norway. In 1964 Mr. Thomas was the local AFS president and in that same year he was president of the Mt. Adams Chamber of Commerce. Donald Thomas was also a driver for starting the first Huckleberry Festival, held annually in the fall in Bingen.

**Back: Don Thomas, Cam, Kris Lien
Front: Sally, Susan, Jean Thomas
in Norwegian sweaters knitted by Kris's mother.**

Don Thomas married Jean Broughton. Their three children are Cam, Sally and Susan. Cam was the builder of the huge NOEL sign that was lit and visible from Hood River and I-84 from Thanksgiving to the New Year. Cam was also responsible for Herkimer the talking pumpkin.

**Thomas, Donald C. and Jean** (cont.)

**Herkimer**

In February 1973 *The Enterprise* reported,

*The stockholders of the Klickitat Valley Bank elected Donald C. Thomas as director. Don is president of Broughton Lumber Co., and will add local representation to the Board of Directors for the people of the White Salmon-Bingen area.*

Cam Thomas relates that his father purchased property on the bluff in Under-

wood from the Zilka family and built a house. In the early 1900's there was a lodge hotel located on the property. Cam and his wife Barbara now live on the property.

**Thornton family**

Moses Jefferson Thornton was born in 1827 in Illinois. He and his wife Sevilia had fourteen children, ten of whom were living at the time of the death of Moses in 1905. Mr. Thornton is the earliest born person buried at the Underwood Chris-Zada Cemetery. Moses and most of the children moved to the Underwood area around 1900. The children were Anna, Loveda, Matilda, Mamie, Mose, Michael, Edgar, Charles, Frank and Jacob. In 1902 among the principal non-irrigated straw-berry growers in the Underwood area were Michael, Charles, Edgar and Jake Thornton. There were enough Thorntons living near each other to name the place Thorntonville. *The Glacier* of August 1903 reported, "Most of the Thorntons from Thorntonville went to Hood River shopping. In Sept. 1904 Jake and Ed Thornton sold 20 acres to Ira Rowland. In Sept 1906 Frank Thornton returned to Under-wood, having disposed of his restaurant in Hood River.

A July 1907 news item said that while camping at White Salmon Falls, the little eight year old son of Moses Thornton (Jr.) was quite badly bitten by a dog. The boy was bitten on the throat and face, requir-ing the attention of Dr. Dumble. The dog was promptly killed.

In August 1908 the Thornton Broth-ers were quite busy hauling wood to the chutes for Hanna, who had a crew at the railroad station loading cars. They have shipped several car loads from Hood. In May 1909 Mr. and Mrs. F.C. Thornton came over from Dee. Frank was laid up for a few days on account of injuries re-ceived in the woods. A news item praised the Thornton Bros. who suspended opera-tions Saturday to gravel a rough place in the road. The reporter stated, "This shows

## Thornton Family (continued)

a great deal more spirit and helps a great deal more than knocking the road and telling how it should be fixed."

In December 1943 Jake Thornton purchased the C.E.Corn property in White Salmon and planned to build a new residence there as soon as materials became available. The Thorntons sold their ranch the previous spring.

### Thornton, Charles H. and Dora

Charles came to the Underwood area in 1895 to join his brother Mike. In 1902 he married Dora Hickman of Trout Lake. They had ten children, seven of whom survived Charles when he died in 1949: Mildred, Selma, Ruby, Dora, Charles E., Fred and Hugh. A Jan. 1904 news article stated that Mr. and Mrs. Charlie Thornton of Vancouver came up to visit relatives and friends at Thorntonville. By 1905 they had a new Underwood area residence and planned to build a hotel, livery and stage. It was nicely situated to take care of the travel along the way to Trout Lake and Underwood. This was a stone house which was torn down when the Underwood Cutoff road was built.

In May 1905 the neighbors all gathered at Mrs. Chas. Thornton's house to give her sister Miss Margaret a 16th birthday party. In 1906 Margaret Hickman married the oldest son of George and Anna Wise, Louis Napoleon Wise. Margaret died the next year of tuberculosis. In Oct. 1906 it was reported that Mr. and Mrs. Charlie Thornton had a fine new girl at their home.

Charles worked during the construction of the S.P.& S. railroad from Cook to Underwood. It took two years to complete and it was all by hand labor. He said, "Even the tunnels were done by hand labor. It was treacherous work, but good work." Thornton for many years has been hobbling about on a game leg, the result of a rattlesnake bite at age seven in

Missouri. (from an interview in the _Mt. Adams Sun_ January 23, 1938)

Charlie was the Underwood mail delivery man until his death in 1949. Ralph Brown recalls that when he was six, he and his sister referred to their mailman Charlie as the postman, because he had a post for his leg (we thought). When he died and we got a new mailman Paul Newell, who did not have a post for a leg, we were a bit confused as to call him a postman or a mailman. Charles actually did not have a post for a leg, but he designed and built a special boot to fit his deformed circular foot.

Charlie had a sawmill in the area of Northwestern Lake. The Thornton cable crossing is referred to in the construction of Northwestern Dam. In July 1912 surveyors for a proposed railroad from Camas to Toppenish slashed both sides of the White Salmon River for a distance of four miles from its mouth. A reporter stated, "One rancher, Charles Thornton, who lives on the east side of the river, says they have saved him the trouble of slashing." Jack Kapp recalls that Charlie had pigs on this property, perhaps partly to rid it of rattle snakes. In his later years, Charlie Thornton lived at Hood, just west of lower Underwood. Charlie's wife Dora lived to be 100 years old.

> _The five railroad tunnels between Cook and Underwood were all produced by hand labor by men like Charles Thornton._

209

**Thornton, Charles H. and Dora** (cont.)

**Charles and Dora Thornton and two of their children.** Photo from John Sylvester Dunlap collection.

### Thornton, Mike and Effie

In November 1903 Mike Thornton of Thorntonville saw a bear on the White Salmon River. A Jan. 1904 news item reported that A.G.Wise and daughter of Chenowith spent Sunday with Michael Thornton of Thorntonville. Also, a surprise party was given in honor of Mike and Flora Thornton of Thorntonville, the occasion being their birthdays.

In Sept. of 1904 Mike Thornton was found in the news to be gathering his prune crop with a large force of men, women and girls picking and packing the fruit. Mr. Thornton had 90 acres - 5 1/2 in strawberries, 10 in orchard, consisting of 800 apple trees, 100 prune trees, 100 peach and 40 acres under the plow. He had a fine spring that irrigated three acres of berries and garden and he could irrigate three acres more from the same spring. Mr. Thornton also farmed 22 acres belonging to his father-in-law, A. Y. Marsh of The Dalles. The new road known as the Cameron Road passed through his place. The road began at Underwood and intersected the road to Camas Prairie (Glenwood) and Trout Lake, 2 ½ miles from the Columbia River.

The next fall when Mike Thornton finished gathering his prunes, he shipped nearly 500 crates. He had promised the champion packer of seven girls a bottle of beer. Miss Elnora Larsen, the smallest girl of the lot, won the prize. She came out 19 crates ahead. But Mr. Thornton said he would keep the bottle until her wedding day and then <u>he</u> would do the drinking act.

In July 1906 Mrs. Effie Thornton had been suffering from the effects of ten teeth which had been extracted. The doctor had been called to her home but "at present she is resting and it is expected that danger of blood poisoning is past." In December of that year Underwood school lost a pupil because Mike Thornton had moved up to his mill and consequently it was too far for his child to walk.

**Michael and wife Effie Marsh Thornton** Photo from John Sylvester Dunlap collection. **John Dunlap is a great grandson of Michael Thornton.**

210

**Mike Thornton's lumber yard in The Dalles**
Photo from John Sylvester Dunlap collection

**Hugh Thornton, son of Michael and Effie**
Photo from John Sylvester Dunlap collection

## Thun, Louis and Emily

Louis was born in 1884 in Austria and Emily Janisch was born in 1888 also in Austria. Louis graduated in landscaping from the College of Agriculture in Vienna and then came to the United States in 1903. He came to Underwood in 1905 to work as a landscaping contractor during the construction of the SP&S railroad along the north shore of the Columbia River. Louis Thun bought an orchard tract on Underwood hill and sold it a year later to purchase part of the Ed Underwood land and house. In 1909 Emily and Louis were married. In 1935 they remodeled the house and in 1937 they added the Morrow-Packard orchards and part of the old Christian Larsen homestead. Their large orchard was always well-groomed.

The Thuns had four daughters: Helen, Martha, Lucille and Dorothy. Mr. Thun was elected to two terms as Skamania County Commissioner from 1921 to 1924 and then again from 1931-1936. After 50 years as Underwood orchardists, they retired and turned the trees over to their daughter Martha and her husband Theodore Lehmann. Louis and Emily are buried at Chris-Zada Cemetery in Underwood.

In August 1928 Louis Thun met with quite a serious accident. He was hewing a piece of timber at the Underwood Fruit and Warehouse Co. building, when his ax glanced, striking his wrist and severing the cords and main artery. He was unable to do much work for two or three months.

A March 1933 news item said, "Miss Helen Thun, a music and fine arts major at Washington State College, was selected to broadcast on the college radio station." In April 1939 Louis Thun drove to San Francisco to attend three Fruit conventions. He expected to attend the San Francisco Exposition before returning home.

After retirement the Thuns got to travel. In November 1953 Mr. and Mrs. Louis Thun of Underwood returned home

**Thun, Louis and Emily** (continued)

from a month's trip to Los Angeles, Nevada and Mexico.

**Thun, Thadeus**

He appears on the 1910 census for Underwood. *The Pioneer* in June, 1911 reported,

*Thadeus Thun, an enterprising young orchardist from Underwood and Aaron Larsen, a strawberry specialist, were down looking at Stevenson real estate. Mr. Thun departed highly pleased with the fine large strawberries which he sampled from Mr. Richards. He bought a 20 acre tract close to said berry patch through Mr. Hamilton and will be a welcome addition to our community.*

And in January 1918, "Thadeus Thun, brother of Louis, and family have gone to Portland to make their home. They will be missed by many friends here."

**Treiber, Otis Daniel**
*By Kathy LaMotte with assistance from Ralph Brown*

The history of Underwood would need to include a colorful figure during the time of ferry boat operations on the Columbia River. This figure, Otis Daniel Treiber, owned three ferries, which he ran between Hood River, White Salmon, and Underwood in the early 1900s.

**The SEAL carrying passengers across the Columbia.** Photo from Gorge Heritage Museum

O.D. Treiber was born in Charlotte, Michigan in 1889 to parents Daniel John and Rose Ellen (Standish) Treiber. He moved to the Hood River Valley with his family from Russell, Kansas in 1903.

**Railroad at Underwood** – photo by *Otis Treiber in 1907. From the Gorge Heritage Museum archives.*

While in school, Otis apprenticed at various trades, including a dairy and a machine shop. Treiber also showed an interest in photography at an early age, taking a well-known photo of friends, three generations of Underwoods: Ellen, Isabella, and Cornelia (See Underwood Family). Treiber went on to take pictures of the construction of the railroad at Underwood, as well as pictures of the young town.

**Spring comes to Underwood** – Photo by *Otis Treiber from the Gorge Heritage Museum archives.*

There is a story told by Treiber's daughter Jeanette. This happening would prove to be a turning point in Treiber's life. While in school he worked for a machine shop in Hood River. During his lunch break he wandered down to the river. A local ferry operator asked if he wanted a ride across the river and back. He was hooked. Treiber went to work for Commodore Dean. Treiber eventually bought the Koburg to Bingen ferry run in 1910, buying the business from Commodore Dean. He then operated the Underwood-Hood River ferry from 1910-1917, buying half interest from Captain Harry Olsen, the husband of Mary Underwood, who ran the Underwood Hotel. Treiber would later on take a well-known photo of Mary Underwood Olsen Lane (See Underwood Family).

Otis Treiber's parents moved away from Hood River in 1911. Otis lived in the Olsen's attic for a time, and later in life refers to Mary Underwood Olsen Lane as Aunt Mary.

**Olive Robbins – 19, Otis Treiber -18**

In 1907 Otis Treiber returned to Russell, Kansas to visit his childhood sweetheart Olive Robbins.

At the age of 18 Treiber built his first ferry, The BEAR. The BEAR was the first gasoline-powered ferry to cross the Columbia. It would hold four cars and many passengers.

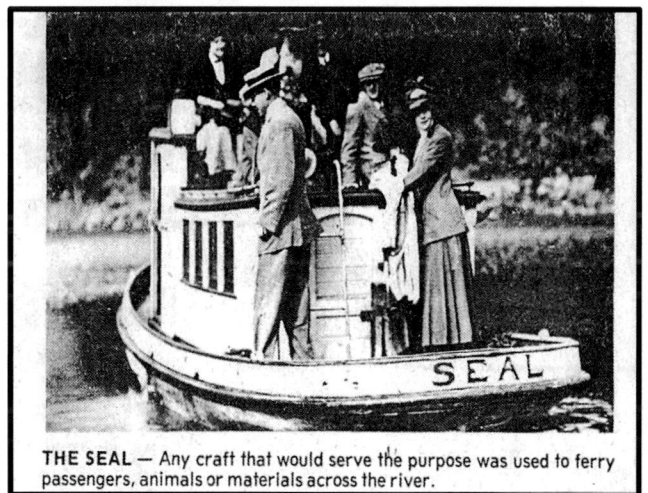

**THE SEAL** — Any craft that would serve the purpose was used to ferry passengers, animals or materials across the river.

**The SEAL carrying passengers to Hood River.** Photo from Gorge Heritage Museum archives

213

**Treiber, Otis Daniel (**continued**)**

**The BEAR**
Photo from Gorge Heritage Museum archives

**The SEAL alongside Trieber's houseboat**
Photo from Gorge Heritage Museum archives

**The BEAR in the White Salmon River**
Photo from Gorge Heritage Museum archives

This was followed by two other launches, the SEAL, and the OTTER. He then built a houseboat on which he lived. It was docked at the Underwood site.

**SEAL and OTTER alongside Treiber's houseboat**
Photo from Gorge Heritage Museum archives

In 1912 Otis went back to Kansas and married Olive Robbins. They came back to Underwood. They were living in their houseboat when their first child was born in 1913. They would eventually have six daughters.

**Otis and Olive (Robbins)Treiber with daughter Georgia Elizabeth (b. 8-6-13) on board the SEAL.**
Photo from Gorge Heritage Museum archives

After Georgia, their other daughters were as follows: Margaret Louise born in 1914, Marion Rose in 1916, Olive Jeanette in 1920, Dorothy Jo in 1924, and Frances Marie in 1924. Dorothy Jo Treiber would live but two years.

> *Captain Otis Treiber built his first boat at age eighteen.*

While still living in Underwood, Treiber was asked to build other boats. In 1914 he designed and built the MARGORY, with an 18 HP engine, to be used on Lake Crescent. In 1915 Treiber designed and built the STORM KING, with a 40 HP gasoline engine to be used on Lake Crescent, followed by the VASHON ISLAND, with a 250 HP diesel engine.

**Treiber's diesel engines in Camden, NJ**
Photo from Treiber family collection

With work keeping him away for long periods of time, Treiber and his family sold their boats in Underwood in 1917. He formed the National Ship Building Company in Seattle. There he designed and built large cargo ships.

In 1926 Otis Treiber formed the Treiber Diesel Engine Corp., in Camden, NJ. He designed and built marine diesels.

Later in 1930 Treiber joined Hercules Motors, in Canton, OH, to develop an automotive diesel for heavy trucks. He held 60 patents and built 27 ships.

In 1956 Treiber retired, but retirement was not for long. Back on the west coast he designed and built the SEA OTTER, a large cruise ship, which he operated in Alaska, the Caribbean, and the Atlantic Ocean until 1970.

During this time Treiber's wife of 49 years, Olive Robbins Treiber, passed away in 1961.

**Treiber, Otis Daniel** (continued)

In 1962, at the age of 73, Treiber received another license. Treiber was now licensed as a master of vessels up to 300 tons on any ocean. Treiber was noted as saying, "Whenever I was doing something for which I needed another license, I'd go out and get it."

The photos below of the SEA OTTER appeared in the August 1958 issue of "The Alaska Sportsman" magazine.

**The SEA OTTER – a large cruise ship**

**The SEA OTTER – a painting
By Marshall Rahn on a 1966 post card**

After his final retirement, his wife now gone, Captain Treiber (as he now liked to be called), often remembered his days on the Columbia, and his friend Amos Underwood, who had helped Treiber as a very young man. He had remained a close friend of the Underwood family. In 1970, after selling the SEA OTTER, Otis Treiber returned to Underwood. He purchased a small house near the river in lower Underwood, which had been the home of Mary Underwood Olsen Lane. The home was being held by Mary's niece Ruth Litton. Captain Treiber remodeled the home and outfitted the Columbia River side with ferry boat windows. This stands just above the pier and warehouses (which are gone today). Also, the home is directly above where the houseboat once docked which was owned by Otis and Olive Treiber.

**The Treiber home still standing in Underwood.**

In 1971, at the age of 82, Otis Treiber traveled to Alaska, to bring Nellie Underwood Howell's body home to be buried in Chris-Zada Cemetery.

**Treiber, Otis Daniel** (continued)

In later years Captain Treiber was often seen in the local area, frequently walking west to visit those working at Spring Creek National Fish Hatchery.

In spanning back over Captain Otis Treiber's life, who knows what path he might have taken if he hadn't wandered down to the ferry as a school boy and taken that first ride across the river.

**Captain Treiber    1976**
Photo from the July 5, 1976 *Columbian*

Otis Daniel Treiber died in 1988, and his remains were placed in Idewilde Cemetery, Hood River. He was 98 .

Still today, his home, with its "pilothouse" overtones sits with a beautiful view of the Columbia River and its river traffic.

References:
Tacoma Public Library
Mid-Columbia North Shore – Keith McCoy
Melodic Whistles in the Columbia River -
Keith McCoy        Gorge Heritage Museum
Ralph Brown        Seattle Daily Times

**Tubbs, C.L.**

In 1905 he was regarded as one of the most successful Underwood farmers. 1908 land records show that he acquired 160 acres. There is a baby Delbert Murel Tubbs buried in the old Chenowith Cemetery. His head stone, dated 1903, is one of two headstones still intact after vandalism.

**Underwood Family**
By Cheryl Mack

The community of Underwood was named for Amos Underwood, who was born in Cincinnati, Ohio on December 10, 1834. At the age of 18 he came west on a wagon train across the Oregon Trail, arriving in The Dalles in September of 1852. He initially settled at the Cascades, near what is now Cascade Locks, Oregon.

**Amos Underwood**
Photo from Gorge Heritage Museum Archives

On October 18, 1855, Amos enlisted as a fourth corporal in Company B of the First Oregon Mounted Volunteers, during what was known as the Yakima War. At the time of his enlistment he lived at what is now Cascade Locks, Oregon. In his enlistment papers he was described as 5' 10½" tall, blue eyes, auburn hair, fair complexion, and a farmer by trade. During his service with the Volunteers he was involved in a 4-day battle at Walla Walla, which resulted in the death of the Walla

Walla Chief Peopeomoxmox. Amos would recount this story many times in his later life. He was discharged on February 16, 1856, and on his return trip to the Cascades in early March he witnessed the burning of the Joslyn house (in what is now Bingen), and joined army troops from Fort Dalles who were sent to protect settlers at Hood River. Amos continued down the Columbia to the Cascades that spring, arriving in time to witness the three-day attack by Yakima Indians on the white settlements at the Upper, Middle and Lower Cascades, beginning March 26th, 1856. He was reportedly present when Chief Chenowith and eight other local Indian headmen were hanged by the army in retribution for the attack. Chief Chenowith and his family had also lived in what is now Cascade Locks, and even though they claimed no part in the attack, they and other local Indians were left to bear the brunt of the settlers' anger.

Following Chenowith's hanging, his young daughter, who had been named Ellen by the Catholic missionaries, was given in marriage to Lt. William King Lear. Lear had served with the Third Regiment under Colonel Steptoe, but had resigned his commission in April of 1856 and became Indian Agent at the Cascades. It is likely that Ellen's family agreed to the marriage in an attempt to forge an alliance with their captors, since all of the local Indians were held as prisoners by the army following the attack by the Yakimas. Ellen's marriage was short-lived, however, and Lear left the area in August of 1856. Their daughter Isabelle Lear was born in May of 1857, at what is now Hood River.

We don't know when Amos Underwood met Ellen Chenowith Lear, but in his pension papers he states that he married her in April of 1857 at Cascade Locks, Oregon, "by the Indian Laws Oregon Territory recognized as man and wife". Around the same time that Amos and Ellen were married, Amos moved up the Columbia to Hood River, purchasing the sol-

dier's warrants of Edwin Stevens and Peter Rudio near Ruthton Point. This had been the Indian village of *Nenoothdedect,* where Ellen's father had been born. Ellen's daughter Isabelle Lear was born at Hood River in 1857, and Amos and Ellen later had three children. Their son Jefferson was born in 1862; their daughter Mary was born in 1864; and their son John was born in 1868.

**Ellen Underwood**
Photo from Gorge Heritage Museum archives, Otis Treiber collection

In 1865 Amos sold his land in Hood River to John Marden, and moved across the Columbia to the Indian village known as *Namnit*, at the mouth of the White Salmon River. His brother Edward joined him there that same year. Edward, who was born in 1846 in Decatur, Indiana, crossed the Oregon Trail in 1864. The two brothers spent the first several years running a wood camp and cutting cord wood to sell to the steamships. They filed their original homestead claims on land up on the flat, and by 1871 they had cleared land for farms and added cattle to their holdings. In 1871 Edward Underwood married his brother's stepdaughter, Isabelle Lear. Edward and Isabelle's first daughter, named Lovisa after Edward and Amos's mother, was born in 1872. Edward and Isabelle ultimately had eleven children, the last one born in 1905.

## Underwood Family (continued)

Edward and Amos were in business together in the early years, and were always referred to as the "Underwood Brothers" in early newspaper accounts. After acquiring title to their two original 160 acre homestead claims, both brothers purchased an additional 160 acres each – Edward up on the flat, to the north of his original claim, and Amos at the mouth of the White Salmon River. The brothers sold apples, strawberries, watermelons and beef, and Amos ran a large sailboat on the Columbia.

Amos and Ellen Underwood's two sons both died young in tragic accidents. Their son Jefferson died in 1881, at the age of 19, in a logging accident. Three years later, in 1884, their son John was shot and killed by a drunk on the streets of The Dalles, at the age of 16. Their daughter Mary married Harry Olsen in 1886, and Mary and Harry made their home in Underwood.

Both Amos and Edward Underwood were civic-minded citizens, with Amos serving as a Skamania County Commissioner for over ten years, between 1884 and 1895. Amos and Edward were instrumental in helping to plan and build the first roads, bridges and ferry landings that would eventually connect the community of Underwood with the outside world. They helped to build the first school house in Underwood in 1897, and donated land for a cemetery after the death of Edward's granddaughter Christina Dark in 1901.

As early as 1893 Amos ran a passenger ferry from Underwood, using his sailboat to haul people, freight and mail to ferry landings at Hood River and White Salmon. His son-in-law Harry Olsen took over the ferry business in 1905.

Amos was involved in many ventures, including mining in the McCoy Creek drainage, in the mountains far to the north. As early as 1895 he sent his brother's son-in-law John Dark and several other men off to the mines for months at a time, in search of the elusive big strike of gold. They continued this venture until 1905, ultimately digging four tunnels, and building a flume and a cabin in the remote mountains. Dark Divide and Dark Meadows (in the Gifford Pinchot National Forest) were later named for John Dark.

In 1898, Amos and Ellen sold their original homestead to Edmund Goddard, and moved down to their land at the mouth of the White Salmon River, building what would be the first home in the future townsite of Underwood. Edward and Isabelle built a new home further north up on the flat, a house which still stands today on Orchard Lane.

Newspaper accounts describe how William King Lear visited his relatives in Underwood in 1903, after spending the previous forty years in Alaska. This was the first time that Isabelle Underwood (now 47 years old) had met her father.

Amos platted the townsite of Underwood in 1904, and offered lots for sale. The first three lots were purchased in 1904 for the construction of a cold storage plant to store fruit prior to shipping. A store soon followed and in 1905 Amos's daughter Mary and her husband Harry Olsen built a hotel at Underwood. After turning his ferry business over to his son-in-law Harry, Amos began operating a saloon in Underwood in 1905. His brother Edward sold off most of his orchard land to the new crop of orchardists arriving in the Underwood area, and joined his brother in the saloon business.

Unlike the rest of the Underwood family, Amos's wife Ellen is rarely mentioned in early newspaper accounts. She died in 1906, at about the age of 68. Her legacy, however, can be found in museums throughout the country. Ellen and her daughter Isabelle were descended from a long line of women who were experts in the art of basket making and beadwork, and they continued this artistic tradition throughout their lives. Family heirlooms donated by Underwood descendants can be found in all of the local museums, par-

## Underwood Family (continued)

ticularly Maryhill, the Columbia Gorge Interpretive Center and the Gorge Heritage Museum.

Edward Underwood died in 1908, at the age of 62, of rheumatism and heart failure. After his death his wife Isabelle sold their home and remaining property on the flats to the Packard family, orchardists who had purchased much land in the Underwood area. According to the 1910 census, Isabelle worked as a servant on a private farm, probably the Goddard's.

**Edward Underwood**

**Isabelle Lear Underwood**

Amos Underwood remained active throughout much of his later life, traveling to California for the winters and making several trips back east to visit family and friends. He was often asked by newspapers to recount his tales of fighting in the Indian Wars. He died in December of 1917, at the age of 83.

Mary Underwood Olsen, divorced from Harry Olsen, continued to operate the Underwood Hotel. In 1921 she married William Lane, who operated a livery service in Underwood.

**Mary Underwood Lane**
3 Photos on this page from Gorge Heritage Museum Otis Treiber collection

When construction of the Bonneville Dam resulted in the disturbance of numerous Indian burials on Bradford Island, Isabelle Underwood was asked by the Corps of Engineers to be one of the honored guests at the reburial ceremony in 1936. She died later that same year at the age of 79.

The Underwood Hotel burned in a massive fire in 1946. Fortunately Mary Lane had previously donated many of her family's heirlooms, primarily baskets and beaded bags made by her mother and grandmother, to the Maryhill Museum. She also donated a necklace to the museum, containing two of the medals handed out by Lewis and Clark to chiefs along the Columbia River in 1805 and 1806. The fact that her family had two of those

220

## Underwood Family (continued)

medals in their possession indicated that Ellen Underwood had been descended from chiefly families on both sides. Mary Underwood Olsen Lane died in February of 1950, at the age of 85. She and her other family members are buried in the Chris-Zada Cemetery in Underwood.

**Newspaper accounts of the Underwood Family:**

*Glacier* October 1898:

*The Underwood brothers have sold to E.C. Goddard of Portland their old homesteads, consisting of 320 acres for $6000. They still have half a section left, some of the most productive land on the Columbia.*

April 1899:

*Ed Underwood was badly injured in a runaway (wagon?), four ribs being broken, one penetrating through the lungs. Hopes are entertained for his recovery.*

*Oregonian* August 7, 1900:

*The Sheriff of Skamania County has been notified that the family of Ed Underwood is afflicted with smallpox. The family has been quarantined, and every precaution will be taken to prevent the spread of the disease. One of Mr. Underwood's daughters, who had been attending a sick patient, carried the germs home in her clothes. The cases are of a mild form.*

*Glacier* July 27, 1905:

*Ed Underwood has a fine home and ranch up on the hill about one mile from Underwood. He has been a resident for 40 years. He is secretary of the Underwood Mining Company and has charge of the liquor store.*

Note: Obituaries for each Underwood family member buried at the Underwood Chris-Zada Cemetery can be found in the book Underwood, Washington Cemetery Obituaries by Ralph Brown. It is available through the Gorge Heritage Museum in Bingen, WA and at the libraries in White Salmon and Stevenson, WA.

**Ellen, Cornelia and Isabelle Underwood**
**Three generations**
Photo from Gorge Heritage Museum archives, Otis Treiber Collection

## Veach, Bert

In 1904 he rented the Goddard farm and moved up from Chenowith. In 1905 he was regarded as an old timer with one of the best arranged ranches.

## Walther, Emil and Rosa
By Kathy LaMotte

Emil and Rosa Walther emigrated from Switzerland to the United States on February 6, 1899. Emil was born in 1867, and Rosa Holtzer was born in 1876. Emil and Rosa Walther arrived as emigrants in the United States on Feb. 6, 1899. The couple homesteaded property up on the west end of Underwood, across from where the county garage stands today. They cleared the land for farming and a small orchard.

**Walther, Emil and Rosa** (continued)

The Walthers would eventually have eight children. The older children, who were young at the time, carried rocks in helping to clear the land. The children were as follows: Herman Emil (1899-1983), Frederic (Fritz) William (1901-1947), Ernest (Ernie) Edward (1902-1931), Olga Rose Walther Kelley (1904-1999), Martha Matilda Walther Kock (1906-1999), Adolph (Bubby) L Walther (1909-1969), Frieda F. Walther Novaria (1914-1981) and Leonard (1916-2000)

This acreage is in the Chenowith area.

At this time Mrs. Walther became very homesick for Switzerland. According to great grandson Greg Kock, the story goes as follows: Rosa had two wishes. She wished for one of two things: to go back to Switzerland or to have a nice home there in Chenowith. She decided to take the children, which would have been the oldest five, and travel to Switzerland to see her family. They were gone for a few months. When Rosa returned she found a surprise. Her husband Emil had provided her with a wonderful home. So she received both of her wishes.

**Left to right: Ernest, Emil (father), Unknown family member in back, Frederic beside dog, Rosa (mother), Olga on mother's lap, and Herman**

**Built in 1909**
**Left to right on porch: Herman, Ernest and Fritz, Emil holding Adolph (Bubby), Olga and Martha. Mother Rosa and dogs below.**
**Photo taken 1911 or 1912**

Sometime around 1908 the Walthers decided to sell off the upper part of their land. They sold this property for $20,000.00 in gold pieces. Unfortunately, most of this money would eventually be lost in the depression. Since the sale of the upper property the land has changed hands perhaps three times. The first owner built a packing shed. The property is now owned by Paul Allen. At the time of the original sale, the Walthers kept 99 acres on the west end of their property.

## Walther, Emil and Rosa (continued)

**Chenowith School -** date unknown
**In photo as follow: Mr. King –Teacher– Top**
**Top left to right: Ernest Walther, Herman Walther, Mr. King's daughter, Albert King, Mr. King's daughter**
**Bottom row left to right: Morhouse boy, Fritz Walther, two Morhouse girls, Olga Walther, Edna King, Mr. King's dog "Tip"**

Rosa and Emil Walther had donated the one acre to be used for the school. It was the original school in Chenowith.

Much of the land had been cleared by the Walthers for farming. Today, it is again covered mostly with timber.

*Glacier* Oct. 6, 1910:

*Emile Walther and family returned home having spent several months visiting in Switzerland and France.*

According to Greg Kock, when his Aunt Olga was 11, and his Grandma Martha was 9, the beautiful family home burned down. A fire started down by the Little White Salmon River and came up the bluff. That would have been in about 1915. A structure was later built on the foundation, but with no-where near the size and elegance of the original home.

Another unfortunate event would happen to the family in only a few short years. In 1917 Emil Walther was suddenly killed in a logging accident. He was 50 years old. Their youngest child, Leonard was just one year old.

Eventually Rosa Walther married George Zulauf, who was also from Switzerland. They moved to the Vancouver area. Olga and Martha attended a convent school in Vancouver for a period of time. Rose died in Vancouver in 1945, at the age of 69. She, along with Emil Walther, and several of their children, are buried in Manor Wilson Bridge Cemetery, Vancouver.

Adolph (Bubby) Walther lived in Chenowith until he died in 1969. At some point the property in Chenowith was sold.

Olga went on to marry William Kelley. They lived in the Mill A area. Greg Kock now lives on his Aunt Olga's property. Adolph was a Pvt. in the Infantry WWII, Martha married John Kock. They eventually lived in Bingen. Frieda married John (known as Jack), Novaria. They moved back from Portland and built a home on the bluff in Underwood, just west of Barry Ternahan's place.

*******************************

The Walthers had relatives living in Underwood. Emil Walther's brother Charles, also immigrated from Switzerland. He married Mary Kellendonk, of another Underwood pioneer family. Charles and Mary had six children. They were George C., Angeline, Catherine, Violet, Frances, and Louise. Many of the Charles and Mary Walther family are buried in Chris-Zada Cemetery.

*********************

*Greg Kock – Great Grandson of Pioneers*
*Photos courtesy of Greg Kock*
*Ralph Brown – Find A Grave web site*
*Thomasina Campbell*
*The Enterprise*
*Robert Dickey*

## Wendorf, William A. and Helen

In 1901 William A. Wendorf acquired a 160 acre Underwood homestead. He was born in 1866 in Missouri. The Wendorfs were fruit farmers here. In October 1903 it was reported, "Mr. Wendorf has no time lately to feel lonesome, as he has one of those companions not generally sought – a felon." (A felon is an infection of the terminal segment of a finger – causing intense itching and pain.)

*The Enterprise* January 1915 :

*Mr. and Mrs. Wendorf had a party at their home for Christmas.*

## Wess Family

"The Journey of My Family"
by Josephine Wess Mason

*(Note: Using multiples of the same name was common throughout generations of the Wess and Zellner families.)*

**John Joseph and Rosa Zellner Wess**
*(Photos courtesy of Jayne Newell Allen)*

My parents were John and Rosa Wess. Leaving the country of Hungary that cold day of January 6, 1914, my father and mother must have had a lot of courage as they boarded a large American ship in the harbor of Hamburg, Germany. They had bid their farewells to family and friends a couple of days earlier. Then they traveled by train from the small village of Paulish, Hungary to the ship in Hamburg.

My father, who was only twenty-four years old, carried my sister Katherine, who was only one. My mother clasped three year old John's hand tightly as they climbed the gang plank of the huge ship. Mom had just turned 21. They were two very brave young people.

My parents brought little with them, as they had few possessions. My mother said that one thing they did bring was goose feathers, so they could have a "docuit" (a feather bed) in America. All our family slept under a docuit for years to come.

Before setting sail for the "Great America" we must not forget the folks they left behind.

My paternal grandfather was John Wess, Sr. He was a colorful character. Legend had it that he could ride a horse bareback faster than any man in Paulish. He was a very hot-tempered person who more often than not settled a dispute with his fist.

My father, John Joseph Wess, started school at the age of six. One day he came home and complained to his father that the young school master had treated him harshly. When my grandfather heard this he lost his temper. He snatched a big knife from the kitchen table, jumped on his horse, and with great speed rode off to the school house. Brandishing the knife, he ran into the school and faced the young school master. The young teacher trembled in his shoes as he stood toe to toe with this wild man and heard him say, "Don't ever treat my son harshly again or I will use this knife on you!" From then on the young school master ignored my father in the classroom. He never attempted to teach my father to read or write.

The next year my father's dad, John Sr., died. My grandmother withdrew my father from school to help push the cart in which she carried flower plants that she peddled each day toward making a living for her family.

My father never learned how to read or write. He did grow up with a love for flowers and plants that lasted him a lifetime. His greatest desire was to own his own farm one day.

On my father's side, my grandmother's maiden name was Rosalie Hock. She lived to see almost all of her children immigrate to America. She journeyed to Cleveland, Ohio with two of her daughters in 1916. However, she didn't like America and returned to Paulish, Hungary to live with her youngest daughter, Rosa. Rosa was the only child not to emigrate from Hungary. She and her husband and children remained in Hungary and had a difficult time making a living. Aunt Rosa's husband died before World War II began. After World War II began in Europe in 1939, we never heard from Aunt Rosa or her daughters again.

Aunt Rosa also had one son, Emil Winkler. He fought for Germany, as all of the Hungarians were forced to do by Hitler. He never saw his family again. He believed that his mother and sisters were forced to cook in one of Stalin's labor camps. Many other families were sent to Siberia, and were never heard from again. After the war Emil Winkler and his young family were allowed to immigrate to the United States in 1946. They settled in Washington, D.C. Emil became a chef and worked in the same restaurant until he retired.

My grandfather on my mother's side was Adam Zellner. He married my grandmother whose maiden name was Sophia Schlecter. By the time all of their children had begun to immigrate to America, my grandmother was widowed. She too saw one child after another leave Hungary to go to the United States. She felt sad as they left that she would never see them again. But, on the other hand, she was happy for them to get the opportunity to make a better life for themselves.

My grandmother's son, John Zellner, and his family didn't find the United States to their liking. A year later they returned to Hungary. Unemployment was high during that time and John Z. was un-

able to find a job. He and his family attempted to return to the US, but because of the quota system they were told they would have to wait for five years.

Uncle John Zellner and his family were able to go to Brazil, in South America, without having to wait. They settled in San Paulo and liked it very much. We received interesting letters from them for many years.

The trip across the Atlantic Ocean, for my parents, in January of 1914 was a very difficult one. The ocean was so rough that my mother was seasick the entire time. That left all the diaper changing and feeding of his family to my father. He must have had good sea legs to care for his family the entire trip.

Because of stormy weather, it took nine days for their ship to cross the Atlantic. When the ship finally sailed into New York harbor and passed by the Statue of Liberty a huge cheer arose from those on board. They had reached America!

The ship docked at Ellis Island where they were detained on board until each person was checked by a doctor. If anyone had a contagious disease they were not permitted to leave the ship. As each person embarked onto Ellis Island large name and destination tags were placed around their necks. Many of the families were advised to alter their last name to make life easier for them in the new country. Our name was changed from Vesz to Wess.

Many of the immigrants were bound for Cleveland or Chicago. My family was headed for the west coast. After a three thousand mile crossing of the Atlantic Ocean, it was another three thousand miles across the United States to Portland, OR, by railway. And what a trip that was for some of them.

Aunt Elizabeth, my father's sister, who had three girls all under the age of four, was put on a different train than her husband, Uncle Raugh Render. She had

## Wess Family (continued)

the three children and the family money. Uncle Raugh had nothing. He said that if it hadn't been for some kind-hearted women who shared some of their food he would have been very hungry by the time he reached Portland.

Aunt Elizabeth said she had a difficult time caring for the three little girls without any help. They were one happy family when they were finally reunited at the train depot in Portland.

When my folks reached Portland, my Aunt Katherine (my mom's oldest sister) was at the depot waiting for them. She and Uncle George and their family had come to America two years earlier. They were helping my folks by loaning them the boat and train fare and by taking them into their home until my folks could find a job and a house to rent.

After the long journey across the Atlantic and the train ride across the United States my parents had no rest. They went in search of work. My father was lucky to find a job right away for a company making ice cream.

My Aunt Katherine took care of my brother and sister, John and Katherine, while my mother was hired as a domestic. Mother laughed in later years as she recalled some of the bloopers she made in trying to learn the English language. At first someone instructed her to just use the word 'yes' when she was asked a question. That turned out to be poor advice. She found herself being laughed at. The same person told her to use the word 'no'. That only made things worse.

My mother said that many of the employers of the domestics were very good to them. They would give them used clothing for themselves and their children. That was greatly appreciated.

When my father and mother were able to pay Aunt Katherine back they found a house to rent. (Katherine and George Reinland were the parents of Teresa Reinland Ziegler, long-time Underwood resident.)

**Rosa Wess Marks**
(*Daughter of John and Rosa*)

During the three years that my folks lived in Portland, my sister Rosa, our mother's namesake, was born, August 25, 1916.

My brother John Adam started school in Portland, OR and was learning to read. My mother would ask him to bring home his pre-primers and point out the words to her and tell her what they were, translated from English. That is how she learned to read our language and increase her speaking vocabulary. Many times I saw her read the newspaper to my father.

My mother's sister, Josephine, and her family, along with her brother, Adam Zelner, and his family, were already in Portland by the time my folks arrived. They all lived close by in what was known as the Woodstock area. Living in such close proximity allowed the cousins to play and go to school together.

Uncle Frank, my mother's youngest brother was only 17 years of age when he joined the rest of the family in Portland. He loved American sports. Baseball, golf, and target shooting were some of his favorites. He was young and lively and became Americanized quickly.

Uncle Raugh, husband to my father's sister Elizabeth, died from a sudden illness. Frank married Aunt Elizabeth when he was only 19 years of age. Uncle Frank and Aunt Elizabeth had two children of their own.

My father kept working and kept looking for a place to work as a farmer.

## Wess Family (continued)

His greatest desire was to own a farm one day. He always said, "Farmers are the most important people in the world. We could not live without them." He loved the good earth.

In the spring of 1918, my father heard that a farmer in Underwood, Washington needed a permanent man to live on his fruit orchard and be in charge. Dad was very pleased to land the job. So my folks left Portland for Underwood, which was about seventy miles east of Portland, on the Columbia River.

They moved into a house which the owner of the farm provided for his top man. It was situated a few feet from the county road. My brother and sister, John and Katherine were lucky. The school bus would pick them up in front of the house.

World War I was drawing to an end in the autumn of 1918. My mother was pregnant with me. She called me, Josephine, the "peace baby." I was born on December 11th just a month after the Armistice Peace Treaty was signed, November 11, 1918.

My father worked hard for the owner of the farm. The owner lived in Portland and would come out to Underwood every now and then to check on his fruit farm.

Two years after my folks moved to Underwood, a thirty acre farm came up for sale. It was just north of the place my folks were farming. It had a ten acre orchard of apples and pears and about five acres of cleared land, just waiting for more fruit trees and strawberries to be planted. My folks went for it. They applied for a loan and got it from the Federal Land Bank in Spokane. At last my dad had his life's desire, a farm of his own.

There was a small, two story white house on one corner of the farm. We moved into the house. My folks would live in this house for thirty years. My sisters Marion, Betty, and Virginia were all born on this farm.

Before writing any more about life on the new farm, I wish to tell you about the little town of Underwood, where we grew up. It is located where the White Salmon River empties into the Columbia River. Lewis and Clark passed by the future town as they headed for the mouth of the Columbia River at Astoria.

Underwood was named after its founder, Amos Underwood. Amos married a young Indian woman named Ellen. Ellen had a daughter, Isabella, by a former marriage. Amos' younger brother, Ed, married Isabella. They had a large family of children. Two of their daughters picked strawberries for my folks many summers.

Amos and Ed homesteaded the land above the bluff, known later as Underwood Heights. They wanted to sell plots and start a town, but the plan didn't work out. Most of the land was sold to orchards during the "Apple Boom" period of 1905-1920.

Amos Underwood was also the owner of the Underwood Hotel that sat on the bluff side of the town. There was a large grocery store, post office, meat market and service station, and later a tavern.

The train depot was on the east side of the town about a hundred yards from the post office. The apple warehouse and the cold storage building lined the west side of town along the railroad track. There were a few Indian families living near the mouth of the White Salmon River.

A two-room schoolhouse was built above the bluff on the flat area of Underwood. There were several apple orchards nearby. The rest of the orchards were located up on the Underwood hills.

Underwood was divided into three sections: the town by the mouth of the river, Underwood Flats, where the schoolhouse was located, and Underwood Heights where our farm was located.

***************************

**Wess Family** (continued)

**Betty, Marion, and Virginia - 1st day of school on Wess homestead.**

The Underwood Grade School was where the social life of our small town centered. The adults had a club known as the Underwood Literary Society. They met at the school house once a month. Why the name was given to the club I will never know. I heard no literature discussed at any of the meetings. But it sounded good and brought all the people of the community together.

They also held dances at the school. While our parents danced, we children played together until we were so tired and sleepy we would lie on the benches and go to sleep. Our folks would cover us up with their coats and we would sleep until the dance was over. The band consisted of a piano, saxophone and a drum. That's where I learned to love the music of a saxophone. After the dances our parents would awaken us and we'd climb into our wagon that was pulled by our two horses and rumble home.

Every year the school children put on a Christmas program for the community and there was a visit from Santa for the children. The town provided a Christmas stocking with an orange in the toe. The rest of the stocking was filled with nuts and candy.

Santa Claus made his appearance each year and asked us if we had been good children. He always had a few gossipy little tidbits for the adults as well. It was the biggest event each year for our small community.

One of our men school teachers was interested in athletics and especially basketball. He was able to get the community to tax themselves for a gymnasium. We had so many wonderful basketball games in that building, and other events as well.

Later the children were bused to White Salmon about six miles away. Eventually the school was torn down. But the gymnasium remained the community focal point for many years.

**Katherine Wess' High School Graduation 1931**

When it snowed in the winter my dad would hitch our team of horses to a homemade snowplow and open the road for us to the highway, so we could catch the school bus. Sometimes we would get snowfalls in the beginning of December and they would last into the middle of March. We had plenty of time to enjoy the snow.

Our summers would get pretty warm. On the hottest days dad would let us take the afternoon off and go down to the Columbia River to swim. His love for the water began as a young boy where he

228

spent many summers in the Mures, near Paulish, Hungary. Dad was a good swimmer. His skills must have rubbed off on my brother John, as he was a very good diver as well.

**Rosa Zellner Wess on Underwood homestead**

We all worked hard together on that thirty acre farm. Our crops brought in good money. My father bought our first car. It was a 1926 Model T truck. We used it for everything from driving to church to hauling strawberries.

All the while my father had his eyes on the eighty acre farm adjoining ours. It had fourteen acres of alfalfa, a big two-story barn, a good well, and a large grazing acreage that could be cleared for planting pear and apple trees. He also wanted to plant a fourteen acre strawberry field.

My mother did not want him to undertake such a big investment and all the extra hard work that would be involved. But my father wouldn't listen to her. After thirteen years of hard work for all of us, we were now finally unable to make the mortgage payments on that second farm to the Federal Land Bank. The bank took it back.

My father went to work for a saw mill about four miles away in a small town called Bingen. They put the farm up for sale and a dentist from Yakima bought it. They moved back to Portland, having lived in Underwood for 28 years.

My parents bought a small, two bedroom house on Rodney St. My dad bought a half acre on Columbia Boulevard, to grow strawberries, raspberries and pansies for the local stores in that area. He also built a small cabin on the property so he could sleep there overnight if he wanted to start picking the berries early in the morning before the day got too hot.

On July 10, 1952 my mother went out to Columbia Boulevard to help my father pick strawberries. He was not there. She looked in the cabin and could see he had not slept there that past night. There were crates stacked up ready for the berries to be picked that day. She walked all over the half acre looking closely for him in the tall grass but found no sign of him. Getting alarmed she called my brother and oldest sister. They too searched the grounds and inquired at the local stores if he had been in with berries. They were told that he had not been seen.

They inquired at the local tavern which my father visited quite often. One person said that he thought my father had been there about 10 o'clock the previous evening. My brother and sister then called the police. The police searched the grounds one more time. There was no evidence of foul play. His body was never found. No one ever saw him again. He was sixty-four years old.

My mother found a job cooking for the Holy Name Sisters at the Holy Redeemer Catholic Church. While she enjoyed the sisters very much, there were fourteen of them to cook for, three meals a day. After several years it became too much for her. She took a housekeeping job for the priest in White Salmon. She enjoyed being there too, as it was the parish she attended all

## Wess Family (continued)

the years that she had lived in Underwood. She liked it because she knew a lot of people and her daughter Betty, and family lived nearby in Underwood.

Unfortunately she had a bad fall at the priests' house and my sister Katherine took her back to Portland to live with her family. She enjoyed living there and being back at the Holy Redeemer Parish again where she had friends. She lived with Katherine until 1967 when Katherine died of cancer. She moved in with my brother John and his wife LaVelle. Again she had a bad fall ending up in the hospital. When she got better my sister Betty took her to Underwood to live.

Mother would have small strokes every now and again and had to be admitted into Skyline Hospital in White Salmon. She lived with Betty for ten years enjoying her children and grandchildren.

Mother passed away in a nursing home in Longview, Washington on October 29th, 1981, at the age of 88. Her great faith and trust in God took her through the trials of 28 years of widowhood. Her strong faith in God was an inspiration to all of us. And so it is in this way that we remember mama.

We laid her to rest on All Souls Day, November 2, 1981 in the White Salmon Cemetery near to her sister Katherine.

**The Mason's**
**Irene, Josephine Wess Mason (author of this story), Marie, Larry, and Carol**

**Marion Wess**

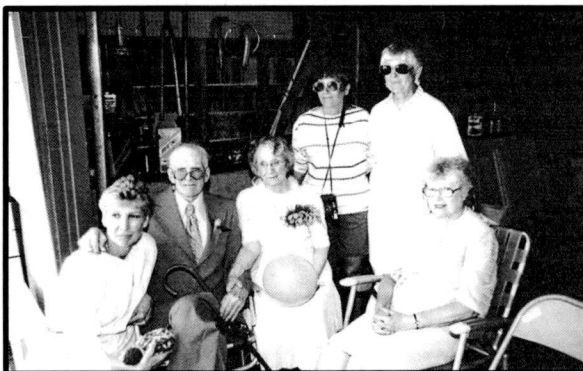

**Left: Betty, John Adam with wife LaVelle, Virginia, Marion and Josephine**

Children of John Joseph & Rosa Zellner Wess:

| Name | Dates | Place |
|---|---|---|
| John Adam | 1910-1992 | Paulish, Hungary |
| Katherine | 1912-1967 | Paulish, Hungary |
| Rosa | 1916-1955 | Portland, OR |
| Josephine | 1918 - 2010 | Underwood, WA |
| Marion | Born 1925 | Underwood, WA |
| Betty | Born 1930 | Underwood, WA |
| Virginia | Born 1932 | Underwood, WA |

## Wess Family (continued)

**All photos from the Wess family collection**

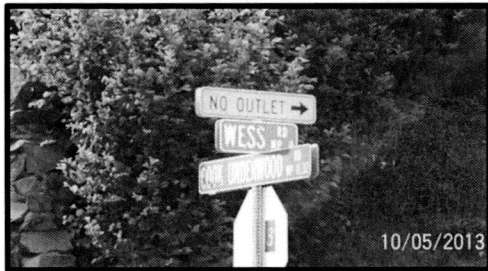

**Road named after the Wess family**

An ad in the *Mt. Adams Sun*, July 30, 1943:

*FOR SALE : 30 acre farm and fresh cows. See John Wess.*

## Whittemore, Melanie Ziegler

### My Life on Underwood Mountain
By Melanie (Ziegler) Whittemore

I was the fourth of five children born to Leroy and Mary Ziegler (Steve was born in 1949, Don in 1951, Melissa in 1955, I was born in 1963, and Kevin in 1965). We lived on 20 acres on the dump road in a building that had once been used as a warehouse. That house had no insulation, so it was very cold in the winter and extremely hot in the summer. Later we lived in a manufactured home my parents bought and moved onto our alfalfa field when I was 12.

My parents had grown up on Underwood Mountain, went to school in Underwood, and raised their children there. The Community Center used to be the gym of the school they attended until they went to White Salmon for high school. They got married December 22, 1947.

My dad was a faller with Broughton Lumber Company for about 40 years. Depending on the weather, he would also work in the orchard where he grew vari-ous types of apples, (gravenstein, newton, ortley and striped delicious), and pears (bartlett, d'Anjou and bosc) as well as cherry and peach trees. We had beef to eat throughout the year because Dad also raised a few head of cattle. When it was deer season, he would usually come home with some venison for us. Dad was a good provider for the family.

My mom helped with expenses by working outside the home. When I was little, she worked in the Hood River cannery in the evenings. Later on she became the Underwood postal clerk when the Post Office was adjacent to the railroad tracks along SR 14, next to the White Salmon River Bridge. When the postmaster retired, Mom became the US Postmaster in the newer location on the corner of SR 14 and Cook-Underwood Road. It was during this time that she was diagnosed with the cancer from which she died in 1984.

When it was time to pick pears, Dad would take on some additional help in the orchard. Sometimes that help included me. There were times Dad would let me learn by experience how to set the ladder against the tree in order to get the fruit from the top; for example, if I had the ladder facing downhill, I quickly realized my mistake since gravity set in and I fell.

I was a good driver on the road, but I never got the hang of driving the tractor on the side of a hill. Once I almost tipped over the tractor, and Dad gave me a different job to do that didn't include driving the tractor. I think he had me move bales of hay in the barn instead.

My normal pastime was playing the piano or reading books. But sometimes I would go on long walks through our woods, sit in "my spot" and dream of the house I would build there that overlooked the Hood River Bridge and the Columbia River. I have very fond memories of that place on Underwood Mountain and growing up on those 20 acres of land.

231

**Mary and Leroy Ziegler**

## Yarnell, Esther Larsen

By Kathy LaMotte

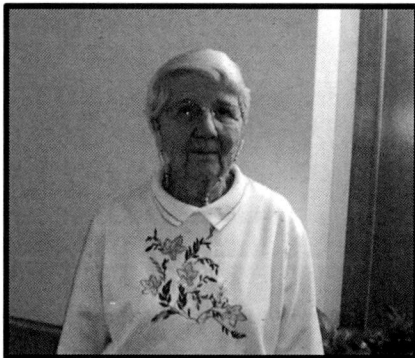

**Esther Larsen Yarnell**

Esther Larsen Yarnell was born to Aaron and Anna Larsen on March 6, 1920. She was born at home. Their home was on property setting by the bluff, just past the Underwood Cemetery. The house is now gone. She had one full

brother named Elmer. Elmer passed away at age 62.

Esther's parents met in somewhat this fashion. Anna's family would follow the fruit harvests. While Anna's family was working here, she met Aaron Larsen. After her parents were married they bought property past the cemetery. On the opposite side of Cook/Underwood Road is Larsen Rd., named after her uncle and aunt, Olaf and Rose Larsen, Olaf being a brother to Aaron.

**Anna Shaw Larsen – Esther's mother**

When asked about the Hood River/White Salmon Bridge opening in November of 1924, Esther had this to say. "Oh yes, I remember. We all rode across when it opened, the whole family. I was four years old. There were my parents, my brother and I, my aunt and uncle, and my cousins. All of us in the car. It cost 75 cents per car, one way. Which was pretty steep in those days. Plus it was 10 cents for every passenger. I was under 7 so I was free. But they hid my brother and cousins under blankets while we went through the toll booth. Because I was under age I got to sit up front and see the whole thing. We very rarely went across because it was just too expensive."

Esther's mother died when Esther was just eight years old. Part of the family lived down by the river. Part of this property is now owned by the US Fish and Wildlife. Esther, her brother, her mother, her aunt, three cousins, and their dog, were in a Model T, getting ready to drive the mile down to Hood, WA (Broughton Lumber area today). As they started to cross the railroad tracks an unscheduled streetcar-like train came through. Esther's mother and two cousins; Jacqueline Cole age eight, and Leona Cole age 18, were killed. Her aunt, Cecil Cole, was injured badly and permanently crippled. Esther also had severe injuries at the time. She remembers the date as August 30, 1928. "There were lots of 8's is the reason I remember. It happened in 1928, I was 8, one cousin was 8, one cousin 18, my mother 28, my aunt 38. And, including our dog, there were 8 passengers in the car. Eight has always been my special number."

Esther attended elementary school at the Underwood School and later graduated from high school in White Salmon, in 1938. While living in their home near the cemetery, she and her brother would walk the distance north to school. Her father would walk down a path to get to the river. There he worked for Spring Creek National Fish Hatchery, as did his father. At that time Highway 14 was still a county dirt road.

Esther's father Aaron built a house down by the river and so when Esther was nine or ten she moved with her father and brother down to property owned by her grandfather Larsen near the river and railroad tracks, just west of the fish hatchery. Their home above was rented out for a while and later sold. Esther does not remember when her grandfather Christian Larsen bought property along the river and built the two-story white house. Part of the property was turned over to the federal government in the late 1940s or early1950s to build residences for hatchery employees.

Sometime later Esther's father re-

married and the family began growing, adding three half-siblings and four step-siblings. (See article - Diane Henry Thomas).

After moving down to the river, a bus would transport Esther and her brother up the hill to school. While attending high school, Esther remembers a bus picked her and Elmer up, then drove down as far as Hood, where it would turn around and proceed into White Salmon.

**Christian E. and Mary Cline Larsen
Esther's grandparents**

In 1934 Highway 14 was built and paved. Before that, as stated earlier, it was simply a dirt road. The road was straightened and altered from the original. The original road actually dipped down behind the white two-story, Larsen house that still stands today, owned by Esther's half-brother Jim Larsen. Don Yarnell, Esther's future husband, worked in construction at the time and drove dirt truck as part of the construction crew. When the new highway was built it split the Larsen property in two.

**Yarnell, Esther Larsen** (continued)

Esther does not know exactly when her grandparents Christian E. and Mary Cline Larsen came to this area as homesteaders. She does know her father Aaron Larsen was born here, and that was in 1894. Christian and Mary Larsen had eight children, six sons and two daughters. They were Phillip (known by Aaron), Amos, Frank, James, Lewis, Olaf, Nora, and Zada.

Esther met her husband Donald Yarnell while attending school in White Salmon. He was from a White Salmon family. She was good friends with two of Donald's sisters. They were married in 1938. The Yarnells have two children. Patricia Curry lives in Brookings, Or. and son Don lives in Mill City, OR. In 1950 Don and Esther moved away for 23 years. They first moved to Brookings. Don was working construction. They moved several times. Their last move was to Medford, where Don was injured, so he retired. In 1973 they moved back to the family property by the river. The house that Esther's father had built on the east end of the Larsen property had burned. Don borrowed a dozer from Frank Hunsaker and worked on the property. They placed their new home on the foundation, where it still stands today.

In 2006 Donald Yarnell passed away. Esther continued living in her home until November 20, 2010, when she moved to Down Manor in Hood River. She gave up her car on her 92$^{nd}$ birthday. She said she misses just "jumping" in and going when she wants. But, with having many friends and the shuttle system provided at her residence, it is working out fine. She is still very active, bowling four times a week.

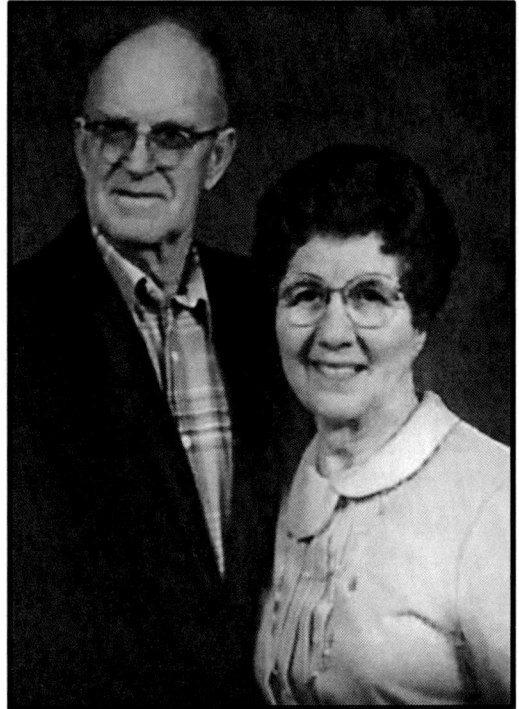

**Don and Esther Yarnell on their 50$^{th}$ wedding anniversary.**

On the following page is a news account of the car/train accident involving Esther's mother. The day following the news account, the *Oregonian* published corrected ages for these people:

Leona Cole , age 18

Jaqueline Cole, age 8

Mrs. Cecil Cole, age 38

Front Page Portland Oregonian August 31, 1928

# 3 IN PACKED CAR DIE AT CROSSING

## Gasoline Coach Strikes Flivver Holding 7.

### ONE OF INJURED NEAR DEATH

### Accident Happens Just West of Underwood, Wash.

### TWO FAMILIES BEREAVED

Sisters With Their Children Make
Up Machine Load Hurled
From Track.

Two sisters and five of their children—the seven packed into a flivver—were struck by a Spokane, Portland & Seattle motor coach at a crossing a mile and a half west of Underwood, Wash., at 4 o'clock yesterday afternoon, and from the wreckage were pulled the bodies of three dead and four injured.

The dead:

Mrs. Aaron Larson, 28, Underwood, Wash.

Leona Cole, 19, 644 Leland street, Portland.

Jacqueline Cole, 10, same address.

The injured:

Mrs. Cecil Cole, 37, 644 Leland street, Portland, St. Vincent's hospital, condition critical.

Charles Cole 6, same address, St. Vincent's hospital, lacerated head and shock.

Esther Larson, 8, Underwood, at Hood River hospital, broken pelvic bone.

Elmer Larson, same address, shock only.

Mrs. Larson was driver of the car. She backed out of an apple shed beside the highway, where she and the others had been sorting fruit. As the car turned, Mrs. Cole is said to have glimpsed the gasoline motor coach bearing down the track. She screamed.

Mrs. Cole Lingers.

## Mrs. Cole Lingers.

Bewildered by the outcry, according to reports, Mrs. Larsen could not get off the tracks.

The coach caught the flivver with the screaming women and children at the crossing and the machine was a mass of wreckage and mutilated bodies before the coach could be brought to a stop.

Occupants of the coach and trainmen ran back to aid, but for Mrs. Larsen and her two nieces no help was possible. They had been killed outright. The usual miracle took place in the comparative freedom from injury of the one boy, Elmer Larsen. The condition of Mrs. Cole and her son Charles appeared desperate, however, and they were taken aboard the motor coach for Portland, while Esther Larsen was sent across the Columbia by automobile to the Hood River hospital.

When the coach got to Portland an Arrow ambulance was waiting and Mrs. Cole and Charles were taken to St. Vincent's. There Mrs. Cole was lingering last night close to death.

### One Left Uninjured.

Two husbands, meantime, received word of the tragedy in their families. Mr. Larsen, long a resident of Underwood, heard at once and was on the scene, but Mr. Cole had to be located at his Leland-street home and then reach Underwood by automobile.

Mr. Cole had been out of work for some time and he had been ill as well; so his wife, with the children, had gone to Underwood, where her sister, Mrs. Larsen, lived, to work at apple-picking while the season lasted.

The crossing where the accident occurred is fairly open, but it is thought Mrs. Larsen found too much to do after just backing from the apple shed and at the same time having the car so full.

Aside from Mr. Cole, there is only one of the family uninjured, and that is a daughter, Olive, who was one of the apple-pickers, but did not get into the packed machine.

235

## Ziegler, Herbert M.

In February 1935 he sold 40 acres on Underwood Heights to Harry J. Card. It had 25 acres of pear and apple orchard and a house. Mr. and Mrs. Ziegler moved to Portland on a half- acre which they purchased on Base Line Road. Mr. Ziegler was an appraiser for the Federal Land Bank of Spokane. Herbert was the son of Samuel Ziegler of White Salmon and related to Isreal Roy Ziegler of Underwood.

## Ziegler, I.R. and Elizabeth (Rosenberger)

By Eva Ziegler Frazer

Isreal (I.R.) Ziegler was born in Reading, Pennsylvania, in October of 1881. His wife Elizabeth (Lizzy) was born in Soudeton or Hatfield, Pennsylvania, in May of 1888. I.R. came west to find a place to help his asthma and found a place in Underwood, Washington. He built a home and in 1911, went back to Pennsylvania and married Elizabeth in March of that year.

The children from this marriage were Reno, born in White Salmon in February 1912; Mamie, born in White Salmon in October 1913; Myrtle, born in Underwood in June 1916; Leroy, born in Underwood in September 1922; Esther, born in Underwood in June 1920; Eva, born in Underwood November 24, 1924.

All six children attended the Climax school, walking the half mile from their home in the Buck Creek area. Even though it was a one-room school, it had exceptional Christmas programs. I.R. said the small schools were the best for learning. After fifth grade, the children all went to Underwood school and then graduated from Columbia Union High School in White Salmon.

The Ziegler family had a big garden and grew hay for their sheep and cattle. I.R. was Skamania County Commissioner and fire warden several years. He helped build the Evergreen Highway to Willard

and Mill A and also the new highway along the Columbia River.

I.R. passed away in March 1950 after health problems caused a move to Vancouver, Washington. Lizzy Ziegler died in 1931. The folks, being Pennsylvania Dutch, were affiliated with the Brethren church.

**I.R Ziegler Homestead**

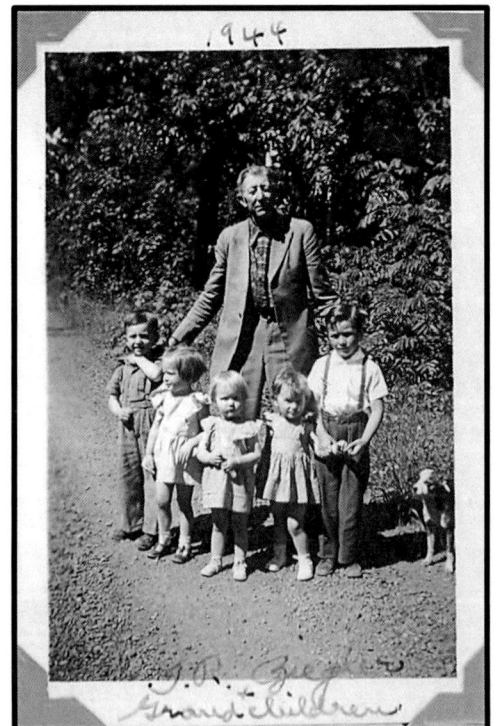

**I.R. Ziegler and Grandchildren-1944**

236

**Ziegler, I.R.** (continued)

News accounts:

June 1917:

*Mrs. I.R. Ziegler and three little children have been suffering with a very painful attack of pink eye. We are glad to report they are very much better.*

January 1928:

*I.R. Ziegler slipped and fell while coming home from work, cutting a deep gash in his head when he struck the ax he was carrying.*

<u>The Enterprise</u>, November 16, 1945:

## HOMESTEADER OF 1903 PROMINENT IN DEVELOPMENT OF UNDERWOOD DISTRICT

*Last month I.R. Ziegler sold his ranch on Underwood heights to Glen F. Fulton, of Underwood, who is now living on the place. Mr. Ziegler, who is in ill health, moved to Portland for medical attention.*

*Mr. Ziegler sold the land on which he had filed a homestead August 11, 1903, and he had resided there until the recent sale. This homestead was one of the last 26 claims filed prior to and around 1903. This locality at that time was known as "Little Norway." Three of the early settlers still live nearby - Gilbert Knutson, who had a claim adjoining Mr. Ziegler, is a jeweler in White Salmon; Frank Hunsaker, who also lives in White Salmon, and Chas. Rosenkranz, who lives in Underwood. The others have moved away or passed on.*

*This ranch Mr. Ziegler had homesteaded was carved out of a dense forest. After 42 years, with little outside assistance, about 70 acres were cleared and put under cultivation and pasture. This land has been developed into a fine stock ranch.*

*While a resident in Skamania County Mr. Ziegler served as County Commissioner from 1924 to 1930 . . . Mr. Ziegler was employed by the county for over 20 years, doing road and highway work. In 1914 he supervised the building of the present Cooks grade and there are very few roads in the Underwood district that he did not help build.*

*Credit is due Mr. Ziegler for other duties which he performed. He was a respected resident in Underwood Heights and vicinity, always ready and willing to do what he could for those needing assistance. He and near neighbors kept a rural school (Climax School) as long as it was deemed necessary. Though this school was small in attendance it had as many advantages and the best of teachers were always secured.*

*Though he has moved from the community he loved best, Mr. Ziegler intends to move back to Washington as soon as his health will permit, but he seems reluctant to give up the fight of making Underwood and Skamania County a better place to live.*

*I. R. Ziegler*

## Ziegler, Reno and Teresa

Reno was born in 1912 in White Salmon to F. Elizabeth ( Rosenberger) and Israel R. Ziegler. He lived in Underwood his entire 82 years, attending a one-room grammar school in the Climax area on Underwood Mountain. He started logging the day after high school graduation in 1931. He worked in Gilmer first and then for Walter Kock in the Willard area. During the winter closure of 1934-35, he worked on the Highway road construction between Underwood and Cook. Reno purchased land next to his father's and married Teresa Reinland in 1935.

Teresa was born in 1917 to George and Katherine Reinland. The family moved from Portland to Underwood when Teresa was six. They lived on the top floor of a packing shed on Little Buck Creek Road and learned to run an orchard and packing house.

After marriage, the couple built a house with the help of their fathers, living in it for nearly 40 years. The home was built from lumber Reno retrieved from Amos Underwood's house that had to be demolished during the construction of the Cook-Underwood Road.

Five children were born to Reno and Teresa: Clark, James, Kenneth, Betty and Linda. Reno worked for Broughton Lumber Company until retirement in 1969. They sold their property on Underwood heights and built a home on the Underwood bluff. After Reno died, Teresa moved to White Salmon and then to Hawk's Ridge retirement apartments in Hood River. She passed away at age 94. Both Reno and Teresa are interred at Chris-Zada Cemetery in Underwood.

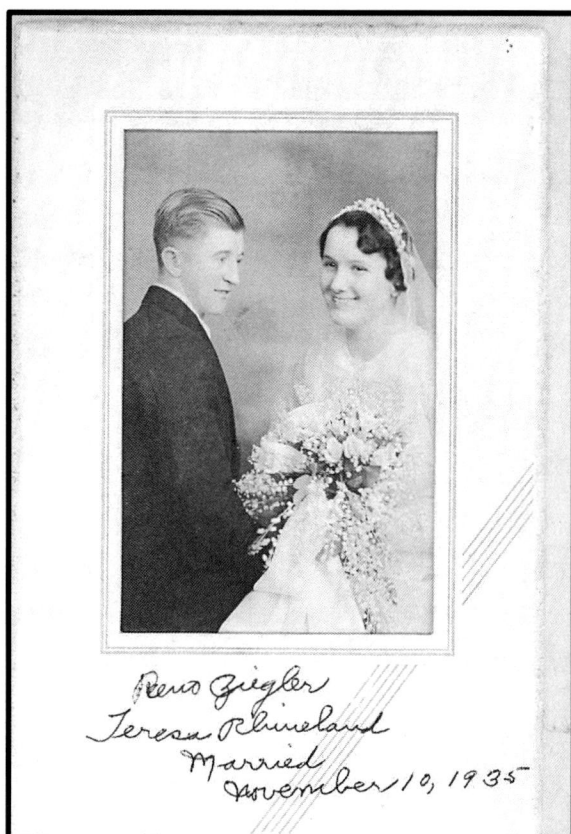

Photo from Gorge Heritage Museum archives, Ziegler family collection

# ORIGINAL LAND OWNERS

**Kow-il-amow-an** was the original name of the area that became Underwood, Washington. Following are Original Land Owners in Underwood, after the government surveyed the land. Information researched and provided by Ralph Brown. Source: Bureau of Land Management web site.

## Township 3 North, Range 10 East

| Name | Section | Acres | Date | Authority How obtained |
|---|---|---|---|---|
| Emma Everrit | 6 | 80 | 7/15/1909 | April 24, 1820: Sale-Cash Entry |
| Emma Everrit | 6 & 7 | 40 | 2/20/1911 | April 24, 1820: Sale-Cash Entry |
| Mattie Franes | 6 | 40 | 6/21/1909 | April 24, 1820: Sale-Cash Entry |
| Daniel Hunsaker | 6 | 160 | 2/4/1905 | April 24, 1820: Sale-Cash Entry |
| Frank Hunsaker | 6 | 120 | 6/30/1906 | April 24, 1820: Sale-Cash Entry |
| William Orser | 6&1of 3N 9E | 160 | 5/5/1905 | March 2, 1899: Exchange-Natl Forest (lieu) (30 Stat. 993) |
| Eliza Schock | 6 | 120 | 9/11/1905 | May 20, 1862: Homestead Entry Original (12 Stat. 392) |
| Charles Tubbs | 6 & 7 | 160 | 9/21/1908 | May 20, 1862: Homestead Entry Original (12 Stat. 392) (12 Stat. 392) |
| Thomas Brotherton | 5 | 160 | 9/5/1906 | May 20, 1862: Homestead Entry Original (12 Stat. 392) (12 Stat. 392) |
| Thomas Elcie | 5 | 160 | 7/26/1907 | May 20, 1862: Homestead Entry Original (12 Stat. 392) |
| Stanton Lapham | 5 | 320 | 4/23/1908 | April 24, 1820: Sale-Cash Entry |
| Emily Butterfield | 5 | 80 | 12/16/1914 | May 20, 1862: Homestead Entry Original (12 Stat. 392) (12 Stat. 392) |
| Israel Ziegler | 5 | 160 | 7/26/1910 | May 20, 1862: Homestead Entry Original (12 Stat. 392) |
| Peter Corbett | 4 | 160 | 11/12/1908 | May 20, 1862: Homestead Entry Original (12 Stat. 392) (12 Stat. 392) |
| Joe Crowe Georgia Williams | 4 | 80 | 8/13/1949 | October 14, 1865: Indian Fee Patent (14 Stat. 703) |
| Mary Edwards | 4 | 160 | 5/27/1907 | April 24, 1820: Sale-Cash Entry |
| Gilbert Knutson | 4 | 160 | 3/19/1904 | May 20, 1862: Homestead Entry Original (12 Stat. 392) (12 Stat. 392) |
| Edith Nickoli | 4 | 160 | 2/20/1900 | April 24, 1820: Sale-Cash Entry |
| Georgia Williams | 4 | 80 | 12/14/1908 | June 15, 1880: Indian Trust Patent (21 Stat. 199) |
| Ellis Breedlove | 3 | 40 | 8/16/1949 | October 14, 1865: Indian Fee Patent (14 Stat. 703) |
| Bridget Sloutie | 3 | 40 | 12/15/1949 | October 14, 1865: Indian Fee Patent (14 Stat. 703) |
| Ann Cameron | | 160 | 9/25/1896 | April 24, 1820: Sale-Cash Entry (3 Stat. 566) |
| ColinCameron | 3 | 80 | 8/28/1896 | April 24, 1820: Sale-Cash Entry (3 Stat. 566) |
| Jacob Claterbos | 3 | 160 | 6/9/1902 | May 20, 1862: Homestead Entry Original (12 Stat. 392) (12 Stat. 392) |
| Sterling Hanel | 3 | 40 | 8/28/1964 | October 14, 1865: Indian Fee Patent (14 Stat. 703) |

## Original Landowners in Underwood

| Name | Section | Acres | Date | Authority |
|---|---|---|---|---|
| Bridget Sloutie | | 40 | 8/7/1893 | February 8, 1887: Indian Allotment - General (24 Stat. 388) |
| Gracie Sloutie | 3 | 40 | 8/7/1893 | February 8, 1887: Indian Allotment - General (24 Stat. 388) |
| Isabel Sloutie | 3 | 40 | 8/7/1893 | February 8, 1887: Indian Allotment - General (24 Stat. 388) |
| Mary Sloutie | 3 | 40 | 8/7/1893 | February 8, 1887: Indian Allotment - General (24 Stat. 388) |
| John Clarkson | 10 | 40 | 6/20/1893 | April 24, 1820: Sale-Cash Entry |
| Derward Davidson | 10 | 40 | 6/16/1904 | April 24, 1820: Sale-Cash Entry |
| Knut S. Knutson | 9 & 10 | 160 | 11/25/1902 | May 20, 1862: Homestead Entry original (12 Stat. 392) |
| Fredrick Luthy | 10 | 160 | 1/10/1901 | May 20, 1862: Homestead Entry original (12 Stat. 392) |
| John Peters | 10 | 160 | 5/10/1884 | May 20, 1862: Homestead Entry original (12 Stat. 392) |
| Charles E. Rader | 10 | 40 | 1/15/1884 | April 24, 1820: Sale-Cash Entry |
| Charles Rosenkranz | 10 | 80 | 6/30/1906 | May 20, 1862: Homestead Entry original (12 Stat. 392) |
| Anthony Schroeder | 10 | 40 | 9/17/1908 | April 24, 1820: Sale-Cash Entry |
| Iver A. Hamre | 9 | 160 | 11/24/1899 | April 24, 1820: Sale-Cash Entry |
| Charles R. Knutson | 9 | 160 | 6/9/1902 | April 24, 1820: Sale-Cash Entry |
| Mattie A. Knutson | 9 | 80 | 12/17/1906 | May 20, 1862: Homestead Entryoriginal (12 Stat. 392) |
| Peter I. Sather | 9 | 160 | 8/16/1904 | May 20, 1862: Homestead Entryoriginal (12 Stat. 392 |
| Clarence E. Dixon | 8,17,&18 | 160 | 10/15/1908 | |
| G.LafayetteKirkpatrick | 8 | 80 | 6/10/1910 | April 24, 1820: Sale-Cash Entry (3 Stat. 566) |
| Nels M. Munch | 8 | 160 | 11/8/1905 | May 20, 1862: Homestead Entry original (12 Stat. 392) |
| George H. Nicolai | 8 | 120 | 2/20/1900 | April 24, 1820: Sale-Cash Entry (3 Stat. 566) |
| Ole G. Tenold | 8 | 160 | 10/1/1908 | May 20, 1862: Homestead Entryoriginal (12 Stat. 392) |
| Northern Pacific Railway Co. | 7 & 8 | 120 | 8/8/1913 | July 2, 1864: Grant-RR Northern Pacific (13 Stat. 365) |
| Ella J. Churchill | 7 & 18 | 160 | 5/17/1909 | May 20, 1862: Homestead Entry original (12 Stat. 392) |
| George Hewett | 7 | 160 | 7/8/1909 | April 24, 1820: Sale-Cash Entry (3 Stat. 566) |
| Nels M.Munch | 7 | 80 | 6/22/1908 | April 24, 1820: Sale-Cash Entry (3 Stat. 566) |
| Alfred Shepler | 7 | 120 | 8/7/1906 | April 24, 1820: Sale-Cash Entry (3 Stat. 566) |
| Washington State | 7 | 40 | 10/29/1092 | March 2, 1853: Washington-Lieu Selection (10 Stat. 172) |
| Millard F. Bennett | 18 | 160 | 9/2/1889 | April 24, 1820: Sale-Cash Entry (3 Stat. 566) |
| William Bennett | 18 | 160 | 9/3/1887 | April 24, 1820: Sale-Cash Entry (3 Stat. 566) |
| Harry T. Coleman | 18 | 160 | 9/10/1910 | May 20, 1862: Homestead Entry original (12 Stat. 392) |
| Claudie B. Airsman | 17 | 120 | 12/21/1911 | May 20, 1862: Homestead Entry original (12 Stat. 392) |
| Edward Ball | 17 | 80 | 9/9/1907 | April 24, 1820: Sale-Cash Entry (3 Stat. 566) |
| Alice L. Brock | 17 | 160 | 5/27/1907 | April 24, 1820: Sale-Cash Entry (3 Stat. 566) |
| George W. Collins | 17 | 80 | 11/27/1914 | May 20, 1862: Homestead Entry original (12 Stat. 392) |

## Original Landowners in Underwood

| Name | Section | Acres | Date | Authority How obtained |
|---|---|---|---|---|
| Maria Rude | 17 | 160 | 8/13/1908 | May 20, 1862: Homestead Entry Original (12 Stat. 392) (12 Stat. 392) |
| James M. Spriggs | 17 | 80 | 6/30/1906 | April 24, 1820: Sale-Cash Entry (3 Stat. 566) |
| Washington State | 16 | 320 | 11/1/1889 | June 5, 1872: MT-ND-SD-WA Enabling Act (17 Stat. 226) |
| Washington State | 16 | 320 | 8/2/1973 | June 21, 1934: State Grant-School Sec Patent (48 Stat. 1185) |
| George Duvanel | 15 | 160 | 4/9/1901 | May 20, 1862: Homestead Entry Original (12 Stat. 392) (12 Stat. 392) |
| William Kellendonk | 15 | 160 | 2/25/1896 | April 24, 1820: Sale-Cash Entry (3 Stat. 566) |
| Edward Underwood | 15 | 160 | 10/26/1892 | April 24, 1820: Sale-Cash Entry (3 Stat. 566) |
| William A. Wendorf | 15 | 160 | 1/10/1901 | May 20, 1862: Homestead Entry Original (12 Stat. 392) (12 Stat. 392) |
| William O. Cox | 14 | 320 | 9/28/1907 | April 24, 1820: Sale-Cash Entry (3 Stat. 566) |
| Clarence H. Cromwell | 14 & 23 | 120 | 11/1/1904 | April 24, 1820: Sale-Cash Entry (3 Stat. 566) |
| Franklin P. Groshong | 14 | 120 | 5/25/1900 | May 20, 1862: Homestead Entry Original (12 Stat. 392) (12 Stat. 392) |
| Christian E. Larsen | 14 | 120 | 3/22/1889 | May 20, 1862: Homestead Entry Original (12 Stat. 392) |
| Jonah B. Turner | 14 | 160 | 5/20/1884 | May 20, 1862: Homestead Entry Original (12 Stat. 392) (12 Stat. 392) |
| Howard C. Cook | 23 | 120 | 3/17/1899 | May 20, 1862: Homestead Entry Original (12 Stat. 392) (12 Stat. 392) |
| James W. Overbaugh | 23 | 135 | 8/8/1897 | April 24, 1820: Sale-Cash Entry (3 Stat. 566) |
| Amos Underwood | 23 | 165 | 7/21/1896 | April 24, 1820: Sale-Cash Entry (3 Stat. 566) |
| Frederick Bueche | 21 & 22 | 80 | 4/1/1901 | May 20, 1862: Homestead Entry Original (12 Stat. 392) (12 Stat. 392) |
| Harry Olsen | 22 | 150 | 5/31/1899 | May 20, 1862: Homestead Entry Original (12 Stat. 392) (12 Stat. 392) |
| Amos Underwood | 21 & 22 | 160 | 1/7/1885 | May 20, 1862: Homestead Entry Original (12 Stat. 392) (12 Stat. 392) |
| Edward Underwood | 22 | 160 | 2/10/1882 | May 20, 1862: Homestead Entry Original (12 Stat. 392) (12 Stat. 392) |
| Henry C. Debo | 21 | 80 | 6/30/1906 | May 20, 1862: Homestead Entry Original (12 Stat. 392) (12 Stat. 392) |
| Alma J. Haynes | 21 | 160 | 6/30/1906 | May 20, 1862: Homestead Entry Original (12 Stat. 392) (12 Stat. 392) |

**Original Landowners in Underwood**

| Name | Section | Acres | Date | Authority How obtained |
|---|---|---|---|---|
| Ed Ramsey | 21 | 140 | 6/29/1908 | May 20, 1862: Homestead Entry Original (12 Stat. 392) (12 Stat. 392) |
| George Sandel Brother Of Valentine Sandel | 21 | 160 | 2/13/1905 | May 20, 1862: Homestead Entry Original (12 Stat. 392) (12 Stat. 392) |
| Benjamin F Beals | 20 | 160 | 6/30/1906 | May 20, 1862: Homestead Entry Original (12 Stat. 392) (12 Stat. 392) |
| Simon Freeman | 20 | 40 | 1/9/1911 | May 20, 1862: Homestead Entry Original (12 Stat. 392) (12 Stat. 392) |
| Emma Goddard | 20 | 120 | 10/10/1904 | April 24, 1820: Sale-Cash Entry (3 Stat. 566) |
| Louis A. Henderson | 20 | 80 | 11/16/1911 | May 20, 1862: Homestead Entry Original (12 Stat. 392) (12 Stat. 392) |
| Richard Jansen | 20 | 150 | 1/7/1909 | May 20, 1862: Homestead Entry Original (12 Stat. 392) (12 Stat. 392) |
| George H. Marsh | 20 | 120 | 10/10/1904 | April 24, 1820: Sale-Cash Entry (3 Stat. 566) |
| Edward B. Perrin | 20 | 80 | 9/1/1904 | March 2, 1899: Exchange-Natl Forest (lieu) (30 Stat. 993) |
| James Crowley | 19 | 160 | 5/25/1900 | May 20, 1862: Homestead Entry Original (12 Stat. 392) (12 Stat. 392) |
| Frederick Fessel | 19 | 160 | 11/11/1898 | May 20, 1862: Homestead Entry Original (12 Stat. 392) (12 Stat. 392) |
| Frank H. Leely | 19 | 160 | 11/11/1898 | May 20, 1862: Homestead Entry Original (12 Stat. 392) (12 Stat. 392) |
| Daniel Moriarty | 19 | 160 | 11/11/1898 | May 20, 1862: Homestead Entry Original (12 Stat. 392) (12 Stat. 392) |

The homestead act of 1862 was one of three United States federal laws that gave an applicant ownership at no cost of farmland called a "homestead" – typically 160 acres. A person could file an application to claim a federal land grant. The occupant had to live on the land for five years, and show evidence of having made improvements. April 24, 1820: Sale-Cash Entry was the other way to own land, and that was to purchase outright the land at $1.25 per acre. There would then be no waiting period.

# References

**Newspapers**

*The Enterprise*, White Salmon, WA

*The Glacier*, Hood River, OR

*The Oregonian*, Portland, OR

*The Skamania County Pioneer*, Stevenson, WA

**Books**

Attwell, Jim
    Columbia River Gorge History, vol. 2.  Tahlkie Books, 1975

Brown, Ralph
    Underwood, Washington Cemetery Obituaries. West Klickitat Co.Historical Society, 2013

Burkhardt, D.C. Jesse
    Railroads of the Columbia River Gorge. Arcadia Publishing, 2004

Fisher, Andrew H.
    Shadow Tribe; the Making of Columbia River Indian Identity. University of Washington
    Press, 2010

Hassell, Barbara,
    Lois; Swiss Roots in Willard Soil  by Lois L. DeWater as told to Barbara Hassell.
    Wilderness Valley Publishing Company, 1985

McCoy, Keith
    Melodic Whistles in the Columbia River Gorge.  Pahto Publications, 1995.
    Mid-Columbia; North Shore. Trafford Publishing, 2003
    The Mount Adams Country. Phato Publications, 1987

Olmstead, Gaelyn L.
    100 Years of Hatcheries Along the Columbia River.

Skamania County History, Vol. I,Second Edition, Columbia Gorge Interpretive Center
    Museum, 2007

Townsend, Homer and Alice
    Obituaries From the Skamania County Pioneer Newspaper 1900-1929, 1985

Ulrich, Roberta
    Empty Nets; Indians, Dams, and the Columbia River. Oregon State University
    Press, 2007

Ward, Anne Markgraf
    Klickitat Saga – 1805 – 1859, 2012

Warren, Esther
    The Columbia Gorge Story, 1977

# INDEX

# INDEX

# INDEX

## INDEX

247

# INDEX

# INDEX

# INDEX

# INDEX

# INDEX

# INDEX

# INDEX

# INDEX

# The Authors

Kathleen LaMotte grew up on the Northern California coast. She attended Humboldt State University, and received her degree from Montana State University. She returned to the Northwest in 1985, moving with her family to Underwood, Washington. After teaching in elementary and middle schools for many years, she retired in 2006. Since, she has dabbled in writing children's books before taking on the project to co-author this book.

Mary Olsen Kapp was born along the Columbia River in Arlington, Oregon. She lived in various towns in Alaska, Washington and Oregon and earned a Master of Library Science degree at the University of Oregon, becoming a school librarian in Central Oregon. After retiring she moved with her husband Jack to Underwood in 2005. Jack had lived in White Salmon and Underwood until leaving for college in 1958.

Mary is involved with the Gorge Heritage Museum in Bingen, which covers Glenwood, Trout Lake, White Salmon, Bingen and Underwood. Noticing that there was not a book written on the history of Underwood, she undertook the project along with Kathy LaMotte.

256